# MEDIEVAL THEATRE IN CONTEXT

*Medieval Theatre in Context* is the first systematic attempt to relate the development of medieval drama – both Christian and pagan – to contemporary society and the Christian church. It provides an invaluable, comprehensive overview of the opinions of modern scholars regarding the content, structure and staging of medieval plays, and clearly locates the drama within its social context.

John Wesley Harris has designed the text specifically to help any reader approaching the subject for the first time. He also provides all the background information needed to appreciate the more detailed social and literary scholarship in this field. *Medieval Theatre in Context* fills a distinct gap in the literature, and will be fascinating reading for all students of the period.

John Wesley Harris is Lecturer in Drama at the University of Hull.

# MEDIEVAL THEATRE IN CONTEXT

## An introduction

*John Wesley Harris*

London and New York

First published 1992
by Routledge
2 Park Square, Milton Park, Abingdon, Oxon, OX14 4RN

Transferred to Digital Printing 2005

Simultaneously published in the USA and Canada
by Routledge
a division of Routledge, Taylor & Francis
270 Madison Ave, New York NY 10016

Typeset in 10 on 12 point Baskerville by
Witwell Ltd, Southport

*British Library Cataloguing in Publication Data*
Harris, John Wesley
Medieval Theatre in Context
I. Title
792.09

*Library of Congress Cataloging in Publication Data*
Harris, John Wesley
Medieval theatre in context / John Wesley Harris.
p. cm.
Includes bibliographical references and index.
1. Drama, Medieval–History and criticism. 2. Liturgical drama–
History and criticism. 3. Theater–Europe–History–Medieval,
500–1500. 4. Theater and society–Europe. 5. Christian drama,
Latin (Medieval and modern)–History and criticism. 6. Christianity
and literature. 7. Theater–Religious aspects. I. Title.
PN1751.H38    1992
792′.094′0902–dc20        92–6559

ISBN 0-415-06781-2
0-415-06782-0 (pbk)

THIS BOOK IS DEDICATED TO
THE MEMORY OF

A. P. ROSSITER

WHO FIRST AROUSED MY INTEREST
IN MEDIEVAL STUDIES

AND WHOSE TRAGIC EARLY DEATH
DEPRIVED THE PERIOD
OF ONE OF ITS
MOST LIVELY ADVOCATES

# CONTENTS

# FIGURES

# PREFACE

This book seeks to set the medieval stage firmly in the context of the society that produced it, by surveying what we know about the plays and their production alongside contemporary social attitudes, particularly those of the Church – a task which seems never to have been attempted before. I hope it will prove a useful introduction for both students of the drama and members of the general public.

A general survey is urgently needed because medieval studies have been very active over the last half-century, on several different fronts. On the practical side, there has been considerable emphasis on bringing the medieval plays back to life, and this has given rise to the re-establishment of various English cycles in their towns of origin, like York, Chester, Coventry and Wakefield, and the creation of specialised groups of medieval players, on both sides of the Atlantic, who have toured medieval farces and moralities with great success. As a consequence, professional and semi-professional actors have begun to feel their way back into the medieval idiom, and this has encouraged a long-overdue study of the plays as practical theatre pieces.

Scholarship in the area is also forging ahead, re-examining old evidence relating to the plays, and constantly ferreting out new data – the Records of Early English Drama project from Toronto is an outstanding example – and this has resulted in a multitude of fascinating and increasingly detailed studies of dramatic activity from city square to parish pump. In the process, though, the larger historical picture has tended to be ignored, so that it is difficult for beginners to find any work that will provide them with the background needed to understand these detailed studies.

So the present work endeavours to take account of the many different theatrical forms that existed in Europe during the Middle Ages, their basic shape and content, their relation to the main trends in their society, and what we know, or can fairly assume, about the way in which they were staged. To achieve that end it has been necessary to disregard the literary dimension of the plays almost entirely, because it would require at least twice the space: interested readers should refer to the many excellent literary appreciations by Axton, Woolf, Tydeman, Davenport and others. There is also unfortunately no room to take account of the new work on local drama, which really requires an independent survey of its own.

Since the book is intended for English-speaking readers, all the texts described in detail are either originally English or readily available in translation – to include continental plays would make the book far too long.

I am deeply indebted to the labours of the many outstanding scholars who have worked, and are still working, in the field of medieval studies, and it is to them the reader should turn for more precise and detailed information. My own objective has been as much as possible to keep the material accessible to the general public, and encourage a wider reading on the various subjects treated, by clearly indicating the main sources I have used for each chapter in the notes at the end of the book. I also record there any comments which would not fit comfortably into the main text, thus avoiding the use of distracting footnotes and references. It goes without saying that everywhere I have tried to be as accurate as possible, and any errors that may remain are entirely my own.

*John Wesley Harris*
Drama Department
University of Hull
21 December 1991

# 1

# THE PASSION OF
# JESUS CHRIST

On Sunday, 1 April, in his thirtieth year, Jesus of Nazareth made a triumphant entry into Jerusalem riding on the back of an ass-colt. He was by that time widely acclaimed as a healer and it was believed by many Jews that he was the Messiah or Christ - the Anointed One - who had come at last to liberate them from the tyranny of Imperial Rome, just as Moses had liberated the Jewish people from their slavery in Egypt; but Jesus rejected the Old Law of 'an eye for an eye and a tooth for a tooth' and taught that there were only two essential commandments: first, to love God without reservation; and, second, to love your neighbour as sincerely as you loved yourself - he had no interest in rebellion.

He had come to Jerusalem because it was the beginning of the Passover week, and he intended to celebrate the feast with his disciples in the heart of the Jewish world. He went straight to the Temple, where he was horrified to find that the courtyards had been turned into a bazaar. He looked sternly about him, but took no action that day, although in the morning he returned and chased the money-changers out of the building, causing a minor riot.

After he had 'purged' the Temple he spent the rest of the week preaching and holding long discussions with his disciples, trying to prepare them for what he knew was inevitable. On Thursday, 5 April, he sent two of his followers to make final arrangements with one of the citizens, in whose large upper room he intended to celebrate the Passover. These arrangements were necessary because, for reasons of his own, he had decided to hold the ceremony a day early. He celebrated the festival that evening, as he had planned.

Eighteen hours later, on Friday afternoon, he was dead - nailed to the Cross as a common criminal, after being betrayed by one of his disciples, put on trial by the Jewish and Roman authorities, cruelly mocked, and savagely tortured, before he was finally condemned to death.

When the body was taken down and buried, the Jewish authorities, fearful that the disciples might steal it and then claim Jesus had risen from the dead as he had prophesied, sealed the mouth of the tomb with a heavy stone and set guards to watch it.

His disciples were all in disarray. But early on the Sunday morning, his mother Mary visited the tomb where his body had been laid, together with two of her friends, only to find that the guards had gone, the stone had been rolled back, and the body was no longer there, although the sheet in which it had been wrapped was still present. They carried this information back to the other disciples, claiming that Christ had risen from the dead, as he had frequently promised them. At this there was great rejoicing. Later, other members of the community claimed to have met the risen Jesus and talked with him, and this did much to reinforce the faith of his followers.

Of the agonising and stirring events of those few days, one picture remained with the disciples very clearly, because Christ himself had given the occasion great weight, and that was the Last Supper, the Passover meal they had shared with him.

The Passover was a very important Jewish feast, celebrating the occasion when Moses had brought the Jews out of their slavery in Egypt. The Jewish God had visited nine fearful plagues upon the country, but Pharaoh had stubbornly refused to let God's people go. Finally Moses received detailed instructions about the tenth, and most terrible, plague: God was preparing to destroy all the firstborn in the land of Egypt and, to ensure that none of his chosen people should suffer, they were to give him a sign. Each Jewish household was to kill an unblemished lamb and use its blood to mark the sideposts and upper crosspiece of the door; they were to roast the lamb and eat it, with a garnish of unleavened bread and bitter herbs; it was to be consumed to the last crumb, and it was to be eaten with the loins girded for travel, with sandals on the feet and a staff in the hand, ready to depart from Egypt; for in the night God would send his Angel of Death to smite all the firstborn of Egypt, but where he saw blood on the doorposts he would *pass over* that house, and its inhabitants would come to no harm – hence the name of the feast.

By the time of Jesus, the Passover had become an intimate family festival, celebrated in April, called the 'Pessach' or 'Pasch', at which the story of the escape from Egypt was recounted and praise and thanks were given to God for preserving the liberty and identity of the Jewish people.

It took the form of a commemorative supper retaining the basic features of the meal in Egypt – the Paschal Lamb, the unleavened bread and the bitter herbs – and central to it were two blessings that were to become central also to the Christian message. Before the lamb was eaten, the head of the household took bread, and broke it, and blessed it, and passed it round the table for all to eat – and after the meal a cup was filled with wine, and the head of the household took the wine, and blessed it, and passed it round the table for all to drink. The blessings pronounced upon the bread and the wine could be quite original, and those that Jesus chose to utter at the Last Supper were solemn and disturbing in the extreme, which made them very memorable.

The earliest account of the Last Supper is provided by St Paul, who describes it in the way those present described it to him:

> that the Lord Jesus the same night in which he was betrayed took bread: and when he had given thanks, he brake it, and said, 'Take, eat: this is my body, which is broken for you: this do in remembrance of me.' After the same manner also he took the cup, when he had supped, saying, 'This cup is the new testament in my blood: this do ye, as oft as ye drink it, in remembrance of me.'

It is obvious that many things were running through Jesus' mind at the time, and led to these strange words of blessing. For one thing, we know he believed he was the 'suffering servant' the prophets had foretold who would die to release mankind from the miseries brought on them by the disobedience of Adam and Eve. He also clearly identified himself with the pure, unblemished Lamb of the Passover - the Paschal Lamb - which was to be eaten to sustain the Jewish people and whose blood was to be the sign that liberated the faithful from death. He may also have seen himself as part of the universal spirit of God, which was just as much present in the bread and wine as it was in himself, and which nourished and supported all things; and lurking somewhere in the background was possibly the folk-memory of a human sacrifice, in which the body of a 'king of the year', who had been ritually slain, was eaten by his followers to allow them to absorb his strength and life and so renew their own vital forces. 'Take, eat: this is my body, which is broken for you . . . This cup is the new testament in my blood': the words could not be plainer or more direct, but their meaning was profound.

When he spoke, the disciples will also have remembered his assurance that his body would be restored to life after his death - for the suffering servant was to be resurrected, the indwelling spirit of God was indestructible, and the Lamb of the Passover, and the primitive human sacrifice, died to ensure the continuing life of the community.

After Christ's death, the disciples obeyed his injunction, and regularly re-created the Last Supper as a memorial meal, which they called the Eucharist, or 'thanksgiving', to celebrate the fact that his death had released all men from their inborn tendency to sin and brought them the promise of everlasting life, confirmed by his Resurrection.

So the celebration of the Lord's Supper, better known as the Mass, became the central feature of Christian ritual, although the whole Passion, or 'suffering', of Christ, the tortures and humiliations he underwent from the time of the Last Supper to his death on the Cross, and above all the joy of his Resurrection at sunrise on Easter Day, were equally important.

The events of the Passion were eventually destined to produce a new form of theatre in Europe several centuries after the collapse of the Roman Empire, and the Mass was the trigger for the process. Nor is it surprising that drama should spring from a story abounding with so much tension and pathos, and containing so many memorable scenes – such vivid images of suffering and rejoicing. What is surprising is that it took so long.

St Paul's advice to the Corinthians on how they should conduct the service of the Eucharist makes it clear that in his day the occasion was still a communal meal like the original Passover, but that the new meaning Christ had given it had turned it into a very different kind of ceremony that required some kind of self-examination and confession of your sins or shortcomings before you approached the Lord's Table. After all, it was to save men from their sins and set them right with God that Christ had suffered torture and death, and it was only proper that you should realise that *you* were one of the sinners that he had died to save.

By that time the ceremony was being conducted in Greek instead of Hebrew, because Greek was currently the most 'international' language in the eastern Mediterranean, and Christianity, largely through St Paul's influence, had become a movement to save all men, not just the Jews.

In due course, the growing Christian communities became too large to hold the Eucharist as a domestic gathering, and the supper element of the ceremony wasted away, except for a single table at which the presiding elder pronounced the thanksgiving over the bread and the wine, now viewed as two different 'species', or physical aspects, of Christ's body.

Because of the warm Mediterranean climate, it was, and still is, the custom of both Jews and Greeks to eat their main meal in the cool of the evening, and the Eucharist had also been eaten at that time, normally on a Thursday, to recall the circumstances of the Last Supper; but once the meal element had disappeared, there was nothing to prevent the choice of another part of the day for the ceremony, or even another day of the week.

The logical choice of day was Sunday, because that was the day on which Christ had risen from the dead, and his Resurrection was the most obvious reason for thanksgiving. The hour was moved to the early morning, partly because it was reminiscent of the rising sun when Mary and her companions came to the tomb, and because the rising sun was also a very apt symbol for the Resurrection; but the main consideration was probably practical: such an early hour was convenient because it fell outside the labourer's usual working day, which often extended far into the evening – and the bulk of the early Christians were slaves and labourers to whom the radicalism of the new religion appealed very strongly because of its call for the equal division of wealth and the common ownership of all possessions (very much the reasons why Communism appeals to the poor and oppressed today).

There was a basic simplicity and informality about the early Greek Eucharist. The service ('liturgy' in Greek) could apparently take almost any form the celebrants liked, providing it contained somewhere the essential account of the Last Supper and the blessing and distribution of the bread and wine, which were known in Greek as the 'canon', or 'standard part', of the service. Water was mixed with the wine, because that was the normal Greek drinking practice, but the custom was usually justified by the report in St John's Gospel that when the dead Christ's side was pierced with a Roman spear 'there came forth blood and water'. In fact one mystical sect, called the Gnostics, renounced wine entirely, and used only water to celebrate the Eucharist, but, when the doctrines of Christianity were set down more precisely by the Roman Church, this practice was ruled heretical.

The ceremony still retained many Jewish features from the disciples' background and upbringing, despite its use of Greek. In particular it borrowed from the synagogue the Sabbath practice of incorporating two readings of the Scriptures – one from the 'Old Law' of Moses and one from the 'New Law' of the prophets – together with the singing of psalms and the delivery of a short address, either explaining the readings or commenting on some current moral or devotional problem. In the Christian ceremony the two readings, or 'lessons', were taken respectively from the Jewish Old Testament and from Jesus' teachings in the New Testament, the elder's address became the 'sermon', and these two features became a regular accompaniment to the central ritual of the Mass. When the new drama eventually arose, each of these three aspects of the service (lessons, sermon and liturgy) would become the inspiration for a different kind of play.

The fourth century saw the beginning of a new and unfortunate trend in Christianity, which developed from the Church's over-reaction to a popular heresy called Arianism and was later to provide the main reason for the coming of religious drama.

Arius, a well-educated priest who lived in Alexandria at that time, believed that Christ must have been created by God, like everything else in the world, and that, though he was doubtless the first and most perfect of God's creatures, he was in no way divine. In short, however holy and inspired Christ's teachings might be, he was basically a man like other men – a very great and good man, but a man nonetheless.

This opinion created chaos in the Church because the worship of Christ, if he was only a man, was plainly a form of idolatry – so the newly converted Emperor Constantine called a Church council at Nicaea near Byzantium in AD 325 with the express purpose of putting an end to the Arian question. The council's job was to make the godhead of Christ quite plain, and, with the help of Athanasius, another very enthusiastic Alexandrian, it drew up a declaration of belief, which clearly affirmed that Christ was 'begotten not made, being of one substance with the father' – and so, Constantine hoped, the problem of Arianism was laid to rest.

However, this was far from the case. Setting aside the new problem of Athanasius – who was so rabidly anti-Arian that he was constantly being exiled by the Church for being too extreme – the main effect of the Council of Nicaea was to split the Roman world. Local nationalism, which had seemed to be dead since the Roman conquest, suddenly revived. The Western Empire enthusiastically accepted the Nicene Creed, and Egypt, too, fanatically supported Athanasius, who was now their bishop; but Constantinople, the new centre of the Empire, and most of Asia, were strongly inclined to Arianism, and the overall result was the emergence of new sects all over the Middle East, preaching more or less Arian doctrines, and serious disagreements between Christians everywhere.

The Church now began to stress the divinity of Christ in order to combat Arianism, and his image began to change from that of a noble God–man figure into a much more unearthly spiritualised being, who exercised the unquestioned rights of a God, and who therefore needed priests to mediate between his divinity and the common people – in this way the supremely human qualities of Jesus began to disappear in a blaze of godhead.

In the meantime, the Latin Mass had gradually taken over from the Greek Eucharist in all the Western parts of the Roman Empire. This happened remarkably slowly, considering that the Latin service had existed since the second century, and that Constantine had made Christianity the official religion of Rome in 312, but, in fact, the Latin Mass does not seem to have achieved its position of supremacy until the fifth century. At that time, first under the threat of Gothic invasion, and later during actual occupation by the Lombards, the Pope – in the absence of any emperor in the West, and quite unaided by any military forces from Byzantium in the East – was forced to take over the helm and become the civil administrator of Rome as well as its spiritual leader.

This explains a noticeable feature of the new Mass: in marked contrast to the Greek freedom of expression, it is absolutely *rigid* in nature and demands a specific order of service. This seems to have been a desperate affirmation of the Roman sense of order, and the universality of Roman influence, at a time when the residents of the Western Empire could see nothing around them but a total collapse of all civilised values. The magnificently theatrical processional elements of the Roman Mass and the elaborate vestments worn by its priests can similarly be seen as a last-ditch attempt to preserve Roman morale – for there was little to stress but spiritual unity at a time when all the material components of the Western Empire were falling into ruins!

In accordance with this policy, St Gregory (the first Pope of that name) made strenuous efforts to establish a common form for the Mass throughout the Western Empire in the sixth century, when independent forms of the service were flourishing everywhere – particularly amongst the Celts. The standardisation he envisaged was not to occur in his lifetime, but his *Sacramentary*, or 'book of rules', was destined to become the pattern for a universal Catholic Mass.

More importantly, though, Gregory was not satisfied with establishing the proper *shape* of the Mass, he also wanted to establish what he believed to be its true *interpretation,* and this he did in another work, called the *Dialogues*, which became the accepted guide to the meaning of the service.

Believing as he did in the doctrine of the Real Presence – which taught that when the bread and wine were united in the Mass, to symbolise the Resurrection, the living Christ became present there in person – he saw the service as literally the re-creation of the Passion of Jesus Christ, a renewal of his act of sacrifice, to obtain a renewed absolution of all Christians from sin.

He also saw the service as a confluence of two worlds, the earthly and the spiritual, in which the radiance and joy of Heaven interpenetrate and illuminate the ritual movements of both priest and people. In a famous passage he says:

> What right-believing Christian can doubt that in the very hour of the sacrifice, at the words of the Priest, the heavens are opened . . . that high things are accomplished together with low, and earthly joined to heavenly and that a union is made of the visible and the invisible.

Indeed, Gregory's successors concurred with him in regarding the Mass, and the Holy Scriptures too, as a fusion of a 'visible' outer meaning, which was often a simple story, with various kinds of 'invisible' symbolic meanings reflecting the purposes of God.

This way of thinking, which is typically medieval, also embraced events in the physical world, which, it was believed, might well possess an inner symbolic meaning far more important than their simple outward appearance. Its origins lay in an earlier Jewish vision of the whole of life as the unfolding of God's divine plan for the world, as it had been exclusively revealed to his chosen people – a viewpoint the Christians had naturally acquired with the rest of their Jewish inheritance.

What is more, because medieval people lacked the kind of detailed knowledge of the universe that was needed to pursue the hidden patterns of cause-and-effect, this belief that a divine plan was woven into the very fabric of existence caused them to place great importance on any

7

analogies or similarities they could see in the world about them, believing that such comparisons had been placed there by God specifically for the instruction of man. God's hand was everywhere, and, as St Irenaeus put it, 'In God nothing is empty of sense.'

This means that they envisaged the world as if it were a giant poem, rich with metaphors and analogies. They looked at red and white roses blooming side by side amongst the thorns and saw there the symbols of blood and purity in the midst of pain and menace, and instantly their minds conjured up an image of the virgin martyrs, shining with glory in the midst of their persecution. In this way the whole of creation was a book provided for man, in which he could read the wonderful works of God.

Dramatically speaking, this attitude was very important, because it brought to the fore the poetic notion of images that are very physical but at the same time rich with emotional and intellectual associations; these are exactly the images that drama always works with, because they combine three things - the theatrical need for display in their sheer physicality, dramatic tension in their emotional content, and thematic unity through their allusive reference to the author's larger vision. Later on, too, when the priest and his helpers could be seen, at different points in the Mass, to be actually *representing* Christ, and his disciples, the liturgy also acquired elements of characterisation, representation and enactment, all of which are equally vital to the theatre.

St Gregory's proposals regarding standardisation of the Mass were eventually put into effect by the Frankish King Pepin in 754, and this created further difficulties, because he decreed that the standard Roman liturgy should be used in all churches. Now, the standard liturgy was written in classical Latin, which was rapidly becoming a thing of the past and being replaced by a host of dialects. These were gradually turning into what are now Spanish, French, Italian, Romanian, and so on, and the different forms of the Mass had mainly developed because local priests were beginning to present it in these new 'vernacular' languages.

It was therefore a serious mistake to insist on the use of the Roman liturgy, because only a tiny fraction of the people could understand it, mostly the educated kings and nobles, and those of the priesthood who had studied in Rome - in short, the upper classes, who still looked upon classical Latin as the only truly 'cultured' language and had not the slightest desire to use the vernacular, which they considered fit only for peasants.

In this way a language barrier was erected between the priests taking the service and their congregations, and this reinforced the rift caused by the new doctrines of Christ's divinity that were being used to combat Arianism - doctrines which were very popular with the Frankish clergy because they reaffirmed the high social standing of the priesthood.

Theoretically, of course, even the lowliest peasant could enter the Church and advance to the highest possible position by dint of hard work and an unshaken faith, but it was observable that by the eighth century most of the higher-ranking priests came from well-to-do families. What is more, members of the priesthood were almost the only highly educated men of their time and acted far and wide as the natural governing class in society, second only to the kings and the nobility. They now began in a very un-Christian way to see themselves as vastly superior to the 'common' people, and unfortunately remade the figure of Christ in their own image, as a kind of divine aristocrat. Throughout the centuries these tendencies were reinforced every time a further disagreement with the Arians arose – which meant frequently. On every such occasion the absolute godhead of Christ and his superiority to all things merely earthly was re-stressed and strengthened, and the gulf between his representatives the priests and the members of their congregation became constantly deeper.

As a result of this continual pressure, a further change took place in the Church's ideas of the Mass. Hitherto it had always been seen as a prayer of thanksgiving to God for the purification of men from sin, achieved by Jesus' death, and the promise of everlasting life offered by his Resurrection, and the thanks of the community had always been extended to God by one of their own number acting on their behalf, originally an elder and later a priest, who ensured that their feelings were translated into a sacrificial offering that was acceptable to God.

However, in the seventh century, Isidore of Seville suggested that the Mass was not a thank-offering made by the community at all, but a *gift* graciously extended by an infinitely forgiving God to an erring mankind, through his chosen intermediaries, the priesthood.

This growing gulf between the priests and their congregations was of the utmost importance for the re-emergence of drama, since it was becoming increasingly obvious that bridges needed to be built, and drama was one of the best ways of constructing them.

# 2

# CHRISTIANS VERSUS PAGANS

The development of early Christianity in Rome was set against a very garish background, provided largely by the entertainments of the time, which the early Christian Fathers learnt to hate and despise. The only plays they might have found acceptable, the lively social comedies of Plautus and Terence, by that time lay far in the past, and the current theatre was devoted to sex and sensationalism – probably in an attempt to woo the crowds away from their two main preoccupations, the Circus and the Hippodrome.

The extremely popular chariot-racing at the Hippodrome was relatively harmless, though it seems to have involved a savage determination to win which often created violence on the track and a corresponding violence amongst the supporters of various racing factions in the streets of Rome – but the 'games' at the Circus were sadistic. The gladiatorial and beast-fighting shows presented there were so brutal that a number of emperors, like Julius Caesar, actually turned their backs on the arena when they had to be present, and devoted their time to administrative work. However, no emperor dared to suppress them – they were an expected part of every national celebration; every major official was supposed to present them at some time during his period of office; and they were sometimes mounted privately by rich politicians in order to win the support of the mob.

Neither of these forms of entertainment could be countenanced by serious Christians, certainly, but in many respects they considered the stage was worse, because the lively street theatre of the mimes and the elaborate performances of the pantomimes were more seductive.

The pantomimes claimed to present Greek tragedies, but they would not have been recognised by the classical Greeks. The original Greek plays had two types of performer, both male – actors, who performed on a raised stage; and a chorus, which performed on a circular orchestra, or dancing-floor, in front of the stage. The number of actors was limited, and each of them usually played two or more parts, changing masks and costumes to do so. They mostly spoke or chanted their lines, but at moments of high emotion they sang. The chorus, at different times, danced, chanted and sang. It partly interacted with the actors, partly created mood, and partly commented on the action, and thus provided time for the actors to change their masks and costumes.

The first change the Roman producers made was to lift the chorus, which now did more singing than dancing, up onto the stage - but the actors were still dominant and the most memorable and important part of the plays were still the *cantica*, or 'musical numbers', delivered by the principal actor. These might be either sections of 'recitative', or full-blown 'arias', to use roughly modern equivalents, and they tended on the whole to contain serious social comment, either on what was happening in the play or upon contemporary life.

Many of the most famous *cantica* were well known to all the citizens, from generation to generation. For instance, we hear that at Caesar's funeral, when Mark Antony revealed that he had willed certain property to the city, the crowd spontaneously sang a verse from Pacuvius' *Trial at Arms*, composed two hundred years earlier, to give voice to their sorrow: it ran, 'Have I then saved them only to perish at their hands?' Britannicus, too, saved himself from one of Nero's plots by singing an aria from *Andromache*, reflecting his own tragic position in that its hero had just been deprived of his throne and his royal rank: it began, 'O father! O fatherland! O house of Priam!', and evoked such a powerful movement of support amongst the guests that Nero thought it wise to defer his arrest and assassination to a later date. Stories like this rather suggest that opera, when it eventually developed, was in some sense natural to the Italian people.

The next modification was made by producers under the Empire, in early Christian times. These began to focus the performance more and more upon the principal actor, who first played more roles than the rest and then began to banish his rivals from the stage completely, taking over all their parts himself, and becoming a 'pantomime' or 'actor of all the parts'. As the supporting actors disappeared, the chorus became more important again and divided into 'pyrrhicists' and 'symphoniacs' - dancers and singers - who reinforced or counterpointed the main actor's movements and choral motifs.

The instrumentalists down in the orchestra, the original dancing-floor, also became subordinated to the principal actor, highlighting his performance with their zithers, trumpets, cymbals, flutes and castanets. It was soon mostly the soloist who filled the stage, singing, miming and dancing his way through the whole piece, and giving life and substance to all the action. This, of course, put an enormous physical strain on the main actors and they exercised constantly to preserve the tone of their muscles, the suppleness of their joints, and the volume and charm of their voices, and also followed a strict diet which called for purgatives and emetics the moment their waistline was threatened. But all the hard work brought its rewards. The pantomimes were the great stars of the Roman stage and inevitably became the heroes of the day and the darlings of all the women in the audience. Indeed they were so popular they even attracted the argumentative and unruly supporters of the racing-track, and were adopted by the different racing stables – the reds, the whites, the blues and the leek greens – and violent battles took place between their respective supporters. Under Tiberius one of these riots became so serious that several soldiers, a centurion and a magistrate were left dead on the streets.

As a result of all this attention most of the pantomimes became vain and pretentious and indulged in petty jealousies and squabbles, preening themselves if they came into royal favour, like Pylades, who was the Emperor Augustus' favourite. At one point Nero, despite his liking for them, had to issue a decree of banishment against them when their partisans became uncontrollable – but he soon called them back, because neither he nor the Roman public could do without them.

Under the Empire, the pantomimes progressively abandoned the attempt to both dance and sing at the same time and stressed the mime and dance in their performance, leaving the *cantica* to be sung by the choir. The pantomimes of this 'new wave' were brilliant dancers; we have many tributes to the fact that they 'spoke' with every part of their body, especially their hands – tributes from men well qualified to judge such effects, like Quintilian the famous orator. By the end of the first century, the performances of the pantomimes were virtually completely mimed, in the modern sense, to the accompaniment of the chorus, and the form was beginning to be known as 'the Greek dances'.

Now a further degeneration set in. Originally the pantomimes had been content to use their dance and mime as a commentary on the *cantica*; now they went on to subordinate the *cantica* to their performance. Managers, musicians and librettists were reduced to the level of mere artisans. Roman poets felt privileged when they were invited to write for a 'star' like the celebrated actor Paris, and it brought them rich financial rewards, but they had to write what he wanted: he now chose the subjects, outlined the various situations, prompted the musicians and even suggested verses he would like to see incorporated in the finished work. The new pantomimes were busy selling themselves to the public, and they were sure they knew best how to do it.

They aimed more and more at catching the eye and stimulating the senses rather than speaking to the heart. The plays became either tragedies of stark horror or sensual episodes guaranteed to titillate the sexual instincts of the audience. The one thing that was certain was that there was always a meaty part for the star: he might be a father whose sons were served up to him in a pie, a hero run mad, a virgin who had been raped and had her hands and tongue cut off so she could not accuse her violator, a father incestuously seducing his daughter (and the daughter as well), or any number of fornicating gods and goddesses, but he would certainly be the undisputed centre of attention.

We hear that the actor's lascivious movements at high points of the sexual pieces often threw women in the audience into an ecstasy. 'Tuccia cannot contain herself', writes Juvenal in one of his satires; 'the Apulian maiden heaves out a sudden and longing cry of ecstasy as though she were in a man's arms; the country-girl Thymele is all attention and even she learns something!' You will see from this brief survey of the form why the Christian Fathers did not take greatly to the pantomimes.

The simple street mime, though, could be almost as bad. This was a much more ancient form of theatre dating from the very early days of Greek civilisation, and the word 'mime' implies full spoken acting, and not miming in our modern sense. The mimes – the actors who performed these pieces – were troupes of travelling players, both male and female, very much centred round one principal actor or actress, who was known as the 'archmime' and who was often, though not always, the manager of the company. The pieces seem to have started as monologues, but gradually other performers were drawn into the action, though never on an equal footing. The performers originally wore masks, but in Rome we hear that they often rejected them and played bare-faced. Many of them seem also to have had tumbling skills.

The companies were quite small, no doubt for reasons of economy, and the titles of many early pieces suggest this clearly. 'The Quack Doctor comes to Town' could easily be a monologue, so could 'A Deserted Heroine Resorts to Magic' and 'The Beggar turned Millionaire', but 'Two Old Fishermen Have a Chat' and 'Two Syracusan Women Attend the Festival of Adonis' obviously imply two actors; while other titles, like 'The Women at the Isthmian Games', probably involved more, though we can safely assume the numbers will have been kept as low as possible. Ovid mentions one mime with a cast of three – a flighty wife, a foolish old husband and a foppish lover – while a mime-scene painted on a lamp also shows three actors but implies the presence of a fourth off-stage.

Most of the titles suggest chatty comedy or farce, and that was obviously the staple of the mime, but two pieces from Egypt reveal a broader range. One is an adventure in which a Greek girl escapes from the unwanted attentions of an Indian king and his followers by making them all drunk – this contains a very vulgar stand-up comedian – and the second is virtually a comic melodrama. A frustrated, power-mad wife tries to wreak vengeance on a male slave who refuses to make love to her because he prefers one of the female slaves; she does everything possible to have the pair killed and later tries to poison her husband, but her clumsy attempts all fail. What she thinks is poison is in fact only a sleeping-draught, and the husband wakes up during his funeral. The piece involves seven characters, but only needs four actors. It interestingly demonstrates the predominance of the archmime, in this case the woman playing the wife, who hogs about 80 per cent of the written text. She will probably have produced and directed the piece as well, and may even have written it.

The mimes the Roman people regularly called for in the streets and market-places were full of kidnappings, cuckoldry and lovers hidden in convenient chests or cupboards, surrounded by a lot of horseplay, dancing, obscenity and bawdy. The sexuality of these romps was reinforced by the right which the people claimed to make the actresses strip on stage and play naked – a practice that started at the festival of the Floralia, where it probably reflected a folk-custom, but which rapidly spread to everyday performances of mimes throughout the Empire, though we hear that Britain disapproved of the practice. There were also mimes who specialised in erotic dancing, including transvestites, and this was taken further at court, where both Nero and later Heliogabalus delighted in nude shows, and the latter – who, incidentally, was a eunuch – often forced mime actors performing adulteries actually to fornicate on stage.

So the performances of the mimes and pantomimes did not endear them to the Christian Fathers, who considered the sadistic horrors and lecherous bawdy they purveyed detestable – as did many Roman moralists and satirists – and, as they gradually gained more say in the running of the city, the Christian elders constantly tried to place some kind of ban on actors and acting.

They were helped by the fact that actors had little political importance in Rome because they were mostly slaves or freedmen. They were not allowed to hold aristocratic rank; they were not allowed to vote or become members of the Senate; and they had no right to take any case to the law courts. Julius Caesar prevented them from holding any municipal posts outside Rome, and Augustus forbade the males of any senatorial family from marrying any woman whose parents had been on the stage or who had been on stage herself. However, when they became favourites, they inevitably gained influence at court, and emperors can break decrees. Caracalla despatched one actor, at his own request, to take up a military command on the frontier; Heliogabalus made another a prefect in the city of Rome itself, and Justinian, in the sixth century, married the famous Byzantine mime Theodora, thus making her an empress. On the other hand, there were limits, and Trajan, who had a love-affair with the second Pylades, rejected with horror the idea that his lover should perform a dance in his honour between two acts of *The Loves of Mars and Venus*!

The Christian Fathers felt rather more strongly on the matter, particularly when the mimes began to mock Christians at the time of the Arian heresy because Arius had a vision of a reformed and purified theatre that could safely be used for the instruction of the faithful – an idea the mimes found hilariously funny.

Amongst the Christians who attacked the theatre most strongly was Tertullian, who wrote an uncompromising treatise *On Entertainments* (*De Spectaculis*) in the year 200. He held that Christians automatically undertook to avoid plays when they renounced the Devil and all his works at baptism. What are these performances but idolatry, he says; they represent pagan gods, they minister to the baser passions, and they take place at the festivals and in the holy places of the god Dionysus, and in his honour! He tells the story of a devil who entered a woman in the theatre and when he was eventually exorcised by the priest apologised for his mistake, explaining that he thought she must be one of his followers since he had found her in the devil's domain. Christians, in any case, says Tertullian, have no business lusting after earthly pleasures, and should take no interest in them. If they need shows, then they can find them in the services of their own Church: there they will find nobler poetry, sweeter voices, wiser maxims and more beautiful melodies than any play can boast – and all of this coupled to truth instead of fiction! He then warms to his subject; if, after this, they still want more sensational shows, he says, then let them wait for the Last Judgement: 'Then will be the time to listen to the tragedians, whose lamentations will be far more poignant in their deserved agony. Then they will see the comedians twist and turn, rendered nimbler than ever by the bite of the everlasting fire . . . What a block-buster of a show that will be!'

But the question of attendance at theatres was trickier than Tertullian suggested. If the Church wholly banned this popular pastime, it was simply asking to have its orders disobeyed; so, while it extended a complete ban to members of the clergy, it only forbade the theatre to laymen on Sundays and Holy Feasts – but if you were caught there then, immediate excommunication followed!

The Church also tended to be cautious about its attitude to actors, because they came from the same slave and freedman class as many of the faithful, and they contented themselves with forbidding Christians to become actors or even marry them, unless the actors concerned were baptised and forswore their profession.

As the Empire became more and more Christianised, the position of the emperors became increasingly difficult. They found themselves caught between bishops on the one side pleading for decency and humanity, and the people on the other refusing to give up their traditional 'bread and circuses'. The theatrical legislation of Theodosius in the late fourth century reflects this dilemma. He forbids performances on Sundays and during the most sacred periods of the Christian year; he forbids actors and actresses to wear gold ornaments or rich fabrics, or to ape the dress of nuns (which suggests that the holy sisters had become objects of satire); he forbids actors to seek the company of Christian women and boys; he forbids them to come into public places, or to walk the streets ostentatiously attended by slaves with folding chairs; and he will not, he declares, have their pestilential pictures polluting the neighbourhood of his own statues. But they are nonetheless to be tolerated. He relaxes the strict laws forbidding actors and actresses from marrying into other classes; he expects the city praetor to spend lavishly on all aspects of entertainment to keep the people happy; and he makes it quite clear that he will not have actors, whom he describes as 'public servants', poached and deported from Rome by rival cities or rich impresarios. In short, the idea of *suppressing* actors is never entertained for a moment.

The Empire was officially divided in 395 into an Eastern and a Western sector, with the Eastern capital, Byzantium, providing most of the laws and bureaucracy, and it was in Byzantium that St Chrysostom preached a bitter sermon on Easter Day 399. He had been attacking the stage for a whole year from the pulpit, he said, and had just seen all his exhortations come to nothing. Early in Holy Week, it was true, there had been an almighty storm, and people had superstitiously flocked to church, but it was a week of entertainments – on Good Friday the Circus had been crowded and on Holy Saturday the theatre had been full to overflowing, and on both days the churches had been empty. He dwelt passionately on the inevitable damnation bound up with all things theatrical and ended his sermon with a threat to enforce a sentence of excommunication upon all those who ever again dared to absent themselves from the church on a Sunday or any Holy Day. This attack produced, typically, two contrasting sets of instructions from the authorities, one insisting that public entertainments must at all costs be maintained, the other forbidding, yet again, any performances in Holy Week or on the occasion of any important Christian ceremonies.

St Jerome and St Augustine, Chrysostom's two great contemporaries at the Western end of the Empire, were at one with him in their condemnation of the evils of the public stage, but they were divided on the question of whether it was proper to *read* plays or not. Various devout members of the Western Church, including one of the bishops, had been encouraging young people to read the comedies of Menander and Terence to broaden their education. Augustine had some sympathy with this tendency. In his *Confessions* he recalls the powerful influence exercised over him by tragedy, particularly erotic tragedy, when he was a young man, and in *The City of God* he draws a careful distinction between the higher and lower forms of drama; and if he does not exactly approve, at least he does not condemn, the use of tragedies and comedies in humane education.

Jerome, on the other hand, who was of an altogether more crabbed and ascetic disposition, saw the whole business as damnable, and a letter he wrote protesting against the reading of comedies by priests ultimately passed into Roman ecclesiastical law.

Salvian, a French Father of the fifth century, made the last known protest against the Roman theatre. He had seen his native city of Trèves laid waste by the Franks when he was a boy, and he attributed the moral weakness of the Romans specifically to their indulgence in theatrical entertainments. Even though his own home city had been destroyed three times by the barbarians, he complains, the citizens were still calling upon their rulers for chariot-races and a new theatre; and with the Vandals at the very gates of Carthage, the Carthaginian *clergy*, let alone the common people, were wallowing in theatrical entertainments, particularly comedies. The inhabitants of the Empire must surely have eaten some root that induced madness, for they insisted on laughing even while they were dying.

However, the theatres were now falling into ruins on every side. The barbarians had sacked half the cities of the Empire and nobody could afford to pay for shows any longer. Rome still had a circus and a theatre and nearby Ravenna had another theatre, but that was about all, and even those were maintained largely by the tourist trade. In the circus, the combats involving gladiators and wild beasts had finally been suppressed, apart from bull-fighting, and replaced by racing, boxing, wrestling and animal acts.

Our last records of the Roman theatre date from the earlier part of the sixth century. Theodoric, king of the Ostrogoths, who by then was ruling over a very mixed population of Romans and Germans, found it necessary to continue to support public entertainments, even though he personally despised them. In his state papers he never mentions the actors without a sneer, but he takes great pains to ensure that all their performances are carefully regulated, together with those of the chariot-racers, who now came under the same general category of *histriones*, or 'entertainers'.

The Goths were superseded in Italy in 553, when the West was temporarily re-conquered for the Emperor Justinian by his brilliant general Belisarius, but in 568 came the Lombards and a new dark age. The Lombards had no interest in entertainments whatsoever, or, indeed, in any part of the ancient Roman culture. The theatre may have endured for a while in provincial Ravenna, but it was of no interest to the authorities in Rome: there Pope Gregory was urgently trying to restore the morale of the Roman people by making the services of the Church central to their lives, and wanted no competition from the theatre, and soon all the theatre buildings that remained in the Western Empire had been converted into barracks or municipal storehouses.

The loss of the theatres meant the end of the pantomimes, because theirs was an expensive kind of show to produce, needed a large stage and, despite its erotic appeal, depended on an artistically cultivated audience which could appreciate the finer points of dance and choral music. It did not appeal to the barbarians, who favoured sword-dances and bagpipes. The chariot-racing went too, for much the same reasons – lack of money and the need for an elaborate arena. The demise of these two forms of entertainment was not mourned by the Christians.

The mimes, on the other hand, continued to travel the roads and perform their farces, together with a host of other general entertainers – jugglers, rope-walkers, stilt-walkers, tumblers, beast-tamers, strong men, and so forth – and they entertained audiences wherever they could – in great halls, at tournaments and archery-contests, at fairs, in market-places and even in monasteries. Basic farce has a permanent appeal, and stories of old husbands, young wives and eager lovers were not likely to disappear after being played all over Europe and the Middle East for the past thousand years. The mimes needed little equipment to survive: a comedian with a ready wit could always make his way in the world with nothing but the clothes he stood up in, and if he could find a female companion and a mat to define the acting area, so much the better; the two of them could play a farce.

Evidence of the mimes' existence is sparse but continuous throughout the early medieval period. In 679 the English monasteries were warned not to have 'revels or plays' staged for their benefit; in 789 a church law threatened any player who dared to counterfeit a priest with corporal punishment and exile (which suggests that the mimes had been satirising the Church again); in 835 mimes entertained the Emperor Louis I, and in 960 Edgar, the reformist king of the English, lamented that the monks had become so decadent that the mimes mocked them in song and dance in the market-place.

In the meantime, from the sixth century onwards, barbarians of different races had been coming face to face amongst the ruins of the Roman Empire, and a new sense of nationalism developed, as each tribe sought to prove its superiority to the rest. The tribal warriors began to fuel their nationalistic spirit with a new form of entertainment, the lays, or epics, about heroes of their race and their mighty deeds, sung to the harp by musicians who were known variously as skops, skalds, gleemen, minstrels, jongleurs or troubadors, depending on when and where they sang.

It seems, too, that lays were not always presented by the solo minstrel but sometimes involved mimetic dance and a male voice choir. A very theatrical example of this technique is reported from the Byzantine court in 953. On that occasion, the 'director of the theatrical games' rode on horseback round the emperor's dining-table and hall to define a 'playing circle' into which he then called two teams of warriors. Each team had a leader and was accompanied by musicians playing stringed instruments. The warriors were clad in reindeer-skin cloaks and wore various kinds of masks, and they carried shields in their left hand and wooden staves in their right. At a command from the master of ceremonies, the leaders signalled their men to engage the enemy, and the two teams danced out a mock battle, rushing together in perfect symmetry and striking their shields and staves together, while they shouted a rhythmical Gothic battle-chant. One party eventually surrounded the other and circled them three times in stylised battle. Then, falling back into two opposed ranks, they delivered an antiphonal chant, which celebrated the achievements of Gothic heroes.

Plainly, though, most minstrels pursued a simpler, narrative form of warrior entertainment, which resulted in the *chansons de geste*, or 'songs of noble deeds', stories that are too sophisticated to be easily captured in a dance-drama; and later they turned their attention to stories of love and courtship, and heroic adventures undertaken by the knights of King Arthur and Charlemagne, thus creating the *chansons d'aventure*, or 'songs of adventure'.

The details of what happened next are obscure, but it seems that the mimes, who already included tumbling and juggling in their repertoire, linked up with the minstrels, creating what are known as 'minstrel troupes'. There is no precise information as to how these combined shows were put together, but it seems likely that they would begin with juggling, tumbling and general entertainment, probably including a short farce, after which the minstrel would provide the more serious part of the show, and the evening would be rounded out with more general entertainment.

The most common term for the performers in minstrel troupes was 'jongleurs', and they can be found travelling the roads of Europe throughout the whole of the Middle Ages, eventually supplanting the mimes, who are no longer mentioned much after the tenth century – indeed, *mimi* seems to have become merely an alternative name for 'minstrels', which is in itself significant. We hear that their clothes were brightly coloured, far gaudier than even a knight could reasonably wear, and that they had shaved faces (which suggests they used full-face masks), close-clipped hair and the flat shoes proper to their profession, which involved a lot of dancing and tumbling. They were presumably identical with 'the usual masked players' referred to in one contemporary account and are represented by many groups of masked dancing figures in the margins of illuminated manuscripts. They are also frequently compared to apes, which implies that they used grotesque mimicry.

By the fourteenth century, entertainers of this kind had obviously specialised in a number of different ways. Thomas de Chabham, the sub-dean of Salisbury, divides them up at that time into three groups. He writes:

> Some transform and transfigure their bodies with indecent dance and gesture, sometimes shamelessly unclothing themselves, at other times donning horrible masks . . . others live like vagabonds, without any permanent dwelling-place; they frequent the courts of the great and say scandalous and shameful things about those who are not present, to the delight of all the rest . . . others, again, play musical instruments for the pleasure of the public, and of these there are two kinds: some frequent common drinking-places and lascivious gatherings where they sing suggestive songs, but others . . . sing the stories of princes and lives of the saints.

It is possible that, from time to time, some kind of silent enactment, or mimed dance, accompanied the bard's narrative, giving more tangible form to the story he told – a civilised variation on the Byzantine hero-entertainment described earlier. The main reason for thinking so is that various lives of Terence written in the Middle Ages assumed, wrongly, but presumably by analogy with the Roman pantomimes, that this was precisely the kind of presentation the poet had in mind when he composed his plays, and this belief may well have given birth to the new form. If such a tradition of 'mimic drama' existed, it would certainly have been reinforced by the customary practice of one or two dancers 'acting out' the story of a ballad as it was sung by the villagers composing the *carole*, or circle, in which they performed, and it would explain the habit in early Renaissance puppetry of having a presenter who described the actions of the dolls, rather than using voices for the individual puppets – as on the famous occasion when Don Quixote became so emotionally involved in the performance at the inn. If that is so, it throws a new light on pieces like *Aucassin and Nicolette* from the thirteenth century, where the narrative is punctuated by songs introducing the separate stages of the story, and where the characters' speeches seem to be planned either for *very* accomplished mimicry, or actually for additional actors: such pieces would be a natural development of the 'mimic' form.

Meanwhile, in the late twelfth and the thirteenth centuries, actual scripted plays on secular subjects began to emerge again, many of them depending on just the kind of material likely to have been used by descendants of the mimes. In France in the twelfth century, for instance, there are descriptions of jongleurs where 'L'uns fet l'ivre, l'autre le sot' – 'one plays a drunkard, the other a fool' – and there are also references elsewhere to playing the part of a whore. This sounds like the kind of basic farce that would not have surprised an ancient Roman audience.

Alternatively, the two-handed entertainment described may have been a kind of dramatic debate, because these were also very popular in the twelfth century and we find them everywhere, under the name of *débats* in France and *estrifs* in England. They are usually simple scripted arguments between two actors, representing two different animals, or objects, each struggling to win the contest. Thus we have debates between Winter and Summer, Wine and Water, the Owl and the Nightingale, and the Fox and the Wolf – but they cover more serious subjects too, including a debate between the Body and the Soul, and one between Mary and the Cross.

In the late thirteenth century a genuine farce in French appears in Flanders, called *The Boy and the Blind Man*. This is a rather cruel little two-hander in which an old blind man is tricked by a young sighted one, and is only softened by the fact that the blind man is an utter rogue. Another farce from the same period is the English *Interlude of the Clerk and the Maiden* (*Interludium de Clerico et Puella*), which involves three characters, the Clerk, the Girl and Mother Eloise, who advises the young man how to get the girl to sleep with him.

These pieces are forerunners of the popular plays known as 'interludes' that were common in the fourteenth century and are dealt with later. The only difference is that interludes were longer, often had a more serious moral or political purpose, and were played by players who were certainly specifically actors rather than all-round entertainers like the jongleurs.

So it could be argued that, despite official and ecclesiastical disapproval, the popular farces presented by the mimes survived the fall of the Roman Empire and did much to provide the general 'tone' for the secular interludes that developed towards the end of the Middle Ages, particularly the bawdy ones. Little else remained of the Roman theatrical heritage, and its real treasures, the lively, and much more substantial comedies of Plautus and Terence, which preceded the Empire, were largely neglected until the Renaissance, apart from the occasional imitation by gentlemanly writers like Vitalis of Blois, which seem to have been intended for private reading and perhaps a mimed performance by a circle of enthusiastic amateurs, rather than for general display to the public.

There was only one, rather unusual, dramatist who wrote imitations of the Latin comic writers that were truly actable, and this was a remarkable woman called Hrotsvitha ('the white rose') who, despite her romantic name, was a canoness attached to the convent at Gandersheim. Admittedly, she was not a nun but a laywoman, with considerable freedom to express her personal views, but as a nobly born and well-educated Saxon lady and a close friend of the Abbess Gerberga, she will certainly have appreciated her moral responsibilities.

Sometime in the latter half of the tenth century, this imaginative woman composed six energetic religious dramas based on the comedies of Terence. She explained that this was an act of poetic justice intended, 'to glorify the praiseworthy chastity of Christian virgins in precisely the same form of composition as was once used to describe the shameless acts of licentious women'. She chose for her plays some of the stories of the virgin martyrs whose chastity had been threatened by evil pagans, thus obtaining a lust-interest which helped to create dramatic tension, while at the same time making the plays morally acceptable. Dealing, as she does, with monkish legends, the actions of the plays are very rapid and compressed, though she embroiders them with a number of comic incidents: the evil governor Dulcitius goes to rape some holy virgins by night, but stumbles into the kitchen and begins kissing the pots and pans thinking he is embracing the girls; the holy hermit Abraham comes to seek his niece Mary in a brothel, but can only gain admission by presenting himself to her as a client; Paphnutius the hermit converts the courtesan Thais from her evil ways but falls in love with her himself, and she in turn has to save him; and so forth.

There is no proof that these plays were ever intended to be acted, though they are great fun and very viable, as has been proved by several amateur productions. Hrotsvitha probably intended them to be either read silently or declaimed, possibly with mimed action as an accompaniment, but it is interesting to note her claim that they were intended to *replace* the over-worldly plays of Terence – an argument which suggests that the nuns at Gandersheim were reading or even 'performing' his plays, or at least agitating to have them read or performed, despite the well-known views of St Jerome and other Church Fathers on the matter.

# 3

# FROM RITUAL TO
# DRAMA

By the early ninth century some Churchmen were becoming very concerned at the alienation the new Latin Mass was causing between priests and their congregations. The Church authorities tried to combat this by instructing clergymen to explain the service to their parishioners and involve them in singing parts of the liturgy which had previously been reserved for the officiating priest and the choir, but some of the higher clergy felt that more vigorous action was needed. One of these was Amalarius, Bishop of Metz - a prominent figure at the court of the Emperor Charlemagne.

Amalarius believed that a more vivid, theatrical presentation of church services would help to communicate their meaning, even when the language was not understood. He began by creating a number of new rituals of a dramatic and allegorical kind. Typical of these was his service for the consecration of a new church, which he turned into a drama reminiscent of Christ's 'Harrowing of Hell' - the occasion when he descended into Hell from the Cross to release the souls of all the righteous non-Christians from the clutches of the Devil. The bishop himself assumed the role of Christ, triumphantly beating upon the great western doors of the newly built church, which represented the Gates of Hell, and demanding entrance - while a member of the local clergy, hidden behind the door, acted out the part of a devil defying him and trying to resist the divine invasion. Then, when the doors were finally opened, the devil-cleric fled out into the crowd, thus visibly demonstrating that the new building had been purged of the evil which automatically attaches itself to all earthly things.

It was inevitable that Amalarius should, in due course, extend this principle to the Mass, emphasising its tremendous dramatic and theatrical potential, and he wrote two interpretations of the service with this objective in mind, his *Pastoral Dialogues on the Roman Rite (Eclogae de Ordine Romano)* in 814 and his more popular *Book of the Service (Liber Officialis)*, which ran to three editions between 821 and 835. He did not, of course, propose to make a *play* out of the Mass, but he showed how every detail of the service could be interpreted as an *image* of one of the events of Jesus' last days and be presented by the officiating clergy with appropriate signs of sorrow, guilt, anguish or joy. The whole story of the Passion was implicit in the liturgy – the triumphant entry into Jerusalem, the betrayal, torture, death and Resurrection – and the ceremony could be seen as a ritual drama whose theme was no less than 'the renewal of God's whole plan of redemption for man' through the life, death and Resurrection of Jesus Christ.

This approach to the Mass was particularly helpful, because it placed great stress on the gestures and movements of the priests presenting it, which were clearly visible and intelligible to everyone. Understanding the actual words of the service was less important if the congregation could be presented with a vivid re-enactment of the key events of Jesus' life, on which their faith was based – one image was worth a thousand words.

To appreciate the setting in which this simple ritual 'enactment' of the Passion took place, we need a mental picture of the church of those times. It was a long building with double colonnades, very like the nave of the usual church, but it had no pulpit, no transepts (the wings stretching out to right and left near the pulpit) and no choir-stalls. The eastern end of the building, which is where the altar always stands, was closed off with a shallow semi-circular apse, which threw the action and sound forwards towards the congregation. A small altar, clearly visible to everybody, stood well forward of the apse, more or less at the point of focus suggested by its curve. Behind the altar, facing the congregation, was a semi-circle of seats for the clergy, with the bishop's chair, slightly elevated, in the middle of them. Directly above the bishop's chair, on the inner surface of the half-dome that crowned the apse, was painted an image of Jesus, sometimes as the Good Shepherd, but usually as Christ Triumphant, often in his symbolic form as the Paschal Lamb carrying the red-cross banner. This image of Jesus was deliberately placed to dominate and overshadow the bishop's chair, implying that its occupant was the agent of the risen Christ.

Round the walls of the apse, behind the chairs for the clergy, were seats for the members of the choir, all clergymen, divided into two half-choirs, one on each side. On the altar would be a bare cross without any figure of the crucified Christ. In front of the altar would be either one lectern, on stage left, or two, one on each side, in which case the one to stage right, from which the Gospels were read, would stand slightly higher than the other and have more steps.

The whole impression was rather informal and far more cheerful than that of a Gothic church, and the altar was absolutely central to the ceremony. The difference in atmosphere is largely explained by the different emphasis of the Mass, which was not focused, at that time, on the Passion, the pain Christ suffered for man on the Cross, but on the wonder of the Resurrection and his triumph over death: 'Be glad, oh be glad, for the Lord is risen!' – a positive emphasis that was later lost.

There was a very strong superstition relating to the two sides of the church. The stage-left side, that on the bishop's left hand as he sat behind the altar facing the congregation, was strongly associated with evil, and 'sinister' events – the word 'sinister' in Latin meaning both 'left-handed' and 'ill-omened' – while the stage right was associated with joy and good fortune. The women of the congregation invariably sat on the 'good' side of the church and the men on the 'bad' side – a practice explained by the argument that women, being the weaker sex, and more liable to temptation, as was shown by the behaviour of Eve, needed the protection of the 'good' side of the church, while the men were strong enough to do without it. This traditional emphasis on the spiritual 'quality' of stage left and stage right was later of the utmost importance for the staging of religious drama.

When the members of the congregation were taking communion, they came straight to the altar and received the bread into their hand, while standing, and similarly handled the cup when drinking. No altar-rail kept them at any distance from the holy table, nor was there any kneeling or genuflecting during the ceremony – the congregation either sat, or stood to show their respect, depending on the importance of what they were hearing.

There was no collection of money; instead, the offerings made before the Mass consisted of whatever gifts people could afford – loaves of bread, flasks of wine, meat, fruit, incense or candles – partly for distribution to the poor, and partly for the use of the church. The bread and wine used for the Mass were selected from these offerings. The occasion would almost certainly remind a modern Christian of Harvest Festival.

More surprising for such an observer would have been the kiss of peace, known as the 'pax' because it accompanied the blessing 'Pax Domini vobiscum' ('the peace of the Lord be with you'). This occurred twice during the ceremony and involved everyone. The first pax occurred at the very beginning of the service, when the bishop reached the altar and turned to face the congregation. After delivering the blessing, he kissed first the priest to his right and then the priest to his left. They each embraced another priest at the altar or in the choir, who in turn embraced another, and so on. As the kiss of peace spread through the choir they stopped singing the Old Testament texts they had been using up to that point, and burst into a hymn of praise to the Holy Trinity.

The last priest on each side of the church kissed the nearest member of the congregation, and Amalarius makes it quite clear that except for the first priest who kisses a woman on the 'good' side of the church no man should kiss a woman, or vice versa – this, he says, might too easily lead to thoughts that are less than holy. And so the kiss of peace rippled out to the fringes of the assembly, until everybody present had been involved.

The second pax occurred at the moment of the service which commemorated the Resurrection, and was much more emotionally charged, because it physically affirmed the fact that the peace brought to mankind by Christ was working amongst the congregation.

Following Amalarius' instructions, the bishop would identify himself with Jesus at certain points in the service, and the deacons and sub-deacons assisting him would identify themselves with the disciples and the holy women, but it is a fluctuating kind of identification which is not yet consistent enough to give rise to any thoughts of independent playmaking. The audience is always aware that these are merely priests demonstrating what happened: as yet there is no identification of the actors with the characters.

It is plain, though, that the new approach to the service caused the priests to put more feeling into their delivery of the words than before, and the congregation could identify emotionally with what was happening. This is shown by the success of Amalarius' two books, which achieved immediate popularity, particularly, we hear, with 'the more simple kind of folk'. His proposals were condemned as heretical by the Council of Quiercy in 838, but their popularity continued to grow and their influence to spread, and the electrifying effect they had on congregations did much to rouse Christianity from the lethargy into which it was sinking.

However, not all the contemporary clergy recognised the need to revitalise the church services – and many of those who did thought Amalarius' methods were quite unsuitable. Anything smacking of the theatre was bound to encounter opposition after the Church Fathers of ancient Rome had proclaimed it ungodly, and Amalarius' opponents felt that this new theatrical treatment of the Mass was literally damnable. Even when the Church eventually recognised its inability to restrain the new movement, there were still many who deplored it, amongst them some, like Deacon Florus of Lyons, who scorned the new trend because it appealed only to 'the simple folk' – an uncharitable observation which shows how far some priests had become detached from their congregation.

More interesting, though, are the complaints of Bishop Agobard, also of Lyons, regarding the 'theatrical mannerisms and stage music' encouraged by the new movement. How far this trend had gone by the twelfth century can be gathered from the complaint of Aelred, Abbot of Rievaulx, in his *Mirror of Holy Love* (*Speculum Caritatis*), that the clergy were singing in a style that involved the mimicry of female voices, sighs, sudden dramatic silences and vocal imitation of the agonies of the tortured and the dying, and that some priests contorted their whole body with 'histrionic gestures' – practices more suitable for the stage than the church. These complaints pinpoint a development in the *music* accompanying the divine service, which paralleled and reinforced Amalarius' dramatisation of the priests' actions.

The favoured music of the Church was Gregorian plainsong, which had achieved great artistic heights, especially in Rome. This derived from Jewish synagogue chants, which were basically an easily understandable, one-note-per-syllable, method of reciting the psalms. However, when plainsong came to be applied to the Mass, it soon began to be enriched at key points, like the Introit (or introductory passage), the Gloria and particularly the Alleluia, by two or more groups of voices singing in parallel at acceptable musical intervals (octaves, fifths and, with some necessary modifications, fourths). Next came the addition of decorations for such passages, known as 'melismas', literally 'melodies', which involved the elongation of single syllables of the text to cover a large number of different notes, creating a joyful and often ecstatic sound. These melismas tended to obscure the text. In fact St Augustine, in the fifth century, found this aspect of Gregorian chant so seductive that he reminded himself that it was a sin to enjoy the music of the service without paying attention to the words.

Some of these melismas proved musically difficult to remember, so *prosulae*, or 'prose passages', which possessed one syllable for each note, were devised for insertion at those points in order to help the singers. In view of the antiquated nature of the classical Latin in the service, the devisers of these passages felt they should use them to reveal in simpler and more vivid language what the associated part of the service was all about: in this way the *prosulae* became 'tropes', a term used by rhetoricians to mean phrases which were used improperly – as these elaborate passages were, in the sense that they had no proper place in the liturgy at the points where they occurred. Nevertheless, they quickly proved that they could powerfully reinforce the mood and impact of the service, and were soon being composed as separate pieces, gradually developing a more dramatic form in which voice answered voice in the choir in the form of a dialogue, making the meaning of the service even more immediate for the listeners.

Relying as they did on the syllabic allotment of notes to enhance their clarity, tropes encouraged rhythmical and emotional variations which reflected the mood of the text – where the material was sad the syllables could be prolonged, where it was joyful they could be sharp and lively, and the music could easily change mood between one line and the next. So it became possible to reflect the emotional and physical action of the text in the music, and the musical characterisation of any biblical personage whose words were being sung became almost inevitable.

It was such tropes that Aelred and Agobard were complaining about, and it is hardly surprising, given the strong trend towards dramatisation that now existed, that one of the tropes should eventually have turned into a new form of sacred theatre, known as 'liturgical drama' because of its close association with the church service.

The trope in question was named after its first words 'Quem quaeritis?', or 'Whom do you seek?'. It exists in many versions, and, for a long time, it was thought that the one from the monastery of St Gall, near the Lake of Constance in Switzerland, was the earliest, because it was the simplest. However, we now know that this was preceded by the more complex version from the monastery of St-Martial in Limoges, which dates from some time between 923 and 934. In its earliest form, the trope seems to have served as the Introit to the Easter Mass, but it was later transferred to the end of Matins, the early morning service just after midnight, where it was inserted after an extra lesson that told of the three Marys' visit to the tomb, of which it was, indeed, an expansion.

It is easy to see why this trope became the first point of dramatic growth in the liturgy, since the visit of the three Marys to the tomb and the joyful message they received from the angels that Christ had risen emphasised the theme of Resurrection that was absolutely central to the early Christian Church. It was logical, then, for this trope to receive the most attention; but in order to demonstrate the full theatrical and dramatic force it possessed at the time, it needs to be displayed in its proper setting, which means the various Church practices that had grown up around Easter by the tenth century.

The Church calendar still preserved the memory of the actual week of Jesus' Crucifixion, even to his eating the Passover one day early: Thursday of Easter week was associated with the Last Supper, Friday with the Crucifixion, the Deposition of the body from the cross, and the interment in the tomb, Saturday with the body lying in the tomb, and the posting of the guards, and Sunday with the early visitation of the three Marys and the news of the Resurrection. These stages in the holy story were reflected in the daily services throughout the Easter period.

For some time there had been a practice of 'reserving the Host' during part of Easter. The 'Host', or 'sacrifical victim', was the term used for the consecrated bread and wine which represented Christ's body, and 'reserving' it meant withdrawing it from the communion. When this happened, three separate Hosts, or batches of bread and wine, were consecrated together by the priest on Maundy Thursday, the day of the Last Supper – one for the Thursday itself, one for Good Friday, when Christ was crucified, and one for Easter Sunday, when he rose again from the dead. Sometimes only two Hosts were consecrated, and the bread and wine given to the communicants on Good Friday was unblessed, and 'empty' of Christ's presence, reflecting the disciples' feelings of loss. On Easter

Saturday, when Christ was lying in the tomb, no Host was provided at all, and there was no communion made during the service.

It had become the custom to place the Host in a special tower-shaped chalice on Good Friday, to represent Christ's burial, and to 'rediscover' and elevate the same Host on Easter Sunday, when it became the symbol of his Resurrection, at which point the napkin, or *sudarium*, in which the chalice had been wrapped, became Christ's empty shroud.

This abstract and ritualised treatment of the death, burial and Resurrection was restrained enough to appeal to even the most conservative members of the Church, but, needless to say, the dramatisation of the events of Easter had become much more extensive than this and embraced the whole church building.

What happened seems to have been more or less as follows: during Passion week, the church was progressively stripped of its finery and darkened. On Good Friday the brethren removed the crucifix from the altar and set up a temporary cross in front of it, appointing two deacons to intone the *improperia*, the scornful reproaches hurled at Christ by the Jews as he hung upon the Cross. The Deposition from the Cross, and the interment of the body in the sepulchre, were also represented in the same ceremony. The temporary cross was taken down and wrapped in a veil symbolising the gravecloths and was then placed in a likeness of the sepulchre – either a receptacle standing on some part of the altar, where there was room for it, with a curtain stretched round it, or, more frequently, a simple curtained structure to one side of the altar and detached from it. As the cross was laid in the 'sepulchre' an actual burial ceremony was pronounced over it.

Two or three brethren were then appointed to represent the soldiers placed to guard the tomb, and these employed themselves in keeping a faithful watch over the 'body', chanting psalms throughout the night. This watch was known as the Easter Vigil. During the Vigil, a single great candle – the Paschal Candle – was the only illumination, and this was placed on the ground in front of the altar to represent the fact that hope was at its lowest point, that the Light of the World was brought low, and that Christ had assumed perishable flesh in order to save man. The Vigil continued throughout the whole of Saturday, when the Host was withdrawn and no communion took place, into the early hours of Sunday morning – that is, Easter Day.

At the second hour after midnight on Easter morning, the bells of the abbey were set joyfully ringing. The great Paschal Candle was lifted on to the altar, and six smaller lighted candles were added to it, three on each side, returning their number to the sacred seven which was usual for the Mass. The bells still continued to ring, whilst a procession formed at the altar and travelled round the building, eventually returning to the 'sepulchre'.

Two acolytes led the procession carrying candles, followed by two more acolytes with thuribles – that is, incense-burners swung on the end of chains; then came two deacons walking in silence, and behind them another two deacons chanting in Latin the account of the visit of the holy women to the tomb: 'And now they said amongst themselves, "Who shall roll us away the stone from the door of the sepulchre?" And when they looked, they saw that the stone was rolled away, although it was very great.' Behind the two chanting canons came the cantor, or chief singer, accompanied by his assistant. The members of the procession up to this point were dressed in white copes, and they formed the core; all the other celebrants then followed in order, two by two, wearing their normal vestments or habits and each carrying a lighted candle.

When the procession reached the sepulchre, two acolytes concealed inside the structure, representing the angels at the tomb, sang in Latin, 'Quem quaeritis in sepulchro, O Christicolae?' ('Whom do you seek in the sepulchre, Christian women?'). The two singing deacons replied, 'Ihesum Nazarenum crucifixum, O Coelicolae' ('Jesus of Nazareth who was crucified, heavenly ones'). Still in Latin, the answer came at once: 'He is not here. He has risen as he predicted. Go! Proclaim the news that he has risen from the tomb!' A priest dressed in a white alb then emerged from the sepulchre carrying the special Easter chalice containing the Corpus Christi, or 'Body of Christ', which was, of course, the preconsecrated Host from Maundy Thursday. Four further acolytes, who had been standing beside the sepulchre carrying a canopy raised high on staffs, now advanced so that the canopy covered both priest and Host. The two acolytes bearing candles took up position in front of the canopy, and those bearing thuribles flanked the priest on either side.

The chanting deacons then proclaimed, 'Surrexit Dominus vere, alleluia! – The Lord has truly arisen, alleluia!', and the cantor and his assistant sang an antiphon – a musical piece in which voice answers voice – expressing the joy of all men that Christ had been restored to them, while the procession proceeded to the middle of the church and turned to face the altar on which, by now, the usual crucifix had been reinstated.

More antiphons and verses followed, concluding with the key words 'Quod enim vivit, vivit Deo' ('He lives because he lives in God'), at which point the priest advanced and placed the chalice containing the Host upon the altar. At this the bells, which had been silent during the singing, rang out again, and the bishop, standing by his throne began the Easter Mass, which would culminate in the Elevation of the Host, when the chalice containing the bread and wine that represented the risen Christ was raised high by the bishop on one side, representing the Church, and the chief deacon on the other, representing the congregation. It must have been a most impressive ceremony.

It was not yet drama, because it was still essentially liturgical in emphasis, and, in some ways, not a great advance on Amalarius' interpretation of the Mass; but it was a start, and when the 'Quem quaeritis?' trope moved to the end of Matins, where it had more room to expand, it soon became more consciously theatrical.

This emerges clearly in the *Regularis Concordia*, or *Agreed Model*, prepared by St Ethelwold of Winchester between 965 and 975 for the use and guidance of the Benedictine monks in England. Here it is no longer two angels and two deacons who enact the trope, but a *single* angel and *three* holy women. The Gospel accounts differ on the number of angels, but they are emphatic about the number of women, and this is now reflected. The choice of a single angel also increases the theatrical effectiveness of the piece by focusing attention on his message and providing a striking contrast between the single figure who represents the unity of Godhead and the three representing fallible humanity. 'Hand props' also begin to appear – the women carry 'spices' to the tomb, which are abstractly represented by thuribles, and the brother playing the angel carries a palm branch, which was one of the distinctive marks of benevolent angels in the art of the period.

There are also instructions as to how the roles should be played: the women are to move haltingly and uncertainly, 'as if they are seeking something'; the angel is to sing 'in a sweet and moderate voice', as befits an angel, so that he does not startle them; when he sings, 'Come and see where the Lord was laid', he is to do so 'as if calling them back', so he presumably beckons, and he then lifts the veil covering the sepulchre to show them the empty tomb; the Marys take up the shroud and display it to the other clergy, who represent the disciples, 'as if demonstrating that the Lord has risen and is not in it'. All these 'as if's specifically demand the kind of imaginative re-creation of the situation which is the basis of acting, so the element of imitation is much clearer here and a further step has been taken along the path to true drama, in addition to which the changes of emotion in the piece are very precisely indicated for the singers in the music.

It was not long before tropes were being used to distinguish other important ceremonies in the Church Year – all of them based directly on the Easter 'Quem quaeritis?'. At Christmas, for instance, the Nativity was hailed with the words 'Quem quaeritis in praesepe, pastores, dicite?' ('Whom do you seek in the manger shepherds, tell me?'); 'Christ the Lord and Saviour, the infant wrapped in swaddling clothes, of which the angel told us'; 'The babe is here, with Mary his mother'; and so on – with the procession this time representing the shepherds. At the Ascension we find it again: 'Quem cernitis ascendisse super astra, O Christicolae?' ('Whom did you see ascending to the stars, Christian women?'); 'Jesus who rose from the tomb, Heavenly Ones'; 'He has ascended as he promised you';

and so on. These imitations bear eloquent witness to the popularity of the new Easter trope.

In point of fact, Christmas and the feast of the Ascension were better suited than Easter to the development of drama, because the Resurrection and its associated Passion were much too sacred to be treated freely by potential dramatists. So, though the *Visitatio*, or visit of the Marys to the tomb, became much more common in cathedrals and abbey-churches during the late tenth and early eleventh centuries, it showed no signs of developing into a fully fledged Easter drama.

Christmas was quite another matter. The stories of Christ's birth felt like folk-tales and seemed far removed from the sombre accounts of the Passion, nor was any treatment of them likely to be heretical. This meant they could be dramatised without serious danger of upsetting the priesthood – so it is around Christmas that we find the next development. Towards the end of the tenth century the play of the *Pastores*, or shepherds, performed on Christmas morning, was joined by the first play about the *Magi*, the three kings bearing gifts to the manger, which was played on the traditional day of their visit – 6 January, Twelfth Night. The eleventh century saw the development of ten more *Pastores* and seven more *Magi*.

King Herod also makes his earliest appearance in two plays during this period. The first is the story of his slaughter of all the young children in Bethlehem in his vain attempt to destroy Jesus – this was designed to follow the service on 28 December, the Feast of the Holy Innocents, or Childermass. The other play in which Herod appears is more interesting because for the first time it shows a tendency to run separate incidents together. The visits of the shepherds and the kings to the stable are here fused with the kings' earlier visit to Herod. The piece has no overall name, and no indication of when it was meant to be performed – any day between Christmas Eve and Twelfth Night might be considered appropriate, but it will certainly have needed to be allotted to a specific feast-day. The extremely dramatic episode of the kings' visit to Herod never stood by itself as a liturgical play because it had no feast allotted to it – a point well worth mentioning, because it underlines the very functional nature of liturgical drama and the limitations placed upon it by the structure of the Church Year.

The end of the eleventh century sees a further development: this is the so-called *Ordo Prophetarum*, or *Procession of Prophets*, often called simply the *Prophetae*. The origins of this rather simple piece are unique. It did not derive from a trope, or even from the Bible – at least not directly. Instead, it was based on a popular sermon, wrongly attributed to St Augustine, delivered to the unbelieving Jews and pagans and the misguided Arians.

This sermon, which seems to have been written in the fifth or sixth century, contains a number of sections where the writer tries to persuade the Jews of Christ's Messianic status by drawing their attention to numerous Old Testament prophecies that were considered to be predictions of his coming. The preacher quotes the authentic prophecies of Isaiah, Jeremiah, Daniel, Moses, King David and Habbakuk - all of whom can be seen as predicting the Messiah. To these he adds the ecstatic outburst of old Simeon when he saw the baby in the Temple ('Now lettest thou thy servant depart in peace, for his eyes have seen thy salvation'); Zacharias' prediction that his son, John the Baptist, should 'go before the face of the Lord and prepare his ways'; the incident when Elisabeth, pregnant with John, visited her cousin Mary, pregnant with Jesus, and the child leapt in her womb; and Nebuchadnezzar's vision when he saw the three innocents he had thrown into the fiery furnace joined by a fourth figure who was 'like the Son of God'.

There are also two unexpected names on the list: one the Roman prophetess, the Sybil, because she made a typically obscure prophecy about God breaking down the doors of Hell and sitting in judgement, and the other Virgil, who wrote in his *Georgics* about a Virgin who should give birth to a 'new generation which descends from Heaven on high' - he was actually flattering his patron, the Emperor Augustus, but Christians took it to be a direct prophecy, and on the strength of it Dante appointed Virgil his guide through Hell in *The Divine Comedy*.

Other prophets were added to the list from time to time, particularly Balaam and his ass, which refused to pass an angel its master could not see, and when he whipped it for not moving, acquired a human voice and scolded him soundly - a lively incident which brought some humour to an otherwise sober occasion.

The long and rather tedious extract from the sermon which contained all these prophecies was originally read as a special extra 'lesson' on Christmas morning, but in the eleventh century it occurred to somebody that it would be more interesting to have a presenter introduce each prophet and then have his prophecy delivered 'in character' by a deacon.

By the end of the eleventh century, then, it is clear that Christmas has become the main point of dramatic development. The versions of the Easter *Visitatio* have so far made hardly any advance on their tenth-century form, while the plays dramatising episodes from the Christmas story are lively and imaginative, and some are already introducing elements that are not in the biblical account at all but taken from various apocryphal gospels.

The twelfth century sees a reversal of the eleventh-century trend - there is not much development at Christmas, though the sheer *number* of plays given then continues to increase, but the *Visitatio* now begins to develop at Easter. Several elements were added, the most common being an anthem for Easter which had existed independently for a long time: it was known as the *Victimae Paschali (Easter Sacrifice)* and is similar in many ways to the 'Quem quaeritis?'. It, too, begins with a question, this time directed to the Virgin Mary – 'What do you see before you, Mary?' – and she replies, 'The sepulchre of the living Christ and the glory of his resurrection.' From then on it is a hymn of motherly pride and exaltation, well suited for the purpose of building an emotional climax directly after the news of the Resurrection, where it is generally found.

To counterbalance it, in some versions, there is a lament delivered by Mary on her way to the tomb before the Resurrection, known as the *Planctus Mariae (Lamentation of Mary)*. This, too, had long existed independently as an Easter tract – a tract was a 'sorrowful anthem' – and in it the Virgin expresses her grief at her son's death very movingly. Where the *Planctus Mariae* is used in conjunction with the *Victimae Paschali* the shift in emotion before and after the Resurrection can be very powerful.

A small, but interesting, addition is found in some continental versions at the point just before the *Planctus Mariae*, when the women, before they visit the sepulchre, stop to buy the spices they need from an *unguentarius*, or ointment-seller, sometimes called simply 'the merchant'. There is no scriptural authority whatsoever for this piece of business, which seems merely to be added to give the whole process an added realism and perhaps to raise tension slightly by delaying Mary Mother's emotional display, which everybody knows is coming. The *unguentarius* was very popular in Germany and sometimes used in France, but interestingly never appears in any English play.

A more active, narrative addition to some pieces was what is often known as 'the race to the tomb'. This was based on the passage in the Scriptures that tells how, when the disciples heard the news of the Resurrection, John and Peter, the youngest disciple and the oldest, raced to the sepulchre to confirm the fact for themselves – 'They ran swiftly, the two of them together, and the other disciple was faster than Peter and came first to the tomb.'

In the presentation of this action, nothing so unseemly as actual running was involved. A presenter merely sang, or chanted, the account from the Gospel, and the two deacons representing John and Peter discreetly mimed 'running on the spot'. However, where this incident is used, it is usually the two deacons playing the disciples who draw attention to the gravecloths, instead of the Marys. They are given one each by attendants, and they display them to the choir, facing east towards the altar and the rising sun which symbolises the Resurrection, and singing, 'Behold, comrades, here are the linen gravecloths and the *sudarium*, and the body is not to be found in the sepulchre!'

It would be wrong to suggest that the liturgical drama ceased to develop after the twelfth century, but, until late in its history, it remained a very inward-looking artistic form, devoted exclusively to reaffirming the faith of true believers by reinforcing their emotional response to the Passion and the Resurrection. It has none of the missionary zeal, or sheer energy, of the vernacular plays that were later written for performance outside the church and it had no direct influence upon them – although, by its very existence it doubtless pointed the way and encouraged imitation.

At its best it was a very beautiful form of music-drama and must have done much to enrich the faith of those who could understand the Latin in which it was written, but it was very processional and static in its nature, and when, in the late fourteenth century, it sought greater theatricality and allowed itself to be influenced by the 'popular' religious drama, it became more vigorous but lost much of its unique artistic quality.

# 4

# THE CHURCH AS A
# THEATRE

Accounts of early liturgical plays constantly refer to the use of a 'sepulchre' for the Easter *Visitation* and a 'manger' for the shepherds' play at Christmas. This structure seems to have been a replica of the Holy Sepulchre in Jerusalem, which, for medieval Churchmen, meant the 'Anastasis', or 'Resurrection', a circle of columns crowned with a conical roof symbolising the vault of Heaven which had been built by the Emperor Constantine on the rocky outcrop containing the cave where Christ was originally buried.

Because of its associations, images of the Anastasis were often used as a means of invoking a blessing. For instance, life-size reproductions of it were built into some English and European churches, usually at the request of a rich crusader returning from the Holy Land. These were incorporated into the fabric of the building, either just inside or just outside the western doors, and their conical cover was incorporated into the structure of the roof. When such a 'sepulchre' was built at the western end of the church, its association with Christ's Resurrection was reinforced by the tombs of local kings and chieftains, which were often built outside the western doors in the early Middle Ages, in the hope that their closeness to a consecrated structure might enhance their chances of eternal life.

The Anastasis used as a sepulchre in the plays was quite small but made its appearance much earlier than the large-scale versions, in fact almost as soon as Constantine had completed the original monument in Jerusalem. At first it seems to have been only a model standing on the altar at Easter to remind the congregation of Christ's Resurrection. Later it was enlarged to hold a chest in which the Easter chalice was kept between Good Friday and Easter Sunday, and eventually the same model became the manger for the Nativity at Christmas, when the Easter chest was replaced, first by an icon of the Virgin and Child, and later by a realistically painted statuette. Around the altar which bore the model was erected what is known as a baldaquin. This was a canopy-like structure consisting of a dome or cone-shaped pinnacle 'floating' above the altar, either supported by four temporary pillars at its four corners, or suspended from the roof. From this hung curtains surrounding the altar on all sides, the front pair of which were theatrically drawn back during the Easter Mass just before the Host was elevated, to reveal the impressive tower-shaped Easter chalice to the congregation.

Gregory of Tours, in the sixth century, describes the arrangements at the Vatican church in Rome. Four elegant snow-white columns supported the domed roof of the structure – a recent improvement on the cone, which reminded Gregory of a large inverted bread-basket – and upon the altar beneath rested a model of the sepulchre, which he describes as an object of rare workmanship. In this instance the sides of the baldaquin, between the pillars, were enclosed with grilles, the one in front having a small window through which the faithful could see the sepulchre as they offered up their prayers. The grilles were there to ensure that the Host should not be touched by unconsecrated hands, and the wording of Gregory's account suggests that they were removed when the altar was in use. They will also have served as a useful safeguard against thieves, who were a very real danger; later, some churches in the north of Europe replaced the insubstantial baldaquin with a permanent stone structure to ensure that the church treasures remained safe, often decorating the stonework with scenes and symbols recalling the life of Christ.

It was not long before the sepulchre became a larger structure, still basically preserving the shape of the Anastasis but detached from the High Altar and often containing an altar of its own. There was no fixed tradition as to where this structure should stand in the church, but it is often described as being in the choir or presbytery (the area lying between the choir-stalls and the altar.) In England it was almost always to the stage right of the altar, on the north side of the choir, the 'good' side of the church. In Germany it is found in many different places in the building but *never*, interestingly, on the north side of the choir, although it was often on the south (or 'sinister') side, near the archway leading into the nave. At other times we find it in the body of the nave – sometimes in the middle, which was an important theatrical location, sometimes at its western end, far from the altar, and sometimes in the aisles, enveloping the altar of a saint. It could also be erected in a side-chapel, or even in the crypt beneath the choir. In France and Italy it might be found in any of these locations, even on the north side of the choir, depending on local practice.

Germany is the only country that furnishes us with an actual picture of a free-standing 'sepulchre', in a late woodcut of 1516 illustrating the merry pranks of Tyll Eulenspiegel: this proves to be not a replica of the Anastasis, but a small wooden house, rather like a tall dog-kennel or sentry-box, with the same kind of saddle roof and an opening in front where the angel is sitting.

By the end of the Middle Ages, a good many continental churches were adorned with *permanent* sepulchres in the form of elaborate stone monuments. These were highly sculptured, with figures on them representing either the entombment, the watchers at the tomb, the Marys making their Visitation, or some other appropriate scene. They are usually very solid, without any space for the concealment of priests performing the part of angels, so they were probably not used for any enactments – but they may well have been used for the 'burial' of the cross representing Christ's body, and for the symbolic Easter Elevation of the Cross when his Resurrection was proclaimed. In South Germany, where the practice lingered until the early years of this century, both permanent *and* temporary 'Holy Graves' were used for the Elevation of the Cross – but not for anything else.

In England the ecclesiastical establishment chose not to model their sepulchres on the Anastasis, except for the large-scale architectural versions built into the famous 'round' churches; nor did they favour elaborately sculptured monuments, but there is abundant evidence for the use of temporary wooden structures to represent either the sepulchre or the manger, and we also have the remains of scores of stone structures used for the same purpose. In this case, the essential part of the Easter celebrations seems to have been a large wooden chest or coffer in which the 'buried' Easter cross and the pre-consecrated Host could be kept safe between Maundy Thursday and Easter Day. This was placed within the sepulchre, where such a structure existed, but more often in an aumbry, which was a deep recess built into the wall of the church to serve as a cupboard. These exist in large numbers in English churches and are of various shapes and sizes and usually located in the north wall of the choir. For most of the year they were used to store food which was to be distributed as alms to the poor, but at Easter-time they were often used as sepulchres, and even had a reminiscent cave-like look about them.

However, the most usual place for the sepulchre, either in England or abroad, was near the altar, because of its association with the Passion, and there it formed part of a pattern linking together all those parts of the church building which had specific symbolic meanings, the 'good' and 'bad' associations relating to the north and south sides of the church becoming interwoven with a similar tradition regarding the eastern and western ends of the building, which were respectively seen as relating to Heaven and earth. These conventions, as we shall see, were consciously used by the performers of liturgical plays to achieve a visual reinforcement of the action.

Christian altars were always located at the eastern end of the church so that the congregation was facing the place of sunrise, which symbolised the Resurrection. This, and the very presence of the holy altar, gave the eastern end of the church powerful associations with holiness, Heaven, salvation and everlasting life and joy; and since the human mind is very prone to think in dichotomies, or pairs of opposites, the great western doors through which the most important people always entered the building became strongly associated with the non-spiritual, material world of mutability, or constant change, of which death was an important part.

As we have seen, the early structures representing the Anastasis, which after all first and foremost covered Christ's *tomb*, also tended to be built at the west end of the church, near the royal mausoleums, and this tended to give the *whole* of the nave an association with the death of kings, the death of Christ, and the material and corruptible world – indeed, the western end of the church was often nicknamed 'Galilee'. A natural extension of this thought was that the great western doors, standing furthest from the altar, represented the Gates of Hell itself – as in Amalarius' consecration ceremony – while the high altar represented Heaven and Paradise, which were incorruptible.

Many continental scholars believe that it was this east–west axis that caused the liturgical drama to expand progressively from the altar into the body of the church. They also suggest that there was a tendency to move towards the western end because all continental cathedrals and abbeys had a tribune, or high balcony, at that end, above the great doors, which was an ideal place both visually and acoustically for angels to sing from – to the shepherds, for instance, in the Nativity plays.

No doubt where a tribune existed it will have exercised a powerful influence on the movement of the drama westwards, but in England, despite a lack of tribunes, performances of liturgical plays still invaded the nave, so we must assume that the cause was more general – perhaps a desire to move these rather materialistic presentations of spiritual truths away from the altar and its holy mysteries, perhaps a realisation that the congregation would see and hear better if the plays were nearer to them, and quite possibly an artistic realisation of the power of the symbolism of east and west and a desire to use it to underline aspects of the plays which the north–south symbolism could not cope with. The idea, sometimes advanced, that drama merely overflowed from the chancel into the nave because it was becoming too expansive to be contained in the eastern end of the church is much too simplistic.

As the nave came more into use, two further important locations established themselves. The centre of the nave, not unnaturally, is the most important, and the action relating to the material world was usually sited there, with occasional forays towards Heaven and everlasting life in the east or death and Hell in the west – but there was often a secondary focus employed at what the rubrics call 'the centre of the *church*' as opposed to 'the centre of the *nave*'. This can only mean the point where the nave is intersected by the two transepts running north and south, forming a symbolical Christian cross – indeed it must mean the precise centre of that cross. It is therefore interesting to find that in the plays this focus is normally used to represent the Church as a force in society; in other words, it is where we find the disciples or the representatives of the Christian community gathering – as they do in the Tours play of the Resurrection.

A demonstration of the distinction made between these two locations is provided by *The Procession of the Prophets* at Rouen, where the instructions to the actors are quite specific. A 'burning fiery furnace' is set in the centre of the *nave*, together with an idol and the seat of Nebuchadnezzar. The ecclesiastical procession which begins the piece, however, is instructed to proceed to the middle of the *church*, where it meets with six Jews and six gentiles, the Jews probably on the 'sinister' side and the gentiles on the 'good'. The choristers as a whole then act as presenters, from their heavenly location near the altar, and, as they are called, the prophets enter through the western door, and each sings his piece, mingling his voice antiphonally with those of the choir. After Virgil's appearance, attention shifts to the centre of the nave, where Nebuchadnezzar orders the three young Hebrews ('the children', as they are often called) to worship the idol and, when they refuse, has them cast into the fiery furnace by his guards, where they are soon joined by the fourth figure, who looks like the Son of God and doubtless carries a small cross. When this is all over, the last of the prophets emerges from the western door. This is the Roman Sybil, whose prophecies call down the horrors of the Day of Judgement upon all unbelievers, including Nebuchadnezzar and his guards, who quail before her. All the participants in the action then become simple priests again and join the procession, which returns to the choir, establishing an easterly, heavenward movement of the blessed which is constantly repeated in these plays.

The play of the *Resurrection* at Tours gives us another example of the use of the church. This time Pilate's judgement seat was the main focus, standing at the centre of the nave, presumably on a raised platform, for greater emphasis. The sepulchre was located in a porch between the inner and outer western doors. It was not seen during the performance, so we do not know whether any physical representation was involved. The soldiers sent by Pilate to keep watch over the sepulchre therefore travelled from his judgement seat in a very worldly, negative direction. The disciples and the holy women were located as a group in front of the choir, in the centre of the church, where we would expect them to be. The three Marys broke away from this group when they went to visit the tomb, and travelled down the 'sinister' side of the church, implying their distress, until somewhere along the side of the nave they met the ointment-seller. They then entered the sepulchre beyond the western inner doors, probably using the small door which is always provided for informal use. After they had re-emerged and displayed the grave-cloths, the *hortulanus*, or 'gardener', episode occurred. This was the incident recorded in the Scriptures when 'Mary Maudlin' mistook the risen Lord for a gardener. This very emotional scene occurred just inside the inner doors on the 'good' side of the church. After this John and Peter detached themselves from the group of disciples, and came running, in a decorous fashion, down the 'good', or triumphant, side of the church to see the evidence for themselves, after which, as usual, all the holy characters, spiritually strengthened, returned to the choir in the east. What precisely happened to Pilate and the soldiers is not clear – perhaps they merely withdrew when their parts were done and, if so, it will surely have been to the western door.

In the *Pastores*, or shepherds' play, at Rouen, as in many others, the shepherds are tending their sheep at the extreme western end of the nave, which represents their condition of worldly ignorance, but, when they hear the news of Christ's birth from an angel singing up on the tribune above them, they proceed eastwards towards the manger, which is located in the choir, thus symbolising their search for enlightenment. When they arrive there, a curtain is drawn to reveal the Virgin and Child, which could have been a picture or a statuette, or even a live priest holding a doll. After their act of adoration, during which the Virgin says nothing – unlike her equivalent in the vernacular plays – the shepherds rejoice and praise God at the altar, and then return to the world, in the west, to spread the news of what they have seen.

In *The Raising of Lazarus* at Orleans we have a new development. It is the earliest piece we know which uses the central area of the nave to represent *two different places* at different times. First it represents the house of Simon in which Lazarus lies ill. Lazarus then dies, and is transported for burial towards a sepulchre, real or imagined, near the western door – the furthest possible distance from heavenly bliss. Christ, when he comes to raise Lazarus from the dead, first descends from the choir in the east to the centre of the nave, which now represents Mount Olivet, where he is found by Lazarus' relatives, and then penetrates with them even further into the world of corruption in order to raise Lazarus from the dead. After Lazarus' resurrection, Jesus leads him back, rejoicing, towards the altar, Heaven and salvation. It is interesting to realise, in this instance, that the sepulchre Lazarus is taken to may well be the same sepulchre as is used on Easter morning, in which case Christ's own Resurrection would be vividly symbolised by his raising of Lazarus.

Finally, it may be useful to consider one piece in greater detail, fleshing out the symbolic movements with words and action. A good example to take is the Rouen version of a very popular play, known as the *Peregrinus*, or *Pilgrim*, that originated in the twelfth century. This was

41

based on the Scriptural story of how the risen Christ met two of his disciples on the road to Emmaus and they failed to recognise him. The actors, of course, sing throughout, as is the case with all liturgical plays.

In the centre of the nave there is a structure representing the castle of Emmaus, which consists of a simple raised platform carrying a table with a loaf of bread upon it and three chairs. After the blessing at the end of the service, a procession leaves the holy altar in the east and proceeds down the nave of the church as far as the castle, thus symbolising the gracious desire of Heaven to extend hope to sinful man, who lives in ignorance. The procession then stops and chants the psalm beginning 'When Israel came out of Egypt'. When the psalm is ended, two sub-deacons, clothed in tunics with copes worn over them and carrying staffs and wallets like pilgrims, enter the church by the 'worldly' western doors and advance slowly up the 'sinister' side of the building towards the procession. They stop when they reach it and intone the hymn 'Jesus our Redeemer'. On the line 'We are contented to see thy face', a priest representing the risen Christ, lightly clad in nothing but an alb and an amice (a long white tunic and a simple neckcloth), with his feet bare and carrying a small cross in his hands, also enters by the western doors, which represent the grave from which he has risen, and comes towards them, up the 'good' side of the building, with his head downcast. All the participants, we notice, are moving in an easterly direction, from materialism towards the light of the rising sun, which implies spiritual revelation and realisation.

When he reaches the two pilgrims, the priest suddenly stops and asks, 'What talk is this you exchange between you as you travel along so sadly?' They look at him with gestures of astonishment and say, 'You must be the only pilgrim in Jerusalem who has not heard about the happenings of the last few days!' 'What happenings?' asks the priest; and the pilgrims reply, 'The happenings at the death of Jesus of Nazareth, who was a prophet mighty in deed and word before God and all the people.' Then the priest looks at each of them in turn and says, 'O fools and slow to believe what the prophets have foretold!'

After these words, he draws away from them, as if he is in a hurry, but the two disciples hasten after him and invite him to share their meal, using their staffs to point out the castle of Emmaus and saying, 'Stay with us, for evening approaches.' As they deliver these words, they lead him towards the central platform, and having mounted it, they seat themselves at the table; the Lord, sitting between the two of them, breaks the bread and blesses it. As he breaks the bread they recognise him, and he suddenly steps back and vanishes from sight. The pilgrims rise, as if they are thunderstruck, and turning to the procession sing an anthem of rejoicing.

When that is done they turn towards the pulpit and chant the first line of the *Victimae Paschali* - 'Tell us, Mary, what do you see before you?' -

to which a priest clad in a dalmatic (an elaborately decorated overgarment) with an amice knotted round his head like a woman, produces and displays two cloths, one in each hand, and replies, 'The heavenly witnesses, the sudarium and the gravecloths.' This clearly symbolises the final acceptance by the two disciples of the truth of the Resurrection. Then, after a pause, the priest representing Mary proclaims, 'Christ, our hope, is risen, and has gone before us into Galilee.' The choir and Mary then pick up the last two lines of the *Victimae Paschali*, after which Mary and the pilgrims retire eastward to the choir and the altar, thus physically demonstrating their salvation, and are followed, after a brief blessing, by the members of the original procession.

It was thought at one time that Christ's disappearance in this play was perhaps effected by a trap-door in the Emmaus platform, but more recently a series of woodcuts illustrating the actual performance has been discovered, and these show him simply tiptoeing away, presumably on his way to the altar. This usefully underlines the basic simplicity of staging in the best liturgical plays. The gross theatricality of the trap-door was to be reserved for the vernacular plays in the market-place; it was not suitable, or necessary, in a drama demonstrating faith.

These few examples, which carry instructions for staging in their text, show clearly how the symbolic geography of the church was used by the actors to underline the meaning of liturgical plays. There is less information available about the settings, costumes and styles of acting used, but what exists is still indicative.

The conventions relating to settings are fairly clear, and very simple, and were later adopted and elaborated in vernacular performances. Presentation of a play clearly involved reserving a space for the actors to perform in. This was known as the *platea*, usually translated 'the Place' in Middle English, and in the liturgical pieces it often consisted of a platform. On this platform, or space, there was often a *sedes* or *siège* - a 'seat', which was simply a chair, possibly a fairly large ecclesiastical chair with arms. This could obviously signify a throne, but it could also represent *any* kind of place by extension - the ointment-seller's shop, for instance, or a palace, or even a town, such as Jerusalem or Damas; it could be whatever it needed to be.

Simplicity of this kind marked all true liturgical presentations. Usually nothing but church furniture was used. The castle of Emmaus, as we saw, was merely a platform with a table and chairs on it, and we find that Nebuchadnezzar's burning fiery furnace was also a simple platform, perhaps painted red, or decorated with flames round the edge. Admittedly, the 'idol' in the same play must have been specially constructed, but for the most part liturgical drama was strictly conventional and did not call for realistic, representational decor.

Similarly, the costuming of the pieces was mostly achieved by ringing variations on the usual vestments of the clergy. They might shed their outer cope to represent poverty or humility, or don it to represent the fact that they were travelling, in which case they were also likely to carry the usual wallet (or 'scrip') and a staff. They might wear an amice knotted round their head to look like a woman's head scarf, or don a dalmatic in order to imply their importance, but all the necessary effects were achieved with a minimum of fuss and a maximum call upon the audience's imagination.

'Special effects' in the early liturgical plays seem to be limited to the presentation of the star of Bethlehem. In some places this simply 'appears', an effect easily achieved by drawing back a screen or curtain which concealed the lamp, but it often travels before the three kings, leading them to the manger in the choir, and this may have involved drawing a lighted lamp along a fixed wire of some kind in front of them. However, in one instance it both rises *and* travels before the kings, which must have required more complicated rigging – unless it was simply carried by a priest on the end of a long pole.

On the subject of acting, the rubrics of the liturgical plays are unfortunately not very revealing, but there are one or two exceptions. Outstanding amongst these is a thirteenth-century *Lament of Mary*, from the cathedral of Cividale del Friuli, a few miles north of Venice. It contains the usual characters – Christ's favourite disciple, John, and the three Marys – and, in addition, there are two groups on opposite sides of the stage, one representing mourning men and the other mourning women. Behind them stands Christ's cross, with a life-sized image of the dead Christ upon it, flanked by two lesser crosses carrying the two thieves.

The rubrics here are remarkably specific. There are directions given for the main actors' gestures virtually at every other line, usually in advance of the line to which they refer. Most frequently the performers strike their breasts, to express their grief, or *point* to whatever is mentioned in the line – themselves, Christ, his wounded side, the Cross, the two thieves, Christ's crown of thorns, the angel nearby, the audience, and so forth. At moments of appeal they reach out their arms to the other characters, or to Christ, to the chorus of men or women on stage, or to the congregation. The Virgin Mary sometimes embraces other characters – on one occasion John, on another both the other Marys simultaneously 'around the neck' – a specific instruction which seems to imply that they were kneeling on either side of her, for they both rise a moment later and stand with their hands outstretched towards her, a very symmetrical composition. Later she embraces Mary Magdalen with both arms, and turns half-round to look at the Cross while doing so. To show despair, the actors are instructed to let their hands drop limply by their sides, and both Mary Magdalen and the Virgin at various times simulate weeping and wipe away their tears.

44

The movement is very formal, almost continuous, and is used, in a rhetorical fashion, to underline the emotions displayed and draw attention to the subjects mentioned. There *are* more personal moments, but they are few and far between – Magdalen genuflects deeply before the Cross, John points disdainfully at the audience when he proclaims that Christ's sacrifice was made necessary by the wickedness of man, and Mary mother of James opens her arms and turns, as if she wants to invite the whole audience to sympathise with her, before she covers her eyes with her hands on the line 'Who is there here who would not weep to see Christ's mother in such deep sorrow?'

However, the *Planctus Mariae* deals with a highly serious subject and it would be wrong to think that all liturgical drama was played in this way. This is clearly shown by the performance of one of the characters in the Christmas play from Benediktbeuern in Bavaria, a piece dating from 1230 or earlier, which is unlikely to have been influenced by any vernacular tradition.

The character concerned is the villain Archisynagogus, the leader of the Jews, and his style of acting is much more informal. When he hears the prophecies about Christ's coming, he replies indignantly, 'agitating his head and his entire body and striking the ground with his foot, imitating with his stick the mannerisms of a Jew in all ways'; at one argument in favour of Christ advanced by St Augustine, he answers with 'immoderate and violent laughter'; and when the saint calls upon the Jews to see sense and embrace Christianity, he 'bawls and shouts, agitating his body and head, and deriding the prophecies'; but when Herod calls for his advice later on, he enters 'with colossal pride' and gives vicious advice with an appearance of 'great wisdom and eloquence'. This is a somewhat more realistic performance, but it is of a large-scale, pantomimic kind, and, as with the Cividale *Planctus*, the object is still mainly to get over the message as clearly as possible.

We should never forget that the actors in liturgical plays were clergymen, not professional performers. True, ecclesiastical law dating from Roman times forbade clerics to act or to associate with actors, but Pope Innocent III ruled in 1207 that plays and entertainments that were undertaken primarily for devotional purposes were acceptable, provided they did not cause the people to miss church services and did not contain bawdy or heretical matter likely to undermine their faith; and this seems to have remained a guiding principle for the priesthood. Gregory IX also accepts the involvement of clergymen in plays representing the Nativity, King Herod, the Magi, Rachel and the Easter story. Admittedly, from 1213 we find many bishops forbidding the clergy to take part in 'ludos inhonestos' ('dishonest amusements'), but these seem to be sotties, dances in churchyards, performances by disguised persons at Christmas, May games, minstrelsy and morris dancing, all of which were considered either irreverent or downright pagan. By contrast, the attitude to liturgical performances seems to have been wholly positive – even, at times, positively beneficial. For instance, in 1313 a scholarly and very worthy candidate for the position of Archbishop of Canterbury was passed over in favour of Walter Reynolds, Bishop of Worcester, who, as a contemporary observes, 'had recently been a mere clerk and was scarcely literate', but who 'excelled in theatrical presentations, and through this obtained the king's favour'.

Though the simple and pious ceremonies described in this chapter are almost all relatively late examples of liturgical drama, they are free of influence from the street and the market-place and have all the directness and emotive power which mark the form at its best. The essence of these plays was the story they told and its spiritual significance, which was clearly underscored by the movements and gestures of the performers, most of which had an accepted symbolic meaning, and above all by the magnificently expressive music which clothed both movement and words. There was no need for vulgar theatricality: even the sepulchre was only elaborate because of the central importance of the Resurrection – otherwise a simple platform and the basic furnishings and vestments of the church were all that the clergy performing the pieces required.

# 5

# THE LANGUAGE OF
# THE PEOPLE

Christian plays written in the vernacular – the language of the people –
proved much more flexible than their liturgical counterparts. The first
complete examples we possess date from the latter part of the twelfth
century, but they seem much too accomplished to be the first of their
kind. One of these plays, called the *Auto de los Reyes Magos*, or *Play of
the Wise Kings*, is in Spanish, and is not yet available in translation, so it
is not dealt with here. The other two plays, the *Mystère d'Adam* or *Play of
Adam*, and the *Seinte Resurrection* or *Holy Resurrection*, originally
written in Norman French, are both available in English and prove to be
very informative – the more so, because they are clearly by different
authors and built on different structural principles.

Neither play stands in isolation. The *Adam* manuscript contains not
only the Fall of Adam and Eve, but Cain's murder of Abel and a very basic
Procession of the Prophets. The *Resurrection* manuscript – which is
incomplete – contains the begging of Christ's body by Joseph of
Arimathea, its Deposition from the Cross and burial in the tomb, and
many surrounding details of the story, but it is plain from the text that it
originally also contained a Harrowing of Hell, a Resurrection, and
appearances by Christ to the disciples both on the road to Emmaus and
later in Galilee – suggesting that the author meant to end his piece with
Christ's Ascension into Heaven, which was a natural climax for the
Passion.

Because they contain closely related sequences of plays, both manuscripts were once thought to be parts of larger 'cycles' that had not been
preserved – but a miracle- or mystery-cycle, as will be shown later,
involves more than merely grouping plays together in a manuscript: the
plays it contains are theologically and symbolically bound together in
such a way that constant analogies are drawn between different parts of
the cycle. These two collections of plays are little more than extended
'Bible stories'. The *Adam* manuscript comes nearest to being a cycle,
because its first two parts, the Fall of Man and the Murder of Abel, both
suggest the unavoidable sinfulness of 'natural' man, while the third part,

47

the Procession of the Prophets, counterbalances this pessimism with a promise of eventual salvation – but this is no more than the shadow of a cyclical structure, and seems to have arisen by chance. The manuscript containing *The Holy Resurrection* has no comparable pattern, and consists merely of the basic events of the Passion.

On the other hand, in their full form, either of the groups of plays being considered would have been far too long to be attached to any service, and it is clear that, rather than underpinning the liturgy, they are intended to dramatise the 'lessons', or Bible readings, given at specific daily services. As a result, they treat their material as religious 'history' – and historical narrative, however elementary, demands a different dramatic approach from the largely descriptive material used to reinforce the liturgy.

Liturgical pieces are unwilling to desert the specific words of the holy texts, which in some sense provide an assurance that the miraculous fusion of the everyday and the spiritual will occur – to substitute other words might destroy the power of the ritual. History, on the other hand, can be told in any words, providing they are vigorous and interesting – and when re-telling a historical tale the author can speculate freely about the feelings and motivations of the characters involved; indeed, the audience will expect it.

So the plays in these collections are the second strand of the threefold cord of religious theatre that runs through the Middle Ages. The liturgical drama arises from elaboration of parts of the sacred ritual; the vernacular drama springs from the 'lessons', or instructive daily readings; and the moral drama, to be considered later, is an offshoot of the sermon, in which the significance of the lessons is expounded by the priest. Thus each part of the daily service finds theatrical expression. The three types of drama also developed in that order, because at first the liturgy was all-important; then, later, the theologians focused their attention on the deeper meanings of holy Scripture, from which the lessons were taken; and it was only with the late arrival of the friars that the sermon became a vital part of the service.

Originally the *Adam* was mistaken for a liturgical play, because, though it is mostly in Norman French, it incorporates Latin 'responsories', which are anthems composed to be sung between the two lessons in the daily service and closely based upon them. The responsories in question had been chosen centuries before by Pope Gregory I for the second Sunday before Lent and appear in his *Liber Responsalis* in precisely the same order as they do in the play. So it is clear that the writer – who was probably a clergyman – set out to dramatise the series of Bible readings proper to the services of that particular day and felt the responsories were an indispensable part of the package.

The author of *The Holy Resurrection* indicates his intentions much more clearly. In the margin, at four key points, he has written quotations from Matthew's or John's Gospel which show that he proposed to dramatise the events of the New Testament from the Deposition to the Ascension – this time basing his play on a series of lessons read on the days surrounding Easter.

In essence, both of the plays were a kind of informative 'picture-book', matching the Biblical stories painted on the walls and stained into the windows of the church, and, like them, they were intended to provide delight and instruction for the congregation. The audience watching them would be quite relaxed, and even disposed to laugh when the material was humorous. The enactment was not fraught with mystical meaning and powerful emotion, like the Elevation of the Host, nor was the 'real body' of Christ present in the image taken down from the Cross, any more than the real power of Jehovah was present in the actor playing God. The plays did not need a sacred place to be performed in, and since the intention behind them was to instruct, they were likely to be most effective outside the church where they could make contact with members of the community who were not well-informed church-goers – that was why they were written in the language of the people, instead of that of the priests. In any case, it is unlikely that local vicars, while welcoming the missionary effort involved, will have wanted to see the plays performed in the church building – not for theological reasons, but because the church was a busy place, with seven services a day following the early Mass – matins, prime, tierce, sext, nones, vespers and compline – and confessions to be heard besides.

The vernacular drama's decor and costumes also cost much more than the makeshift theatrical arrangements for liturgical plays, and in the twelfth century the Church had no money to spend on expensive costumes or special properties – its surpluses were very firmly earmarked for the help of the poor, the support of widows and orphans, and the purchase of impressive status symbols – like rich copes and precious church plate – or land for the establishment of new monastic foundations. In short, there were strong reasons for non-liturgical drama to be performed outside the church building.

There seems to have been no direct association between early vernacular drama and its liturgical predecessor. This can be clearly demonstrated from *The Holy Resurrection*, which handles the same subject-matter as the liturgical plays. The two forms differ very obviously in their choice and presentation of material. To list some examples from the play: Joseph asks permission to take down Christ's body before his side has been pierced by the spear (this never happens in liturgical drama); Pilate is reluctant to grant his request (whereas in liturgical drama he never hesitates); blind Longinus, who thrusts the spear into Christ's side, is a beggar hired for the purpose by the soldiery (in the liturgical drama he is always a soldier); when the blood from Christ's side falls on his hands, and he puts these to his eyes, his blindness is healed (this only happens in very late liturgical drama, where it is borrowed from the vernacular tradition); Pilate has Longinus imprisoned because he does not want the news of the miracle to be spread (which never occurs in liturgical drama); there is no mention of the grave-cloths during the Deposition from the Cross, nor are the three Holy Women present (in sharp contrast to the liturgical drama); Pilate's soldiers volunteer to stand watch over the tomb, when their liturgical counterparts have to be either ordered or bribed to do so; and, finally, Caiaphas, the high priest, who goes with the soldiers to the tomb, makes them swear an oath on the Scriptures of the Old Testament (not only is this not known in any liturgical version, but it seems to be unique to this particular play and has no Biblical authority whatever).

Another feature of vernacular plays is their originality. The liturgical drama had no place for originality: it was concerned only with what the sacred texts recorded and what that signified. By contrast, the vernacular plays were interested in character and motive, on an elementary level. In *The Holy Resurrection*, for instance, Pilate's reluctance to let Joseph of Arimathea have the body turns him into a cautious administrator or bureaucrat, unwilling to act until he has checked the facts. It is not a very developed characterisation, but it goes beyond the Biblical source, and creates extra dramatic tension between the two men.

Similarly, the pathos of the Longinus incident is magnified in order to play on the emotions of the audience – though here the author seems more likely to be borrowing from a folk-tradition than using his own imagination: plainly some kind of legend had arisen out of a conflation of the centurion who witnessed Christ's death and acknowledged his divinity and the soldier who actually pierced Christ's side (both only brief references in the Gospels), together with a feeling that the Crucifixion ought to have some associated miracle. In addition, Longinus' acceptance of bribes and later conversion implies a contrast between greed and faith which is reminiscent, in some ways, of Judas selling Christ for thirty pieces of silver and then regretting it.

Again, the fact that Pilate's soldiers volunteer is in no way essential to the plot, but seems to be an attempt to make these colourless figures more interesting by characterising them as boastful and over-eager. Unfortunately we do not know whether this idea was developed further by the author, because the manuscript comes to a premature end just after they have been sworn in on the Old Testament. That action, too, ties up with a new characterisation of Caiaphas, who now not only suggests that a guard should be placed over the tomb, but vindictively goes with them and swears them in because he is convinced they will let the Christians slip by and steal the body. Again, this is crude characterisation, but the swearing-in on the Old Testament is a nice touch, made theatrically larger and more important by having a lesser priest bring in the Scriptures for them to swear on. Incidentally, this episode would probably have been sacrilege if it had occurred in a liturgical play.

To sum up, because the object of the vernacular drama was to teach by entertaining, it had to entertain in order to teach – and to entertain it had to have a certain psychological realism and novelty. It could no longer present events in Scripture simply 'because they were so'; it needed to explain them in human terms. Above all, the characters must be believable – which means that however remarkable the circumstances in which they find themselves, their behaviour must feel right to the audience.

So the vernacular drama goes in for characterisation, though it does not go much beyond types: Pilate is cautious and political, the soldiers are ferocious and boastful, Caiaphas is malicious, and Joseph and Nicodemus are pious. Longinus is the only character whose motives change, and that is a simple conversion, from greed to devotion when his blindness is cured. There is no ambivalence, no ambiguity, no moral complex investigated in any of the characters, no sense anywhere of two separate impulses, no little saint and little devil pulling simultaneously in opposite directions, no internal tension. Each character shows a single emotion or motivation, and shows it quite openly.

Conveniently, *The Holy Resurrection* also provides a very full account of the conventions of popular staging at the time. There is a long, rhymed list of instructions at the beginning of the manuscript telling the presenters what kind of locations are to be prepared for the play, and how they are to relate to one another. The instructions are interesting because they describe for the first time the normal medieval method of staging plays. It is a method we now call *décor simultané*, or 'simultaneous staging', and seems to have evolved from the liturgical drama, although here it is already much more refined. Basically it involves creating a number of different locations for the actors to appear in, which are all present on stage at the same time, and moving the actors from location to location as necessary. The text clearly distinguishes three types of location, which later prove to be the norm for this kind of staging: simple 'places' ('lius') where things happen, 'stations' ('estals'), where groups of characters stand at the beginning of the play, and 'houses' ('mansions'), which are usually buildings like a prison or the sepulchre, but in this case also include the Cross; so the term means any 'place' on which a structure stands.

The layout is simple. Imagine five structural houses, or mansions, arranged in a curve at the back of the playing area, with you yourself standing at the centre of the circle which creates that curve. Directly in front of you is the Cross: to its right from your point of view, on the

51

'sinister' side, stands first a prison and then Hell, probably already represented by an elaborate, monster-like, Hell Mouth. To the left of the Cross, on its 'good' side, stands first the sepulchre, quite possibly a replica of the Anastasis, and, to the extreme left, counterbalancing Hell, the mansion of Heaven.

In front of each of the four mansions other than the Cross there is a related station, with the characters appropriate to it. From the audience's point of view these are: in front of Heaven, to the extreme left, the naturally virtuous Joseph of Arimathea and Nicodemus, together with some servants; in front of Hell, to the extreme right, Pontius Pilate and his knights; to the left centre, in front of the sepulchre, the disciples and the Marys, apparently standing decorously in two separate groups; and to the right centre, in front of the prison, the high priest Caiaphas supported by a party of Jews. Nobody actually stands in front of the Cross at the beginning of the play, but there are two 'places' in front of it which become significant later in the action: near the spectators is a spot understood to be Emmaus or Galilee at different times, and midway between it and the Cross, is a lesser 'place' which is used as a meeting point, first for Longinus and later for other characters.

A simple imaginative transposition will make the association with liturgical staging in the church obvious. If we imagine, for a moment, the Cross standing in a church building, directly in front of the altar, where the Elevation of the Host occurs, we can see that everything falls into place. The audience, like the church congregation, is facing east, the holiest part of the stage is furthest from them and 'Galilee' is nearest, so they are clearly in the domain of sin and death and in urgent need of salvation. The other stations are also allocated as would be usual in the church, on the 'good' or the 'sinister' side as appropriate.

The only new feature of the presentation, which we find repeated in later stagings, is a stronger sense of formal balance: Heaven is balanced by Hell, and the sepulchre by the prison. The character-placements at the beginning of the play reflect the same tendency: closer to the Cross we have the two conflicting religious interests of Christianity and Jewry represented by Christ's followers and Caiaphas and his Jews, while on the outer flanks stand the representatives of heavenly and earthly authority, the merchant Joseph standing for those who act from a natural sense of goodness, and Pontius Pilate representing the earthly power of Imperial Rome. This conflict between heavenly and earthly authority is picked up at the beginning of the play.

Unfortunately, though, all these mansions and stations dominate the dramatist's thinking. He sees his piece rather like a series of chess moves: 'Joseph to Herod's seat', 'Herod's knights to the central station with Longinus', and so forth. He also finds it impossible to let any movement pass without a few lines of dialogue, even if it is only to say, in effect,

'Now we are certainly here, having travelled from there with much toil.' And he is very unwilling to split lines, or even to work in any unit smaller than a rhymed quatrain. All this obscures the proper focuses of action and makes the piece rather tedious.

Characterisation, too, is hindered by the fact that all the characters use exactly the same language. Pilate speaks just like his soldiers, vicious Caiaphas precisely like pious Joseph, and what later writers called the 'decorum' of speech is not observed, it is not 'made proper' to the situation and personality of the character uttering it. The writer employs a kind of neutral 'high style' which makes the play feel scrupulously 'correct' and rather bloodless, as if it had been intended for a highly refined finishing-school for young ladies.

This criticism would be very unfair if it could be shown that nothing better was possible at the time, but the author of the *Play of Adam* proves that much more could be done; indeed, the piece is arguably the best treatment that the Fall of Man ever received in medieval times. The language used is very varied, ranging from the frigid respectability of God, via the cultured smoothness of the Devil, to the vigorous expressions of the peasantry; nor does the author let the verse form dictate to him: he splits up not only stanzas but rhyming couplets, and even individual lines when he feels like it, giving half to one character and half to another. As a result he gets his focus where he wants it, though the focus he chooses sometimes seems strange to us, because it is theological and not humanistic. For instance, he focuses strongly on Adam's regrets and the reproaches he heaps upon Eve after they have been cast out of Paradise. This is absolutely typical of plays of the Fall, but a modern audience finds it too long and uninteresting, because nowadays characterisation is the main source of interest and the theme of a play is expected to be psychological. The medieval audience was quite different: Adam and Eve spoke on *their* behalf, and they accepted the lamentations as a heartfelt expression of the repentance they felt for their own constant backsliding from God's commandments. Nowadays a political play might provide a comparable satisfaction for socialists, by giving voice to their feelings about the situation of the poor and the inadequacies of the social services – and would probably appear just as dull to any uncommitted spectator!

The characterisation is strong. Eve is rather pert, and keen to be independent, contrary to God's plan, which requires her to subject herself to Adam – a weakness which gives the Devil his chance. Adam is rather stuffy, over-assertive and unimaginative, and at the key moment – the plucking and offering of the fruit – he is so flabbergasted by Eve's performing an independent act that he does not know what to do or say, and when she calmly proceeds to eat some of the apple and then offer it to him with the equivalent of 'It tastes fine, now you have a bite', he really has no course open to him, if he is not to lose the initiative for ever, but to say, in effect, 'Okay, I trust you. You're my partner after all', and take a bite as requested. The Devil is suitably slippery: his language is highly polished, very superior to Eve's simple country French, and he gives the impression of being an idle philanderer from the court. Adam does not take to him at all, and when he sees Eve talking to him he reacts like a typical jealous husband.

Physically, the presentation of the play is much simpler than that of *The Holy Resurrection*, requiring only a central 'Place', where most of the action occurs, and two 'mansions', a Paradise and a Hell, on opposite sides. However, the decor seems to have been quite impressive. At the beginning the stage directions read:

> Let paradise be constructed in a prominent high place; let curtains and silken hangings be placed around it at such a height that those persons who are in paradise can be seen only from the shoulders upwards; let sweet-smelling flowers and foliage be planted there; within let there be various trees with fruits hanging on them, so that the spot may seem as delightful as possible.

Then follows an instruction reminiscent of the acting-directions in the Cividale Passion: 'Whenever a character mentions paradise, let him look in that direction and point it out with his hand.' Within the garden, God similarly points out the 'forbidden tree', which must have had practicable fruit because it is picked and eaten. It was probably the traditional apple tree.

Later on the Devil withdraws to 'the Gates of Hell'. This location is mentioned again when Adam and Eve die:

> Then the Devil will come and three or four other devils with him, carrying in their hands chains and iron fetters which they will put on the necks of Adam and Eve. And some will push them and others drag them to Hell; still more devils will be standing near Hell waiting for them as they come, and these will make a great dancing and jubilation over their damnation; each of these other devils will point at them as they come, and they will take them and put them into Hell. And therein they will cause a great smoke to arise, and they will shout to one another in Hell rejoicing, and they will bang together their pots and cauldrons, so that they may be heard outside. And after a short while the devils will issue forth, scattering across the Place, although some of them will remain in Hell.

In fact the devils in the piece are quite active and scatter about the Place more than once. For instance, when God has just shown Adam and Eve the garden, and they are 'walking about virtuously' taking delight in it, 'devils run to and fro through the Place, making appropriate gestures;

and . . . come, one after another, close to Paradise, showing Eve the forbidden fruit as if tempting her to eat it'. After his first rebuff by Adam, the Devil withdraws, gathers together some of his companions, and 'makes a foray through the Place': but after his second rebuff by Adam he first goes sadly back to the Gates of Hell 'to hold conference with the other demons', and then almost immediately makes 'a foray amongst the *people*', which clearly means the audience – and in view of the superstitious belief in devils, and the 'magical' quality of the masks, we can imagine how frightening this tactic would have been.

Apart from these demonic outbursts, indications of gesture and movement in the play are relatively few. The initial rubric says that Adam stands next to God with a peaceful countenance while Eve on his other side – presumably his 'sinister' left – is 'not quite humble enough'. Adam is to be well rehearsed, so he is not too hasty or too slow in answering: and all the actors are to receive similar coaching so that they speak in the proper place, deliver their lines in the right order, and 'make gestures appropriate to the things of which they speak'. The Devil is to address Eve 'fawningly' and when Adam scolds her he is instructed to seem annoyed with her. When he later blames her for their misfortune he is instructed to raise his fist to her, and so on. This suggests a mixed acting style, ranging from the purely indicative pointing at important things when they are mentioned, by way of rhetorical gestures 'appropriate to the things of which they speak', to quite detailed, realistic effects, like the devils' 'appropriate gestures', which are presumably vulgar, and the requirement for Eve to stand in a manner which shows that she is 'not quite humble enough', which would be quite a test for even a skilled actor.

Costume is simple but effective: Adam and Eve in their original innocence are dressed in red and white clothes respectively, and Eve has a matching white wimple on her head. Cain and Abel in the next play are also dressed in red and white respectively, so the conclusion must be that red stands for blood and passion, and white for innocence and purity. When Adam and Eve fall, they stoop down in Paradise, change their costume, and finally emerge in 'poor clothes sewn together out of fig leaves'. At the opening of the play God the Creator wears a dalmatic, as the risen Christ often does in liturgical plays – in which God, incidentally, never appears. However, when he walks in the garden in the cool of the evening, he appears only in a stole, giving a strong impression of enjoying the coolness. Presumably the devils wore devil costumes and masks, as in later vernacular plays, and since Adam's and Cain's costumes were red, theirs were probably black.

Properties are equally few, and either intended to create a realistic impression or to be functional. The trees in the garden, as already mentioned, seem to have real fruit attached to them, or at least the Tree of

Knowledge does. There are also an 'ingeniously contrived serpent', which arises alongside the trunk of the tree; a flaming sword for the angel clothed in white who bans the re-entry of Adam and Eve into Paradise; a spade for the fallen Adam and a rake for the fallen Eve, with which they pretend to till the ground; thorns and thistles for the Devil to scatter amongst their crops; chains, as we have seen, to drag all the characters to Hell, two great stones to act as altars for Cain's and Abel's offerings; a lamb and incense (to make smoke) for Abel's offering; a handful of corn for Cain's offering (which doesn't burn); a pot hidden under Abel's clothes for Cain to break with his fist, creating the cracking sound of the fatal blow; a bench for the prophets to sit on; and various symbolic props by which they can be known, like a long white beard for Abraham, a staff and the tablets of the Law for Moses, a bishop's robe and mitre together with a rod bearing flowers and fruit for Aaron, royal robes and crowns for David and Solomon, an ass for Balaam, and so on. Looking at all this, we can hardly doubt that the play was much livelier than any liturgical play, and much more theatrical than *The Holy Resurrection*.

Insofar as we can draw conclusions about the staging, it would seem likely that it occurred at the top and bottom of a flight of steps near the church, which suggests the western steps. Paradise, after all, is to be in a 'high place', God is said on several occasions to come 'from the church', and the choir can also be heard singing, but is apparently not seen, suggesting they are just inside the western door. The most likely arrangement is with Paradise on the top of the steps on the left-hand side as the audience sees it (that is, on the 'good' side) and Hell at the bottom of the steps on the spectator's right-hand, the 'sinister' side. The Place, or main acting-area, would be at the foot of the steps, with the audience gathered round it. The two 'great stones' acting as altars for Cain's and Abel's sacrifices would be positioned in the Place when needed, with wicked Cain's to the right, and later the bench for the prophets would doubtless be placed at the top centre of the steps, since their message is divinely inspired. The great western door behind the top of tl e steps is plainly Heaven, from which God emerges, since, seen from outside the church, it leads directly to the altar inside, and the choir is a kind of heavenly commentator heard from beyond the great divide. There is also evidence, incidentally, that Cain kills his brother Abel on the stone altar on which Abel himself has earlier sacrificed the lamb, which immediately brings to mind the image of the sacrificial Paschal Lamb and makes us realise that the pure Abel is being compared to Christ, and Cain to the wicked Jews who destroyed him. This relates to the concept of *figura*, or specific analogy, which will be more fully considered later on.

It is almost impossible to overemphasise the importance of these two early plays, because they show very clearly that there was already a flourishing vernacular tradition in the later twelfth century, a tradition which owes very little to the liturgical plays in its approach and subject-matter even at that early date. They also show that the staging of vernacular pieces was already much more sophisticated than that of the liturgical drama, although it probably originated from it, and describe for the first time a method of staging which later proves to be the most common way of mounting plays of all kinds throughout the whole medieval period.

# 6

# THE VILLAGE AND THE COURT

Whilst the jongleurs wandered the countryside entertaining both rich and poor and the new Christian drama slowly developed in the churches, the villagers of Europe were eagerly seizing on every possible occasion to interrupt the drudgery of their daily lives by holding fairs and festivals to mark events like the safe gathering-in of the harvest, the end of winter, the reappearance of plants and animals in spring and, of course, all the local weddings and saints' days. On these occasions the people forgot their troubles for a while and indulged themselves in heavy drinking and uninhibited merrymaking.

The seasonal events celebrated were all basic to an agricultural society, and the festivals marking them were extremely ancient and seem to have involved traditional ceremonies or rituals – usually short plays or mimetic dances which symbolically enacted the death and resurrection of the 'spirit' of the corn, or the triumph of spring sunlight over the darkness of winter, or the wooing of the spirit of the new year by the son of the old, or the casting out of characters representing the sins and shortcomings of the community – all ceremonies stressing the sheer continuity of life and the well-being and preservation of the society. In these performances – if the 'hero combats', 'sword-dance plays' and 'wooing plays' of modern times are anything to go by – masks and disguises will often have been used by the presenters, ranging from the primitive horns and hide of a wild beast to more or less elaborate costumes representing either 'wild men' or fools.

We can also fairly assume that these 'ritual' dramas will have been treated not with ponderous solemnity but with ribald humour and careless familiarity, just as they are today – because, though the plays are certainly an important reminder that life and the community persist, the fertility they celebrate, which is central to the continuity of life, centres upon sex, which is, and always has been, both vastly enjoyable and in many respects utterly ridiculous.

We can also safely assume that, like modern folk-plays, both the simple village celebrations and the 'ritual' enactments will have mixed their action, such as it was, with a lot of deliberate gobbledygook, anarchic disruption of the accepted order, random assaults on the audience and eventually the collection of gifts of food or money. Elements of this anarchic kind were a feature of a number of ceremonies like the Roman Saturnalia, which occurred at our Yuletide - festivals which embraced a temporary return to chaos so that order could clearly be seen to be reborn.

On occasion, the performances given are likely to have been much more basic, like the visitations of the Mari Llwyd in Wales, where the carrying of the mare's head from inn to inn is an excuse for verse-combats between rival rhymers representing the mare and the local publican, which usually result in the defeat of the publican's champion and a good deal of free drinking. But there were also many local plays about saints on appropriate days, particularly the feasts of St George and St Nicholas, together with a number of less easily classified entertainments, the most popular of which, in both Scotland and England, seem to have been Robin Hood plays. These were largely parish-based and associated with May Ales and morris dancing, and often seem to have involved actual wrestling and quarter-staff fighting. Local landowners were even willing to release servants from their duties to play Robin and Marion in these plays, so they were clearly more important than they seem, and may have been another form of fertility ritual - certainly, in Stratford in Shakespeare's boyhood, a Robin and Marion were paraded through the town in the spring, 'copulating' in a cart.

We cannot know whether the people of those times took a more serious view of such performances than their successors do. 'Folklorists' of the last century were convinced that they did, but modern mummers are likely to claim that the play is primarily played because it always has been, and that, in some sense, it is the continuity of the *custom* that is important because it is a thing done by 'us', the community, that distinguishes 'us' from 'them' (the 'foreigners' or outsiders) and welds 'us' together into a self-sufficient body.

Certainly, viewed in the wider context of myth and ritual, such performances seem likely to have provided an essential reassurance for the people who performed them, a promise that they would continue to survive in a difficult and dangerous world, which is why they are linked by common themes - the need to propitiate the gods, to ensure the fertility of fields and flocks, and to promote the health, vitality and continuity of the 'tribe'. Underlying them, too, is a common cyclical imagery - images of the sun which sets every evening only to return at dawn, of the light that retreats each winter only to be restored in spring, and of the corn which dies in the fields only to be born again from the seeds it releases in the hour of its death.

There is a current inclination to reject this ritual approach, yet the cyclical patterns involved seem to have provided man with his notion of spiritual rebirth, and, as one scholar has recently observed, the theory 'appeals on a metaphorical level to unconscious patterns and longings in our own psyches' so that 'we find drama considered in its terms a richer and more satisfying experience than it might be otherwise'. It is dangerous to neglect this fact, particularly when considering the responses of a society accustomed to thinking mainly in symbols, like that of the Middle Ages: nor is it helpful to force the evidence into a scientific frame of reference, which involves a totally different way of thinking, or to take the word of modern mummers, who have lost the medieval facility for symbolic thought.

If the people who presented these performances indeed had a ritual purpose, then they were periodically employing magic to improve the fortunes of their community. Magic, at this level, was not *opposed* to religion but an essential part of it, and it could be either 'sympathetic' or 'contagious'. Sympathetic magic involved the tribe symbolically enacting what they wanted to happen and thus 'ensuring' that it would occur – building ritual fires, for example, at the end of the year to call back the sun, or copulating in the ploughed field in order that 'mother earth' might be impregnated with new life at the same time as the women of the community, with whom 'she' was identified. Contagious magic involved gaining control over something by being in contact with some part of it – for instance, the local sorcerer would assume the horns or skin of an animal killed in the chase and induce a trance in which he became 'possessed' by the spirit of the animal, and was able profitably to 'guide' the herds into the tribal hunting-grounds. Often contagious and sympathetic magic were mixed together in the same ceremony – for instance, after he had become 'possessed' the magician would enact the stalking, hunting and killing of the animal, thus creating the mystical assurance that the hunting of the tribe would be successful.

There are many such rituals, which are found repeated in different forms all over the world, but only a few of them are relevant to the development of drama in Europe. Amongst these, one of the earliest is likely to have been an enactment of the local gods visiting mankind, which involves the use of both mask and personification. In recent versions of this ceremony, the gods are represented by masked tribesmen, each of them 'possessed' by the spirit of the particular god he is representing. These performers process solemnly round the village and visit all the important sacred venues. They accept offerings made to them by the tribe, and usually respond with gifts of their own – gifts that could only be provided by supernatural beings – such as a corn ear which ensures fertile harvests, a spear representing triumph over enemies in battle, and so forth. A modified form of this gift-giving by the gods seems to have become a central part of many social entertainments in medieval times, and it lingered on in the Tudor and Stuart masque. There are many popular relics of these divine visitations: the dark stranger who crosses the threshold with a lump of coal at New Year, for example, or the mummers who come at Christmas or Easter to perform their 'hero-play' of St George conquering the Turkish Knight, which is probably a combination of the old death-and-resurrection play and a St George play.

Ceremonies intended to purge the community of the bad luck it had accumulated during the year usually took the form of a 'scapegoat' ritual, where all the evil and unlucky forces which had been plaguing the tribe were induced by magical ceremonies to take up residence in one chosen individual, who was then driven out of the settlement, taking all the negative influences with him. Often he had to run the gauntlet of his fellow-villagers, who beat him with sticks, sometimes very severely. He would then take refuge in a kind of crude hut in the forest, well away from the tribe's usual hunting-grounds, until the end of an appointed period, after which he was allowed to return. Evidence of this practice is to be found in the 'Mad Tom's lanes' which lead out of many villages into the wilds. Eventually, in some of the more sophisticated societies, an animal came to be substituted for the expelled tribesman – the Jews used a goat, and gave us the word 'scapegoat'. The driving-away of evil or disruptive forces was later to become central to some forms of social theatre, like the sixteenth-century anti-masque.

This kind of ceremony sometimes took on a more cosmic scale when groups of villagers enacted the struggles between the elemental forces that brought the people on the one hand abundance and safety and on the other starvation and danger – forces such as darkness and light or winter and spring. These mock combats, which took the form of war-dances, usually occurred early in the year, and the two forces gradually turned into the spirits of the old year and the new, or Lent and carnival – the times of scarcity and those of abundance. In due course the dancers' swords turned into wooden sticks, and the whole dance became intermingled with rituals of death and resurrection, like the King of the Year play, or the northern sword-dance play, to be considered in a moment. A similar ceremony at the early Byzantine court has already been described, and it is interesting to note that there, too, it had become intermingled with another form, namely the narration of hero-legends. The morris dancers derived from this tradition and carried it into the courts of the great, where it had a marked influence on the development of the court masque – but that was much later, and will be treated in its proper place.

Linked with the idea of the emergence of light from darkness or spring from winter is the idea of the emergence of order from chaos, and this, too, was regularly celebrated all over Europe, usually at midwinter, when the sun was at its weakest and most distant, and bonfires were lit and prayers and sacrifices offered to ensure its safe return. This time of year became associated not just with the re-emergence of life, but also with the purification and regeneration of society. The ceremony took the form of sympathetic magic: chaos, or disorder, was recreated for a brief period so that it could clearly be seen to be overcome and order restored. The occasion seems to have had elements of the scapegoat ritual about it, too, in the guying of figures of authority, particularly on Twelfth Night, the festival of the winter solstice, and suggests that by the rebirth of order from disorder all the incompetence and corruption associated with the old regime of the dying year has been wiped away and a new start made.

At this season, in most Indo-European countries, it was customary to elect mock figures of authority – mock bishops, mock kings, mock officials – from amongst the lowliest members of society and for a few days put the rule of their fellows into their hands. An early example of this was the Roman Saturnalia mentioned earlier, a feast when slaves commanded for a few brief hours while their masters obeyed, and when, in the army, officers served the men their meals – a custom still observed in most European armies on Christmas Day or its equivalent.

The first actual record of the establishment of such a mock figure of authority, or 'Lord of Misrule', is in France in the twelfth century, but the practice had probably been more or less continuous since Roman times. In France the period of disorder was known as the 'Feast of Fools', and the Lords of Misrule had a variety of names associated with that idea, such as the Abbot of Fools, the Prince of Sots, and so on. In England, in Elizabethan times, the Lord of Misrule was known as the 'King of the Bean', because he was selected originally by baking a bean into a batch of cakes and the person who found it became the 'King'.

Accounts of the French festivals of misrule suggest that they went much further than the mere inversion of order in the twelfth century. Usually the lesser clergy elected one of their number – often a choirboy – to be the Bishop, or Abbot, or even Pope, of Fools, after which they would celebrate the occasion by heavy drinking-bouts, by riotous masquerading in beast-heads or women's clothes through monastery, church and town, and by burlesquing the ceremony of the Mass, using puddings and sausages as censers to 'perfume' the church and playing dice upon the altar. All these practices had their equivalents in the folk-festivals of Yuletide outside the church, but inside it they seem to have acquired an additional note of satirical self-conscious mockery. For this reason they were intensely disliked by serious-minded clergymen, and towards the end of the fifteenth century the ecclesiastical authorities took steps to suppress them.

Most significant of the 'ritual plays', though, and apparently the most widespread, at least in Indo-European countries, was that of the death and resurrection of the King of the Year, or Corn King, or whatever he might be called locally. This ceremony seems to have linked the success and fertility of the tribe with the strength and well-being of a single individual. It seems that each tribe viewed its chieftain as a kind of god-king who magically represented the state of the whole tribe – if he was strong and healthy and fertile then so were the crops and herds and the families of the tribe. To ensure his continued health and strength he was challenged every year by a vigorous young brave; they fought, and the loser appears, originally, to have been eaten by the tribe to prevent the spiritual 'power' his flesh contained being lost to wandering demons or wild beasts, and to allow it to be reabsorbed into the bodies of his fellow-tribesmen.

Eventually the ceremony became ritualised and the actual contest and cannibalism were dispensed with and replaced by a simple play, which is preserved for us in many European examples, like the St George, or 'pace-egging', plays in the south of England and the sword-dance plays in the north. These two types of play differ only in detail. In the 'pace-egging', or 'Easter-egging', plays, the hero, St George, is challenged by the Turkish Knight and killed, but is then restored to life by a comic Doctor. In the sword dance, the story is about not a physical fight but the competition of an old man and a young man who are both courting the same girl (what is usually called a 'wooing play'); however, it has become fused with a hero play, in which a symbolic 'death' once again takes place and a 'resurrection' is again effected by the doctor.

It is worth noticing that a further presentational feature links almost all the ceremonies considered here, and that is the use of dance. Dancing is a very apt accompaniment to these life-enhancing performances, because it is itself a revitalising activity, a means of 'firing the blood' and accelerating the heartbeat by the rhythmical repetition of movement. It is suitable for many purposes – as a prelude to sexual play, for instance, or to setting out for war or the hunt – and it particularly associates with the masked medicine-man working himself up into a state of possession, where he can identify with a god through ecstatic dance, sometimes aided by drugs.

The strength of such pagan ceremonies, even after Europe had been officially converted to Christianity, is clearly to be seen from the trouble vicars had with parishioners in their churchyards. This partly arose from Pope Gregory's deliberate attempt to assimilate the old heathen festivals to the new patterns of Christian worship by ensuring that the dates of the new Christian festivals coincided with those of the principal heathen ceremonies and by establishing churches on the sites of heathen temples. The Venerable Bede records the Pope's instructions to St Augustine of Canterbury, when he was sent out to Britain as a missionary in 596. He was to destroy the idols, but the temples were to be sprinkled with holy water, altars were to be set up there and relics enclosed in them:

For if these temples are well built, they are to be purified from devil-worship and dedicated to the service of the true God. In this way, we hope that the people, seeing their temples are not destroyed, may abandon idolatry yet still resort to these places as before, and thus come to know and adore the true God.

– an admirably sensible approach to the problem, which later Protestant missionaries would have done well to heed in Polynesia and Africa.

The heathens, however, were not so easily beguiled – hence the problems in the churchyards, where people continued to celebrate the pagan rituals where they had always celebrated them, giving rise to frequent complaints about 'wanton' dance and song occurring on holy ground. One priest, at Koelbigk in Saxony in the eleventh century, was disturbed at Christmas Mass by the pagan revelling outside the building, and laid a curse on the revellers, including his own daughter, which, according to the story, compelled them to continue dancing for a whole year without intermission.

An unhappy vicar in Worcestershire, at about the same time, who had been kept awake all night by the amorous songs and dances in his churchyard, began the morning service in a misguided spirit of modernisation by singing a pagan ditty, 'Sweet leman, thin are' ('Sweet lover, have mercy'), instead of 'The Lord be with you'. This caused his bishop to reprimand him severely and pronounce anathema upon anyone ever heard singing the song again in the whole diocese.

Sadder still was the case of Father John at Inverkeithing in Scotland in 1282, who compelled the young girls of his parish to join in a processional dance-song in honour of the Roman god of sex, Priapus, during Easter week. He led the dancers in person, carrying a pole topped with a phallus, and stirred all the spectators to wantonness 'by mimed actions and shameless words'. Nowadays this would surely have made the front pages of the popular newspapers.

An important aspect of all folk-rituals was that they were not restricted to the common people: the nobility enjoyed them just as much, particularly when society became wealthier in the later Middle Ages, and the upper classes began to lay emphasis upon entertainments rather than war, and develop their own form of theatre, which is known today as the 'Theatre of Social Recreation'. This embraced dancing and 'amateur dramatics' of various kinds, including the 'momerie', the 'disguising', the court masque, and also the *pas d'armes*, or 'passage of arms', which will all be described in due course.

A number of theories have been advanced to explain why the aristocracy of Europe plunged so vigorously into every conceivable kind of pageantry and semi-dramatic activity, in the fourteenth and fifteenth centuries, but the most plausible of them invoke the common tendency to self-dramatisation found in both individuals and societies in times of doubt and insecurity.

Late medieval society was very unstable. On the one hand much more wealth was being generated, both on the lords' estates and in the newly prosperous trading-cities that were springing up all over Europe, and in this respect the spectre of starvation had been laid pretty firmly to rest; but on the other hand the strength of the new craft guilds and the spirit of independence in the towns was beginning to undermine the feudal system.

The lords saw townsmen beginning to exercise more power in the land than they did, and they saw the king gradually becoming richer from new taxes levied upon these same townsmen. It was obvious that political power was slipping through their fingers, since the king no longer depended on their support, and, if necessary, could hire mercenaries to fight for him with the money raised from his city taxes. Indeed, kings tended to look upon powerful lords as a threat and soon began to limit their private armies by passing edicts against their keeping excessive numbers of retainers, thus reducing the likelihood of their launching the usual kind of civil war that disgruntled feudal barons tended to wage against their overlords.

On the battlefield, too, the days of the armoured horseman were rapidly waning. At Crecy and Poitiers, and later at Agincourt, the English longbowman proved more than his match; in the Middle East the Saracen horse-archers shot him down before he could reach them; and at Mortgarten, Granson, Morat and Nancy the Swiss pikemen held him at bay with their 18-foot pikes, while large companies of crossbowmen picked him off at leisure. Gunpowder, too, was beginning to appear, and, although it was used only against walled cities at first, the threat that it would eventually present to the mounted horseman was plain.

As if this were not enough, kings like Henry V began to urge a policy of 'total war'. Whereas in the old days a knight was very unlikely to be seriously harmed in war, and if he was captured would in due course be ransomed, at Agincourt Henry gave instructions that no ransoms were to be granted, and that all prisoners taken, whatever their rank, were to be killed; the French, on the other hand, took prisoners in the old fashion – hence the remarkable, and more or less accurate, list of casualties read by Henry V in Shakespeare's play. Similarly, at Courtrai, when the French begged to be held to ransom, the Flemish replied 'We don't speak French' and slit their throats: some 4,000 knights are said to have died in that battle. It seemed that, for aristocrats, the pursuit of military glory had ceased to be either a privilege or a pleasure.

In the face of this loss of prestige, nerve and influence, the reactions of the nobility were interesting: their way of life became much more clannish and internalised; they re-asserted their superiority to everybody else (particularly the rising bourgeoisie) by laying out money right and left with conspicuous magnificence, even to the point of occasionally bankrupting themselves; and they began to turn their daily life into an art-form; their emphasis upon the ideals and elegancies of 'courtly love' became general; they learnt to read and to play musical instruments; and they fostered a new interest in deeds of high, knightly courage like those of King Arthur and his knights or the Emperor Charlemagne and his paladins.

Particularly interesting is what happened to the tournament. When the Normans invaded England this had been simply a training-exercise for war, in which two parties of knights fought out a mock battle, using their usual weapons, but not trying seriously to kill one another. However, weapons being weapons, not a few knights did actually die in the process, much to the dismay of the Church, which periodically forbade all tournaments as a sinful waste of life and God's good time; but because it was a pastime of the nobility, and considered essential training for war, which was then the most important source of income and power, the Church was consistently ignored.

However, once the military value of the mounted horseman declined, his individual social importance increased, and the tournament was superseded by the one-to-one combat – either the 'joust' between two individual knights on horseback, or the 'barriers' fought between two individual knights on foot and often indoors. In both cases a wooden barrier separated the two contestants, stressing the 'sporting' quality of the fight, and the weapons used were blunted and, in the case of jousting spears, made deliberately fragile, so that they would shatter before they pierced anybody's armour. Although such occasions were still called tournaments, and indeed usually included one, the joust was by now much more important – if you entered for the joust you could freely take part in the tournament, but entering the tournament did not qualify you for the joust.

People were still killed occasionally, of course – a fall from a horse in full armour was still dangerous, a spear-hit under the chin could break a neck, as could a spear that got caught in the increasingly elaborate metal crests that began to surmount the tilting helms – but intentional killing disappeared; and, it is interesting to note, as the real threat of death receded his figure appeared symbolically in a little shrine set up at the side of the arena, usually as a skeleton dressed in black, either with his traditional scythe, or wearing a crown and carrying a sword.

By now the tournament had become a lively and colourful social event, where nobody suffered much more than a bruising, and bookies took bets on the outcome – rather like a racing meeting at Ascot. But the nobility soon began to enhance the drama of the occasion, by developing what was known as the *pas d'armes*, or 'passage of arms'.

In the *pas d'armes* a knight made a formal entry into the noble's or king's court where the tournament was taking place, and proclaimed, in true story-book style, that he proposed to hold a ford, or a well, or some other 'perilous passage' against all comers for the sake of his lady's love, or some other reason. Everybody would then repair to the tiltyard, where a wooden castle, or mountain, or well, or some other appropriate device, had been erected, and the principal knight would be challenged to single combat there by various individuals in turn. Then, in the evening, after the jousting was finished, there would be a great banquet in the castle hall, with dancing and other entertainments, rather like a modern hunt ball, and the lady of the castle would award prizes to the most successful competitors in the jousts.

The *pas d'armes* became more and more elaborate as time went by, particularly the entry of the knights, which, largely under Italian influence, became a big occasion, not unlike the entry of the toreadors in Spain, involving highly decorated chariots or triumphal cars, a host of elegantly dressed attendants, and a set of armour for the champion which was usually much too elaborate to fight in – for which reason the fighting often took place on the next day.

Partly to support this extra display, and partly independently, the story element was also increased, and more and more elaborate and lengthy incidents were described which were supposed to be the reason for the knight's challenge. Sometimes a 'maiden' or 'damsel' would play the principal part, and in that case, as often as not, the challenging knight would cast himself in the role of a villain who had abducted her and carried her off to his castle.

As time went by, the evening dances and entertainments also became more elaborate, and symbolic characters like Dame Fortune, Lady Hope and Good Companionship began to appear in allegorical displays that preceded the dancing. On other occasions giants appeared, or the Seven Champions of Christendom, or, more and more frequently as the Renaissance took hold, classical gods and goddesses, or Circe the enchantress from Homer's *Odyssey*, or shepherds and shepherdesses from the ideal world of pastoral tradition.

Inevitably, in the increasingly elaborate and refined artistic society of the time, the all-male tournament was soon outshone by the dancing and other social amusements in which the ladies could participate, and by the later Middle Ages a number of folk-rituals had also been adopted by the courts and began to appear amongst the evening's festivities and to receive more expensive forms of presentation.

Mumming was a case in point. 'Mumming' was a general term covering several different kinds of performance: not only folk-mumming, like the St George play, which was certainly a lower-class, peasant entertainment, but also the 'mummery', or 'momerie', which was very much an upper-class pastime.

The mummery was an aristocratic version of the visitation of the black-faced stranger on New Year's Eve – generally known throughout Britain as 'the first footing.' It consisted of a procession of well-to-do people wearing masks who paraded the streets, usually at Christmas or New Year, and entered their neighbours' houses to provide simple dances for their entertainment and to play a game of dice with them in which the dice were always rigged so that the hosts won the prizes. This little ceremony clearly implied that fortune, or the gods, or whatever you care to call the outside forces that govern men's lives, were well disposed to those who won, and it was to be hoped they would continue their favours throughout the coming year.

The use of masks by the visitors was crucial to this ceremony, and in fact the words 'mumming' and 'mummery' and the like all derive from the old Germanic word *mommen* meaning 'mask'. Even the rural performers of the St George play used to wear what became known as 'papers' – costumes which covered the whole body and head, with strips of paper sewn or stuck on to them all over, which gave them a very strange, almost frightening, appearance, rather like great shaggy gorillas. The significance of this strange body-mask was no doubt the same as the corn-stalks or leaves on many African ceremonial costumes, where the rustling of the stalks, as if they were moving in the wind, was supposed to encourage the growth of the crops by sympathetic magic.

The dice-game played on the New Year visits to the well-to-do was called 'mumchance', which could be loosely interpreted as meaning 'masked, or hidden, fortune', that is, the secret disposition of Dame Fortune towards the owners of the house, which was to be revealed by the dice. And the visitors made the occasion very impressive by performing all their actions in a mysterious silence, at least until the music for dancing struck up. This led to our modern expression 'mum's the word', meaning 'don't say anything', and as a result has also led, unfortunately, to a misunderstanding about the words 'mumchance' and 'mumming': namely, the idea that the performers in them were always silent, which is quite untrue, as the St George play, and the northern sword-dance play show quite clearly, both being very dependent on their traditional text.

Mumming, then, of which the court mummery was a part, involved the visit of masked 'strangers' at the turn of the year to entertain their hosts with dances and bring them gifts. This is quite enough to establish the close links of the form with the primitive visitations of the tribal gods and the later court masque, which was essentially a dance incorporating a blessing, and involved the presentation of gifts to the current sovereign by Dame Fortune or some divine power.

It is important to note that mummings or mummeries always took place between people of the same social rank, whether they occurred in the countryside or at court, and those who went mumming to the king, who technically had no peer, were either the most important members of the nobility or the wealthiest members of the city guilds.

The impressive form these New Year celebrations could assume on important occasions can be seen in the account of an elaborate mumming made by the richest citizens of London to the young King Richard II shortly after his coronation in 1377. According to the record, 130 disguised men rode from Newgate through Cheapside 'with great noise of minstrelsy, trumpets, cornets and shawms and great plenty of wax torches lighted', attracting a large crowd of Londoners. The procession was composed of forty-eight squires clothed in red silk and wearing masks, forty-eight knights similarly clad, an emperor, a pope, and twenty-four cardinals, the tail being brought up by eight or ten devils with black masks which appeared 'nothing amiable'.

The procession rode over London Bridge to Kenyton, where it alighted and proceeded on foot to the Hall. There they were shortly joined by the young prince, his mother, and several lords. The mummers saluted them,

> showing a pair of dice upon a table to play with the prince, which dice were subtilly made so that when the prince should cast he should win, and the said mummers set before the prince three jewels one after another – a ball of gold, a cup of gold, and a gold ring – which the prince won with three casts of the dice, as was intended, after which they set a gold ring before the prince's mother, and one before each lord present, and these also won the prizes. The prince then called for wine and music, and the prince and the lords danced on one side, and the mummers on the other, a great while, and then they drank and took their leave and so departed toward London.

Observe that when they danced, the mummers and the members of the court did not mingle, but danced apart from one another. This was not because of any social gulf which existed between the townsmen and the royal party: it was a peculiarity of all mumming that the masked visitors and the hosts never danced together, perhaps because it was not felt proper for mere mortals to mix on equal terms with those who were ambassadors of the gods, or, at the very least, the emissaries of Dame Fortune.

The kind of lavish expenditure revealed in this visit to the young King Richard was typical of many other civic celebrations in the Middle Ages, when the cities of Europe were growing rich and powerful through their trading. The principal citizens loved to display their wealth for the honour of their guild and their city, as will be apparent when the time comes to consider the cycles of mystery plays that grew out of the procession of Corpus Christi towards the end of the fourteenth century.

They also spared no expense to show their loyalty to their ruler on the occasions when he visited them, perhaps bringing with him a lively new queen, or a young prince, or news of victories abroad or a newly concluded peace. These were times when they rolled out the pageant-wagons belonging to the guilds, decorated the whole city with bunting, and built triumphal arches along the king's route, where they could address him with suitable speeches of welcome, or loyalty, or advice – for they now felt quite independent enough to advise him on matters of statecraft. These occasions were known as 'royal entries', and they were another important form assumed by the Theatre of Social Recreation – a form in which rich townsmen could compete with the nobility.

Royal entries were naturally on a far more lavish scale than the New Year mummings, even the one made to Richard II. Consider the reception prepared by the loyal citizens of London for Henry VI when he returned from France in 1431, after being crowned king of the French. On that occasion not only were all the streets lined with marquees and decorations, and all the conduits, or water-towers, which were low enough to be used as convenient stages, thronged with symbolic personifications of the Virtues, who were sumptuously costumed and lectured the king in verse, but 'At the conduit in Cheapside were ordained various wells – a well of mercy, a well of grace, a well of pity – and at each well stood a lady who provided water from the well for such as asked for it' – the 'water' being in fact good wine. 'Around these wells were set divers trees with flourishing leaves and fruits, which were so cunningly wrought that, to many, they appeared natural trees growing.' A little further on there was a wonderful tower which, by means of artificial trees, which were at the same time genealogical trees, showed Henry's claim to the throne of France. The whole affair was clearly very expensive, and must have been most impressive, even though it has something of that pompous and rather self-satisfied feel that so often attaches itself to civic ceremonies.

These accounts of the tournament, the mummery and the civic entry will provide some idea of the nature of court entertainments at about the time of the early vernacular drama. In due course, they were to be transmuted into first the 'disguising' and then the court masque, but that occurred much later and will be treated in its proper place.

# 7

# THE COMING OF CORPUS
# CHRISTI

By the time Amalarius took steps to revitalise the Mass in the ninth century the ideological schism between the priests and the people was beginning to be reflected in the architecture of the church building, where a physical line of demarcation was gradually drawn between the altar and the congregation. This development produced the familiar groundplan of the 'gothic' church.

The altar was moved back to the rear wall of the apse, and the bishop's throne, which had faced the congregation from behind the altar, was shifted to its stage right, the 'good' side. The choir, which had sat behind the altar, was now placed in front of it, and its two halves sat facing each other in the newly built choir-stalls. The altar could still be seen from the nave, of course, but there was now a much greater distance between the priest and his congregation, who could see less of the service and hear very little of the quieter prayers.

The officiating priest now assumed a new position, in front of the altar, rather than behind it, implying that he did not preside at the Lord's Table and identify himself with Christ, but was merely the humble minister of God mediating between his sinful parishioners and the Almighty – being the only person who was authorised to do so, by virtue of his sacred office.

At this point a number of procedural changes occurred in the Mass. About the middle of the ninth century, the type of bread used in the service changed from leavened bread, which too easily became mouldy, to unleavened bread in the form of small circular wafers, which were less subject to deterioration. This change was probably accelerated by the growing reverence for the Host, since the officiating priests were becoming more and more sure that the doctrine of the Real Presence was true, and that the bread and wine miraculously became the actual physical body of Christ when they were blessed, and, for that reason, were becoming obsessed with not losing a single crumb of bread or a single drop of wine.

A pile of the new unleavened wafers could be divided at the 'fraction', or breaking of the bread, rather like cutting a pack of cards, without needing to worry about the loss of any crumbs, and, similarly, the individual wafers could be given to the communicants without any fear of crumbs falling to the ground and being lost – though priests began to think it better that they should place the wafer on the communicant's tongue themselves in order to be doubly sure. In any case, no uncleansed, unpriestly hands should be allowed to touch the holy mystery of the consecrated Host – and, because of the difficulty of actually placing the wafers on the tongues of the communicants when they were standing up, and because of the great holiness of the wafer, it was only proper that the miserable sinners receiving communion should be required to do so kneeling meekly upon their knees.

The priest, too, no longer shared his bread with the communicants. Instead he used a tiny paten, or bread-plate, which fitted exactly over the mouth of the chalice, while the wafers intended for the congregation were transferred to a new chalice-like vessel called the *ciborium*, or 'bread-basket'.

With the coming of the unleavened wafers, which were prepared specially for church use, the offertory procession of the faithful with their gifts of bread, wine and candles died away, to be replaced for the first time by the collection of money which could go to swell the coffers of the increasingly prosperous Church, now hovering on the brink of inventing banking and double-entry book-keeping.

As with the bread, so with the wine. At first communicants were not permitted to drink directly from the chalice, because they might spill some of the precious Saviour's blood. For a while a straw, known as a *calamus* or *fistula*, was used to stop their profane lips actually touching the sacred cup, but by the twelfth century the clergy were beginning to think that Christ's command to both eat *and* drink in remembrance of him was adequately satisfied by the communion of the priest alone, acting on behalf of the congregation – at least so far as the wine was concerned.

Eventually, with the theological decision that the total nature of Christ was incoporated in *each* of the two species, the bread and the wine, independently, the cup was withdrawn from the laity and reserved for the priest, and the people were left to communicate on bread alone – but it is interesting to note that this particular reform was not easy to bring about, probably because Christ's words in the Scriptures were so explicit, and chalice communion was retained for a long time in the Catholic Church, in some cases even beyond the Middle Ages.

With the priests in front of the altar, and the communicants now kneeling, it became inconvenient to have them coming to the table itself, and the altar-rail sprang into existence. In due course, too, the dividing line between the holy choir and the profane nave of the church building turned into an actual dividing wall – the rood-screen. The rood-screen did not usually shut out the view of the altar completely, but consisted of a lattice-work of bars, through which the service was now watched, with even greater difficulty. The area beyond the rood-screen began to be known as the 'chancel', because of the *cancelli*, or bars, that closed it off. Soon the altar-rail began to be placed *outside* the rood screen, so that no profane feet might trespass upon the Holy of Holies, and eventually a separate rood-altar was placed there in many churches to serve the people, the original high altar being reserved for the use of the priests. The alternative to a rood-altar was to place lesser altars for the congregation in side-chapels of the building running parallel to the choir.

So the Mass became even more distanced from the people, and was increasingly treated as a mystery – the mystery, or sacrament,of God's descent to man to release him from sin – which was not so much to be participated in as to be adoringly wondered at by 'the simple folk' and contemplated from afar. And because the priests knew that they were being looked at, and were difficult to see behind the bars of the chancel, and because their holy office as mediators was now of such importance, their vestments became more and more magnificent and took on regular symbolic colourings – white for festive occasions, red for martyrs' days and Pentecost, black for days of penance and Masses for the Dead, and green for days without a specific character. A new kind of theatricality, or display, was beginning to develop in the Mass – but it had none of the humanity of Amalarius' dramatisations.

The altar, too, began to grow larger, so that it could be better seen. The modest table that had served satisfactorily for so many centuries had been 3 or 4 feet long, but in the eleventh century it began to grow, and had soon reached a length of 12 feet. The back of the altar – the part which could be most easily seen from the nave – also began to be built up, now the priest no longer needed to stand behind it facing the congregation.

This elaboration at the back of the altar consisted at first of only a few reliquaries, arranged in no particular pattern, but these were soon replaced by a permanent altar-piece, known as the 'reredos', which in its turn grew until it sometimes reached an immense size, and eventually a 'retable', or frame enclosing the decorated panels, began to rise from the ground above the back of the altar-piece, rather like a theatrical back-cloth.

The increased size of the altar had another rather unexpected effect on the service. Up to the twelfth century it had been customary to have two lecterns for the reading of the lessons, one on the stage left of the altar, the 'sinister' side, for readings from the Old Testament, which was written by men who had not received the enlightenment of Christ's teachings, and a slightly higher one on the stage right of the altar, the 'good' side, for the readings from the New Testament. Since the same Bible was used for both readings, partly because of cost and partly to symbolise the indivisibility of God's Word, the weighty book had to be moved from the altar, where it was blessed, to the left-hand lectern, from there back to the left-hand end of the altar, then from the left-hand end of the altar to the right-hand end of the altar, so that it could be taken from there to the right-hand lectern without causing a clumsy and unartistic hiccough in the service.

While the altar remained small this was quite feasible, but when it reached a length of 12 feet it began to be very inconvenient to move the heavy book from one end of the altar to the other between lessons, so by the middle of the twelfth century the lectern on the stage left of the altar, where the first lesson was traditionally read, tended to be used for both Old Testament and New Testament readings, and its companion lectern disappeared.

This change clearly demanded a reinterpretation of the allegorical meaning of the lectern's position. Why should the Gospel be read on the less honourable side of the church? Ivo of Chartres provided an acceptable explanation: it was the Jews who had originally been the 'chosen people' of God, so the Jews should be seen as associated with the stage right of the altar, but they rejected Christ's ministry, so he had to preach instead to the gentiles, who were *not* God's 'chosen people' and who should therefore be seen as associated with the altar's stage left.

The importance attached to this apparently trivial alteration of Church practice strikingly underlines the tremendous significance of that 'invisible' meaning which medieval man believed God had woven into the universe. Indeed, in medieval terms, Ivo's explanation makes good Christian sense, for Jesus said himself that he did not come to preach to the converted, but to call sinners to repentance, and symbolically sinners must surely be related to the dishonourable side of the church.

Finally, as a result of the growing emphasis on Christ's godhead, and his great goodness in coming to earth in order to save poor miserable sinners, there was a shift in the whole emphasis of the Mass: away from the Resurrection, which offered an equal hope to all believers, because they could identify with Christ who had himself risen, to the Passion, or sufferings, which Christ had undergone to save man, and which none but he, the only Son of God, could possibly have undertaken on man's behalf. This shift of emphasis was again partly a matter of theological politics, for the Passion, being unique to Christ, was clearly a matter for the officiating priest to present to the congregation, making them aware of the gratitude they should feel for Christ's supreme sacrifice – it was not something they could share in.

The distancing of the people from the Mass was now complete, and they saw it as a remote theatrical performance, replete with rich costumes, soft lights and sweet music, played against the backcloth of a decorated altar, far in the distance beyond the fretwork of the rood-screen and the length of the choir-stalls.

Thus it came about, in the late Middle Ages, that the Consecration of the two species, which were both elevated, and particularly the Elevation of the Host itself – actions which were *visible* to the congregation – became the climax of the Mass.

The people had been progressively deprived of participation in any vital part of the ceremony, and had even been denied the holy wine. In this state of spiritual starvation, with so much emphasis being placed upon the divine and gracious sacrament of God's descent to man, the Host took on the aspect of a potent celestial mystery, and this reached a climax in the legend of the Holy Grail, which suddenly makes its appearance at this time amongst the popular Arthurian romances, and in which the religious longing of the Middle Ages increasingly found its poetic expression.

As happened in the stories of the Grail, people expected to be abundantly filled with grace at the mere sight of the mystery. To look upon the sacred Host while it was elevated by the priest became for many the be-all and end-all of the Mass, equivalent to the act of communion itself – in fact, much more important than the communion. At the Elevation, the Host had become the real body of Christ nailed high upon the Cross – see the body of Christ and be saved!

Bishops became alarmed, fearing that people might adore the bread and the wine when the priest first lifted them up in the act of blessing, while they were still mere bread and wine, and thus commit idolatry – and they gave stringent instructions as to how the priest was to proceed in order to avoid such an unfortunate occurrence.

In the cities people ran from church to church to see the elevated Host as often as possible, since they assumed that the more Elevations you saw, the more grace you would acquire. At the end of the twelfth century stories began to circulate of miracles that had occurred at the moment of Elevation – people had seen visions, the Host shone like the sun, a tiny child had appeared in the priest's hands, and so forth. In some congregations the majority of the faithful waited for the ringing of the sance-bell, which signalled the approaching consecration, before they even deigned to enter the church, and then, as soon as the Elevation was concluded rushed out again as quickly as they had come in. People started lawsuits to ensure that they obtained pews which provided a favourable view of the altar, and some priests even took bribes to protract the Elevation.

This scandalous situation greatly troubled the church authorities. It could obviously not be allowed to go on, and the first movement towards finding a remedy was advanced by Pope Urban IV in 1264. He proposed a new feast to celebrate the joy of the Passion, at which the Host could be carried around the town and publicly displayed to all the people – a kind of safety-valve, in fact. At the same time, he obviously intended to tighten up the rules about attendance at Mass – by insisting that people should not be allowed to run in and out simply to witness the Elevation, but must attend the whole service and participate in the communion.

He also felt, quite rightly, that the Lord's Supper was no longer receiving sufficient emphasis. Partly he blamed this on the additional activities that had come to surround the Mass on Maunday Thursday, the day properly associated with the Last Supper. On that day, he says, the Church 'fully occupied as she is with the reconciliation of penitents, the ritual administration of holy oil, the fulfilling of Christ's commandment concerning the washing of feet, and other matters, does not have time enough for the proper celebration of this greatest sacrament'.

He was also aware that the laity was becoming too obsessed with its sinfulness. In the whole of Passion week, he says, Christians are busy meditating on God's terrible sacrifice and the sorrow and shame of human sin that requires such an extreme expiation, but somewhere in the Church Year there should also be scope for the good Christian to express his *joy* at Christ's promises, revealed to him at the Last Supper, because the Mass is a 'glorious act of remembrance, which fills the minds of the faithful with joy at their salvation and mingles their tears with an outburst of reverend jubilation'.

Sadly, Pope Urban died before he could put his plans into effect, and the establishment of the new festival was shelved for half a century until Clement V realised how necessary it was and formally ordered its adoption at the Council of Vienne in 1311, as the feast of Corpus Christi – the feast of the Body of Christ.

Clement also solved the problem of where to locate the new feast in the Church calendar: if it was to be truly memorable it would need to be at a time when there were no other important religious events to distract the worshippers' attention, and that suggested a date just after Pentecost, when the yearly story of Christ's birth, ministry, death and Resurrection had been brought to its natural conclusion, and there was a kind of limbo in the Church Year before Advent announced the coming of Christmas. He also wanted a date in the summer, when the weather ought to be good enough to allow celebrations out of doors and thus make the occasion a genuinely public one. The day eventually chosen was the Thursday after Trinity Sunday, a movable feast determined by the full moon, which, since the old calendar was then in use, fell sometime between our modern 4 June and 6 July.

A hundred years after its foundation, the festival of Corpus Christi was being celebrated throughout the whole of Europe with huge civic processions, containing dozens of pageant-wagons which, in some areas, had become a focus for the presentation of impressive cycles of vernacular plays, based on both the Old and the New Testaments, which recounted the whole story of man's fall from grace and God's plan for his salvation.

Did the plays spring into existence quite independently of the Corpus Christi procession and later get drawn into it, or was the procession an important first step in the creation of the plays? This is a controversial question, which is still being debated, but it must be said that the argument that favours the existence of play-cycles before the establishment of Corpus Christi was based largely on the assumption that they grew directly out of the earlier liturgical drama, which is now known to be false. Consequently there seems to be every reason for thinking that the Corpus Christi procession played a significant part in the development of the European play-cycles, wherever they arose, and it is easy to see how this could have happened.

Since the feast was religious in nature but deliberately located outside the active part of the Church Year, it is likely to have been seen as a suitable occasion on which to recall the whole story of the Redemption incorporated in the daily readings of the Bible – from the time when Adam and Eve damned themselves by their disobedience to the moment when God's Son 'bought back' their souls from the Devil – and this could best be done by carrying pictures or models in the procession which underlined the important parts of the story. In this way the actual *material* of the cycle-plays became incorporated into the celebrations.

Further impetus was provided when the procession became the central feature of the festival, despite the fact that a very beautiful service had been specially composed for the day by no less a person than Thomas Aquinas, the celebrated theologian. The civic leaders of the community joined the religious leaders in an elaborate parade, which toured the town, halting at various religious establishments along the route for the purposes of worship, and the occasion was crowned with a service in the parish church or cathedral. Present were officials of all the craft and trade guilds and all the religious fraternities of the town, accompanied by armed men to guard the Host, retainers of the rich and noble carrying lighted torches and banners, and guildsmen carrying on poles models or specially painted pictures representing aspects of the Bible story.

France, Spain and Austria provide examples of all the separate stages in the evolution of plays from these simple showpieces in the Corpus Christi procession, including the transition to mimed action, and eventually to speech. Ironically, there is no evidence available in England, which seems to have been first in the field.

For instance, in Spain the Corpus Christi plays began as a series of static Scriptural tableaux composed of wooden figures mounted on draped floats which were carried in the procession by men hidden under the draperies. In 1400 the Corpus Christi parade at Valencia included not only figures of angels, apostles, prophets, patriarchs, virgins, saints and dragons, but also images of Noah's Ark, St Nicholas' ship and St Peter's Keys. In 1404 a float depicting the Garden of Eden carried carved wooden figures of Adam and Eve, and in the same year men were paid to dress as lions to accompany the figure of Daniel as he walked in the procession.

The parade at Barcelona in 1424 involved 108 'displays' of various kinds, including several Scriptural tableaux and many Christian saints on foot, together with banners and crosses from the local parish churches and trade emblems representing the guilds. This was plainly not enough, for in 1453 several new pageant-wagons were constructed, amongst them one for the Nativity which was very elaborate. It displayed four angels on pillars supporting a heaven set with stars and clouds, with God in the middle, from whom rays of light or fire descended to touch the Christ-child in the manger, where Mary and Joseph knelt on either side. This time there was definitely physical action – the three kings rode up to the float, dismounted and climbed up to worship the child – but as yet no dialogue was involved.

Ample evidence of both living Scriptural tableaux and mimed religious plays is also to be found in France, where much is heard of mimed mysteries (*mystères mimés*). For instance, in 1313, when Philip IV of France welcomed Edward II of England to Paris, the civic entry presented living tableaux along the route, some of which depicted incidents from the life of Christ. About a hundred years later, in 1424, John, Duke of Bedford, witnessed 'a very beautiful mystery play of the Old and New Testament, which the children of Paris put on: it was staged without speech and without movement, just as if they were figures set up against a wall'.

These pieces were still immobile, but in 1437, when the French King Charles VII made his entry into Paris, the Brotherhood of the Passion (Confrèrie de la Passion), an association of the citizens of Paris formed in 1402 specifically to present religious plays, offered a similar show in which, though the characters did not speak, they used gestures to portray Christ's Passion and the treachery of Judas. At first sight, this suggests that France was lagging seriously behind England in the development of spoken plays, but it is quite possible that mime was already being viewed there as a separate art-form.

So far as spoken plays are concerned, closer analogies with England can be found in Austria than in France and Spain, where dialogue was very late appearing. For instance, the earliest Corpus Christi play from Innsbruck, in Austria, in 1391, contains 756 lines consisting of a series of monologues by Adam, Eve, the Disciples, the Prophets, the Three Kings and the Pope. This relatively brief play with its thirty set speeches, many illustrating prophecies of Christ's coming, seems ideally suited for delivery in a procession at one or more pre-arranged stations on its route through the city.

The development of cycle-drama in the way just outlined seems to have occurred much more quickly in England than elsewhere and to have started at a much earlier date. In fact many medieval towns and cities in the British Isles mounted Corpus Christi processions like those in Spain from as early as 1318, and we know, for instance, that the Water-Drawers of Dee, at Chester, carried a banner or model of Noah's Ark on foot long before they ever used a pageant-wagon to present the play of *Noah's Flood*; but unfortunately all the *detailed* evidence is very late.

Dublin possesses a list, dated 1498, which describes a parade of figures walking in the procession, including 'Adam and Eve, with an angel following them bearing a sword; Noah, with his ship, apparelled accordingly; and the Three Kings of Cologne, riding worshipfully with their offerings, with a star before them.' Hereford possesses a much fuller list, from 1503, of twenty-seven guilds and their dumb-shows, which include 'Adam and Eve, Noah's Ship, the Nativity, the Three Kings of Cologne, the Good Lord riding on an ass, Jesus hanging on the Cross, several Burial and Resurrection episodes, knights in harness, and St Catharine with three of her tormentors'.

However, there is no evidence that either Dublin or Hereford ever possessed any Corpus Christi *plays*, and considering that, by the dates mentioned, the principal play-cycles at York and elsewhere were already long established and very successful, it seems likely that in some places the processional figures and pageants were converted into plays and in others they were not.

Although they are certainly much earlier, there is still some uncertainty as to the exact date at which plays made their first appearance at York. Some guildsmen there must have been parading with more than banners and pictures in the last quarter of the fourteenth century, because an item recorded in a memorandum book in 1376 suggests that storage space was already required for quite elaborate pageant-wagons: 'For a building in which three Corpus Christi pageants were – 2s rent per year.' Certainly pageants of considerable size are implied by the amount paid for the building, and they must have been used to present something substantial, though this was not necessarily plays. It is too easy to go along with the assumption made by many scholars that this entry implies that the York cycle-plays were already being acted: it should be remembered that actual indications of *playing* at York are not found until the next record from the city, in 1394.

Admittedly that record refers to the playing places as *antiquitus assignatis*, or 'previously assigned', implying that it was not the first year of performance, but eighteen years had elapsed since 1376, allowing time for several performances to have taken place without necessarily implying that the pageants carried actors at the earlier date – they could equally well have carried scenes of the life of Christ using painted figures made of wood or clay. It is also possible that pageants built for other civic occasions, like the York Fishmongers' fully rigged ship of 1313, may have been absorbed into the Corpus Christi procession as part of the ceremonial, and it may be these pageants that are referred to in 1376, not acting-wagons at all. By contrast, the record of 1394 provides unequivocal evidence that plays were being performed by that date.

Having plays to present on Corpus Christi Day was not an unmixed blessing, because there was always the danger they would hold up the procession. This is clearly reflected in a document of 1558 from Draguignan in south France which reads:

The said [pageants with speeches] shall be performed on the occasion of the procession as in previous years, employing as many episodes as possible and keeping them as short as possible, and they shall be declaimed while the procession proceeds, without anyone involved in the play coming to a halt, so that undue length and confusion may be avoided in both the procession and the play, and so that visitors can watch the proceedings without inconvenience.

This definitely shows us that in some parts of Europe *mobile* performances of short plays were given as an integral part of the Corpus Christi procession, and suggests that in England short dramatic dialogues or monologues recited from moving pageant-wagons could have supplied the germ from which the cycles grew.

The inconvenience of having to slow down what was already a time-consuming procession in order to give performances caused the clergy in some playing towns in England to separate the plays from the procession and perform them at a different time, sometimes on another day, or days, of the same week, sometimes at Whitsuntide – though, interestingly, even when they were performed at Whitsun they were still usually called 'Corpus Christi plays'.

It was undoubtedly in the northern parts of England that the Corpus Christi plays enjoyed their greatest popularity and underwent the most extensive artistic development. Elsewhere in Europe it was large-scale Passion plays that dominated the field of religious drama, and they were almost always presented at Whitsun, the Corpus Christi procession being thought of as something quite separate and unrelated.

# 8

# AN ACUTE SENSE OF SIN

In the late fourteenth and early fifteenth centuries, religious drama of all kinds suddenly leapt into prominence, both in England and on the continent. From being largely an occasional affair in Latin taking place in or near a few major churches on important religious festivals, it suddenly blossomed into a large number of impressive performances in the vernacular, drawing huge crowds, in most of the major cities of Europe. Sometimes these consisted of specially mounted shows which received only a single performance, but more often what was involved was the annual presentation of a complete cycle of plays, either stretching from the Creation of the world to the Last Judgement or, more often, surveying Christ's life from his birth to his death and Resurrection, with reference to only a few major events from the Old Testament.

At the same time a vigorous form of moral drama also sprang up throughout the whole of Europe, consisting at first of large-scale community plays, which we know as 'moralities', and later of small-scale 'moral interludes', which were mostly performed by troupes of professional actors and had a great influence on the Elizabethan stage.

Some scholars have been unwilling to believe that there could be such a sudden and widespread outburst of dramatic activity and have tried to prove there was a continuous tradition of vernacular religious drama – even actual play-cycles – from the time of early pieces like *The Play of Adam*. Such scholars have ferreted about extensively in the records of the early fourteenth century, but have found little relating to vernacular drama, other than a few brief references to single plays, and odd fragments of what may possibly have been plays, but which equally possibly may not.

For want of more substantive evidence, some have tried to prove the existence of early cycles by reference to the Holkham Picture Book, which is a sequence of pictures illustrating events in the Bible story, with a brief Anglo-Norman text explaining them. It is divided into three sections, separated by blank leaves, and the choice of incidents involved is very similar to the play-cycles. Part One contains the story of Genesis, from the creation of Adam and Eve and their Fall up to Noah's safe emergence from the ark after the Flood; Part Two contains a short review of the life and ministry of Christ; and Part Three contains a visual account of the Last Things - namely, the Fifteen Signs which, according to the prophets, will announce the Second Coming of Christ and usher in Doomsday, when he will judge both the living and the dead, and assign the good to Heaven and the bad to eternal torment.

It has been argued that because the Holkham Picture Book contains a similar arrangement of material to the cycles, it must mean that early cycles already existed - but this is quite unsound. A book cannot be used to prove the existence of an early cycle of vernacular plays just because it has captions in the vernacular and shows Bible stories in a particular order. It certainly proves the existence of a popular way of looking at biblical history, which goes some way to explaining the structure of the cycles - but no more than that. So the vigorous attempts to discover early vernacular cycles merely served to confirm what the scholars involved were hoping to disprove, that secular dramatic activity of any kind was very spasmodic indeed before the upsurge of the later fourteenth century.

However, one thing that it proved about that tremendous outburst of dramatic activity is that it was not just a consequence of the new wealth in the cities, because if the cycles had been linked to civic prosperity they would have started in a simple form and grown progressively more elaborate as the years went by. Clearly, then, there was some powerful religious impulse that developed in the society of late medieval Europe and fuelled the desire for large-scale dramatic demonstrations of faith, and this must have been the same impulse that caused people to run frantically from Mass to Mass to see the elevated Host which would ensure their salvation, and that obsessed them with the debt they owed to the tortured Christ hanging upon his Cross. Late medieval man had suddenly become very aware of his sinfulness and his vulnerability.

This attitude may have been promoted, and will certainly have been reinforced, by the development of the new sacrament of Penance, involving the acknowledgement, confession and forgiveness of sins, as it became institutionalised within the medieval Church.

It will be remembered that even in the time of St Paul it was accepted that you must not approach the Lord's table until you had acknowledged your unworthiness and your need to be saved by Christ, and had attempted to purify your heart and mind by making a confession of your sins and repenting what you had done.

In the early Christian era, when the outlook was still essentially Greek and informal, this confession had been a public ceremony where individuals came forward and confessed their sins before everyone, undertaking some act of penance which would give public proof that they were sorry for what they had done and earnestly desired to reform their way of life. The penance would be imposed by the officiating elder, for the good of both the sinner and the community, and it was looked upon as a means of easing the burden of the sinners' bad conscience and reconciling them both with God and themselves - indeed, it was viewed in many ways as a renewal of the original act of baptism.

However, when the Roman Church took over, it tended very much to stress the virtues of authority and obedience, and sinfulness was viewed much more severely - as disobedience to authority rather than as a personal matter. Consequently, by the third century a system had already evolved according to which the penitent wore special coarse garments, like hair shirts, to punish the flesh for its shortcomings, and performed arduous duties of fasting and prayer to help to subdue sinful inclinations. It was still a public ceremony, though, and came to be performed traditionally on Maundy Thursday, the day of the Last Supper, in memory of the torments Christ had to undergo in order to purge away the accumulated sins of a thoughtless mankind.

As time wore on, the Roman Church became steadily larger, and it became inconvenient to have everybody confessing their sins together publicly on Maundy Thursday. There was a sharp cut-back on public acts of confession, which eventually came to be seen as a means of pardoning only the most serious offences against God and was usually only allowed to each sinner once in their lifetime. Understandably, to maximise the ceremony's insurance value, most sinners chose to postpone this to the last possible moment, and deathbed confessions became the norm - but many Christians felt their spiritual welfare was being neglected under this more limited system of public confession, and that the eventual destination of their soul was placed in peril, since they might well die unshriven - so ultimately the system proved unacceptable and it gradually fell into disuse.

As it did so, another system arose to supplement it: a personal form of confession which took place secretly and in private, the brainchild of a missionary in the sixth-century Celtic Church. The sinner disclosed his transgressions to a priest who questioned him at length to determine his spiritual condition and then set him appropriate punishments as a discipline. Such penance, to use a medical analogy which we often find applied in literature and the drama, was a prescription for the afflicted soul and a purgative that cleansed it and made it function more efficiently.

This Celtic system of private confession and private penance proved extremely successful and eventually spread through the whole of Western Europe, as it became clear that this more personal care of the soul was far superior to anything that had preceded it. As a consequence, by the twelfth century, theologians like Peter Lombard were promoting the idea that personal confession should be recognised as a sacrament - that is, a ritual essential to ensure the passage of the soul after death from this world to the more desirable parts of the next.

Eventually, after a period of debate, the Fourth Lateran Council of 1215-16 accepted the new system and indeed made it a sacrament, because it harmonised with the growing emphasis on the power of the priesthood and was obviously another powerful addition to the priests' social and spiritual armoury. Eventually it came to be symbolised in what was called 'the doctrine of the power of the keys': this was derived from a passage in the Scriptures where Christ delegated his authority to bind and loose all souls to St Peter, later the first leader of the Roman Church – that is, he symbolically gave Peter the keys to Heaven and Hell and the power to allocate people's souls provisionally to one or the other in anticipation of the Last Judgement. This authority was now understood to apply to all anointed priests because they were St Peter's direct successors. So, after the Fourth Lateran Council all adult Christians were required to confess their sins privately to their parish priest at least once a year usually before they took communion at Easter.

It was not easy to implement such a sweeping decree. Before parishioners could confess their sins, they needed to know which sins they were expected to confess, what kinds of penance they could expect to receive, who exactly was authorised to hear their confessions, and, above all, what advantages would accrue to them from regular confession, and what punishments would be imposed on them if they remained unrepentant.

The task of conveying all this information to a largely illiterate population proved formidable, particularly in country districts, let alone the problem of enforcing obedience to the new decree and detecting any abuses that might arise. By the terms of the decree, the responsibility for instituting private confession was laid squarely on the shoulders of the parish priest, and unfortunately all too often the poor fellow was wholly unequipped to bear such a responsibility. He was often ignorant of many of the basic doctrines of the Church, and sometimes barely literate.

The seriousness of the problem is brought home to us strongly by a series of guidelines drawn up by local bishops to help parish priests to handle confessions. In these, the offences they were expected to deal with were listed – usually simply as the Seven Deadly Sins, which were already traditional: after all, pride, anger, envy, lust, gluttony, avarice and idleness together provide a fairly comprehensive catalogue of human shortcomings. To these were added the basic prayers in which their parishioners were to be instructed – the Creed (which now came into its own), the 'Hail Mary' (or 'Ave Maria'), the Lord's Prayer (or 'Paternoster'), the Ten Commandments, and an account of the other sacraments – Baptism, Confirmation, the Mass, Holy Orders, Matrimony and Extreme Unction (the Mass for the dying).

Some conscientious archbishops, like John Pecham at Canterbury, circulated a detailed programme of instruction that all priests were required to give to their parishioners at regular intervals, thus ensuring that all Christians in the diocese were well enough informed to make proper confessions and that they were all provided with the minimum supply of prayers and orthodox beliefs needed to sustain their faith.

In further pursuit of this admirable aim many books of penitential instruction – known as 'shrift manuals' – were written in the thirteenth and fourteenth centuries and widely circulated in manuscript. Some were official, and written in Latin, like William of Pagula's famous *Oculus Sacerdotis*, or *Guiding Light for the Priesthood*, but most parish priests had only a very sketchy knowledge of Latin, so there were many translations and vernacular adaptations of the official accounts, like Mirk's *Instructions for Parish Priests*, which was a fifteenth-century version of the *Oculus*.

Soon a general concern with confession and Penance began to permeate all the activities of the Church. In the collections of sermons that now began to be published for the first time, and in popular devotional works written for the lay public, like the *Cursor Mundi* (*The Guide of the World*) or *Handling Sin*, to give only two famous examples, confession and Penance are almost constantly the focus of interest, and a similar preoccupation extended throughout most of later medieval literature.

Reinforcing this movement to self-purification were the various attempts made to reform and purify the Church itself – some official and some not. By the late twelfth and early thirteenth centuries the Church had become very aware of its own wealth and power; as a result it had come to meddle extensively in politics and had grown more and more worldly and corrupt. This came to a head in the papacy of Boniface VIII, between 1294 and 1303. Boniface embodied all the pretensions of the papacy at its most worldly and its most arrogant. He was a lawyer by training and far from spiritual in his nature: he quarrelled violently with the kings of England and France because they would not submit to him, and in the Jubilee of 1300 had two swords carried before him in procession to symbolise his possession of both spiritual *and* temporal power. Two years later he asserted that a belief in the worldly sovereignty of the Pope over every human being on earth was necessary for spiritual salvation. It is hardly surprising that all the rulers of Europe intrigued to get a more pliable successor elected, and a few years later the papacy was so weak that the kings and the emperor were using it as a kind of diplomatic bargaining-counter – the French even established their own Pope in Avignon for a while, as a rival to the Pope in Rome.

The worldliness of the Church drew increasing criticism during this period, and the whole Church organisation was overrun with lawyers, who were needed to resolve legal squabbles with the laity, and bureaucrats who could ensure that the Church did not die from a lack of circulation of funds, while, sadly, some of the higher clergy, who should have known better, spent lavishly on banquets and even maintained expensive mistresses.

Under these circumstances, the first, and predictable, reaction was a new batch of heresies – involving a refusal to accept either the Church's authority or its teachings. The most interesting, and most widely supported, of the heresies that became current – all of them directed against the wealth and pomp of the Church and striving to return to a plain, simple form of Christianity – was that of the Cathars or Albigenses (the Pure Ones) in the south of France. They were originally an Eastern sect who believed that everything material was created by the Devil and should be renounced by the faithful. They also believed in the transmigration of the soul after death, and particularly that the souls of the wicked were reincarnated as animals – for which reason they were strict vegetarians, abstaining from even eggs, cheese and milk. For them everything in the Old Testament was the work of the Devil, and Jehovah was a wicked demiurge, because he created the material world – Christ alone was the one true God – and they lived literally by the dictates of the New Testament: poverty, communism, pacifism and the avoidance of oaths.

The Albigenses were very vocal about the sins of the Christian clergy, particularly the bishops, and thus drew down the fury of Pope Innocent III, who persuaded the king of France to embark on a crusade against them in 1209. This crusade was conducted with incredible ferocity, and after the taking of Carcassone, in south France, the main Cathar town, there was an appalling massacre. Even so, the Albigenses survived the persecution and were one of the main reasons why Gregory IX founded the Inquisition in 1233.

To show how similar the basic aims of all heretics were at this time, we need only take one other example, that of the Waldenses. These were the followers of Peter Waldo, who started a personal crusade in 1170 to promote observance of the Law of Christ. He gave all his goods to the poor, and founded a society called the 'Poor Men of Lyons', who practised poverty and a strictly virtuous life. Unlike the Cathars, they originally had papal approval, but they too soon came into disfavour because of their forcible attacks on the immorality of the clergy, and were condemned by the Council of Verona in 1184. Thereupon they decided that every 'goodman', as they called themselves, was competent to preach and expound the Scriptures and act as a minister to the people, and they renounced the Catholic priesthood. They too suffered during the Albigensian persecution and fled to Piedmont and Bohemia. In Piedmont they were still being viciously persecuted in John Milton's day – they are the 'slaughtered saints' he refers to in his famous sonnet 'On the Late Massacre in Piedmont'. In Bohemia (modern Czechoslovakia) they found a much more militant leader in the revolutionary John Huss, who met military force with new and effective defensive tactics, and there they became the Hussites.

Both Hussites and Cathars still exist, despite centuries of persecution: the Cathars, in particular, occasionally get into the papers on account of their habit of stripping themselves naked from time to time and burning their houses and other possessions.

Contemporary efforts to reform the Church from within are seen in the emergence of the orders of begging friars, or Mendicants, at about the time that heresy reached its peak. They were inspired by the same desire as the heretics to bring about a simple and uncorrupt Christianity. St Francis, for instance, came from a well-to-do family and was very worldly as a young man, but one day as he was riding in the city he saw a leper and a sudden impulse of pity led him to dismount and kiss the man. Soon after, he decided to forgo all worldly goods and devote his life to preaching and good works. His father, a respectable businessman, was furious but could not stop him. Francis soon gathered a band of followers, all vowed to complete poverty, and his movement became very popular. At first the ecclesiastical authorities viewed it with suspicion, because it looked like another branch of the Poor Men of Lyons, and the early Franciscans were held to be heretics because they actually lived by their vow of poverty rather than merely paying it lip-service like the monks of the time; but in 1209 Pope Innocent III gave recognition to the order, and despite occasional persecutions from the Church later on, when they became too radical or too critical of authority, the Franciscans flourished.

St Dominic, who founded the Dominican order, another community of friars who lived strictly in accordance with their vows of poverty, was more or less a contemporary of St Francis, but very different in nature. He was a Castilian Spaniard by descent, though born in Italy, and had a fanatical devotion to orthodoxy. His main purpose in life was to combat heresy, and he was present in south France throughout the Albigensian crusade, of which he approved in principle, though we hear he disapproved of some of its worst atrocities. His order was founded, again by Pope Innocent III, in 1215 and was particularly active in the work of the Inquisition. St Dominic originally decreed, in the interests of orthodoxy, that his friars should not learn any secular sciences or liberal arts, but, by an irony of fate, the Dominicans later became devoted to learning in all its forms, and in 1259 the rules of the order were changed to make a life of study as easy as possible for them.

The two orders soon acquired popular names – the Franciscans, who wore mousey grey-brown habits, being known as the 'Grey Friars', and the Dominicans, who wore black, as the 'Black Friars' or 'Friars

Preachers'. The members of these orders constituted a kind of mobile priesthood, zealously devoted to propagating the faith among all orders of society. They were particularly involved in the new movement to instruct the general public about private confession and penance, which they did through vernacular sermons of great power and the distribution of shrift manuals. Their comparative effectiveness is clearly shown by the large number of papal rulings during the thirteenth century seeking to soothe the ruffled feathers of parish priests who resented the encroachment of the friars upon their prerogatives, and they obviously deserve the greatest credit for the rapid popularisation of the sacrament of Penance. As priests they had 'the power of the keys', so they could hear confessions and give absolution. Moreover, people were more ready to reveal their secrets to them, knowing they would not be long in the neighbourhood, and were more ready to be confessed by them because they were known never to demand harsh acts of penance. In fact scholars who have studied their work believe that *compulsory* private confession could never have been achieved without their help, because many parish priests adhered far too strictly to the harsh recommendations of the shrift manuals, and a light penance which the people would perform was much better than a heavy one which they would not.

The Dominicans and Franciscans were also closely associated with the universities that were beginning to be founded all over Europe to teach sound Christian doctrine, produce effective new preachers and develop arguments to confute the heretics. All the great thinkers of the day belonged to one or other of the two orders, the two greatest, perhaps, being Dominicans - Albertus Magnus, popularly believed to be a magician, who founded the study of the biological sciences, and his more famous pupil St Thomas Aquinas, whose *Summa Theologica* for the first time fused together the traditions of Plato and Aristotle with those of Christianity to produce a more or less harmonious whole. This work, which was completed in 1273, is still the main pillar of Catholic theology.

Perhaps the most important aspect of the two orders, though, was the fact that they were first and foremost *preaching* orders: they each, in their own way, saw man as being in a perilous condition, teetering on the edge of damnation: they both expected the Second Coming of Christ at any moment, and considered it vital to get over the message of salvation in time to save men's souls. Only their approaches were different: the Franciscans taught that salvation could best be achieved by a faith centring upon love and service to your neighbour, as Christ himself had both taught and practised; the Dominicans, who were the order that actually acquired the *name* of 'Friars Preachers', taught that it could only be brought about by a strict devotion to the orthodox doctrines of the contemporary Church, and they preached 'Hellfire' sermons to scare the wicked into obedience and move them to repentance. The Dominicans were also more worldly than the Franciscans and moved much more freely in society. They were not only at the new universities but also in the schools; they were not only the confessors of kings but were also to be found in the market-place amongst the poor – and it was often the same preacher who was to be found in both places. They were zealous men, quite without fear or favour, and drew no distinction in their sermons between the rich and the poor, or the powerful and the weak – except to underline the fact that the rich and powerful were far more likely to find their way to Hell.

Regarding miracle plays and moral dramas, the friars' attitudes were purely personal and varied widely: on the one hand, there were persistent rumours of friars actually writing plays, and even acting in them, while on the other the famous Dominican preacher John Bromyard reckoned that people should not be diverted from attending the services of the Church by these 'new shows . . . which they call Miracles', which were written by 'foolish clerics' – although he did not positively forbid people from watching them, as some of Wycliffe's more puritanical followers did. Midway we find William Melton commending the plays at York because they instructed the common people in the elements of the faith, but asking for them to be moved to the day after Corpus Christi because their performance led to feasting and carousing which drew people away from the church services, particularly early Mass. We should also note that the Franciscans regularly used drama later to teach Christianity to the natives of Mexico and South America.

So the friars' influence on the religious drama is likely to have been a mixed one. It is nonetheless of the greatest importance, because they were responsible for creating an atmosphere of urgency and lively spiritual concern, and for 'dramatising' Scriptural and moral matters in all sorts of ways, both visual and verbal, to make them more immediate to the people. What is more, the kind of vivid sermons they preached provided the playwrights with a great deal of vigorous moral comment, which they often borrowed verbatim, and also many examples of powerful popular rhetoric, which they used to drive home the opinions of their characters. Besides, the preachers used all sorts of devices in their sermons which were useful pointers for dramatists – moral allegories and parables, lively descriptions of everyday life, and, particularly 'exempla', or 'examples', which were popular stories with a moral emphasis, stories which could be sensational or comic, fantastical or strongly grounded in everyday life, but which were, above all, vivid and memorable. The use of these 'examples' had been encouraged long before by St Gregory as a means of getting through to the common people, on the model of Christ's parables, but they were very little used until the new need for preaching sprang up at the time we are considering.

Importantly, the use of exempla suggested to the authors of the cycles ways in which they could effectively mix different styles, expressing the morally profound in a humorous or bawdy tale, and mixing serious and farcical matters, and high and low language, in a distinctively Christian way. So we find the cycle writers drawing upon legends and contemporary short stories, known as 'fabliaux', almost as much as on the Bible itself.

Furthermore, while sermons on the Scriptures and the life of Christ reinforced the lessons read in church which led to the cycle-plays, sermons on moral matters led just as logically to the moralities and moral interludes which were the other important form of contemporary drama. Indeed, the low-life incidents of many of the morality plays feel very much like direct borrowings from exempla in contemporary sermons, and their sheer dramatic power is well illustrated by the sensational story of the young men who decided to kill Death, in Chaucer's *Pardoner's Tale*.

The early fourteenth century was, then, a restless and uncertain age, seeking the solutions to many pressing problems. Then, suddenly, on top of the turmoil created by the new sense of sin, dissatisfaction with the Church, growing heresy, crusades against heretics, the Inquisition, friars preaching hellfire sermons and a growing preoccupation with self-examination and purification, a final factor was superimposed that gave the whole process a new urgency – the shadow of the Black Death.

Nobody knows exactly where it came from – as happens with so many epidemics which apparently start in Asia – but in 1347 it suddenly struck the seaports of Italy, carried by merchant ships trading with the Black Sea. It was the worst scourge man has ever known. In that same year it ravaged Naples and Sicily. In 1348 it spread like wildfire across Europe. In the winter of 1348 it invaded England but lay dormant till the spring of 1349, when it savaged the population. By 1350 it was in Scotland and Ireland, in Portugal, Scandinavia and White Russia.

A quarter of the population of England died in that dreadful scourge, but the rural areas on the whole suffered less than the towns, where losses were sometimes as high as almost one person in every two. At least 25 million people died in Europe in this visitation, and it was only the first of many, for from that time on the Plague struck regularly, often with only short intervals, until the latter part of the seventeenth century.

There were some grotesque by-products of the fear that the Black Death instilled. One was an attitude of bravado, similar to that of Elizabethan whores when they were first faced with syphilis, and took to wearing rings with a skull on them as a reminder to get the best they could out of life while it lasted. Typical of this ambivalent attitude was the fact that in Paris many prostitutes chose to pitch their booths in the cloisters of St Innocents' churchyard, which were stacked with the rotting flesh and bones of the newly dead – though not, it should be said, those who had died of the Plague. They chose the area because people flocked there in crowds, laughing and joking and holding social dances. Friars preached there regularly, too, because of the place's popularity. The people obviously found pleasure in mingling with the remains of the dead. It seems to have been a process of familiarisation with the inevitable, a way in which they could steel themselves for what might come tomorrow by surveying their inevitable end with an ironical and macabre humour.

It is the same mocking attitude that is to be seen in the fifteenth-century Dance of Death, which is best known from Holbein's magnificent but gruesome series of pictures. It seems that the idea may have originated in an actual mimetic dance in which Death comes to take away people in all ranks of society, one at a time – the King, the Pope, the Emperor, the Cardinal, the Doctor, the Lover, the Old Man, the Child – everybody! The performance was probably used to drive home a sermon about the inevitability of death – certainly such a Dance of Death occurred under Franciscan auspices at Besançon in 1453; another may well have taken place in St Innocents' churchyard itself, because there was a Dance of Death painted on the walls there.

It is difficult to realise fully the horror of the Black Death: bubonic plague was a putrid typhus – it started with huge boils under the armpits and then the body rapidly turned black as it decayed and its victims died raving and in agony. People fled before it into country retreats; whole Jewish communities migrated to try and avoid it, and a second 'diaspora', or 'scattering', of the race resulted; but run as they might, nobody could escape it.

Faced with a sudden ghastly death in this guise, the whole process of preaching and repentance took on a more urgent note. Till then people had been threatened with death catching them unawares, but hardly believed it – now suddenly they saw neighbours caught unprepared all around them and dying unshriven, their souls surely on the direct route to Hell. It was in this new, urgent atmosphere that the cycles and the moralities suddenly became a reality, and money was poured from civic coffers into the celebration of the promises of salvation to mankind as a whole and forgiveness to the sinner who repented.

Ironically, the Black Death also created the wealth with which to produce the new drama. Those who survived it prospered because the resulting shortage of manpower favoured both skilled and unskilled workers. The old feudal slavery was destroyed by the new demand for labourers, who could now claim both greater independence and higher wages, while in the towns the shortage of skilled craftsmen put a premium on their products and provided the guilds with a much stronger bargaining position in their negotiations with the corporation. As a consequence the guilds flourished and, in return for the town's protection of their local monopolies, were prepared to undertake civic responsibilities like the mounting of pageants for the Corpus Christi or Whitsuntide festivals – an undertaking for which they now had ample funds and which, in any case, was a lively advertisement for the products of all the local guilds.

# 9

# THE STRUCTURE OF THE CYCLES

The freshness and immediacy of the Corpus Christi plays must always have appealed to viewers and readers, but it took time for scholars to realise they were not simply naive folk-products, but carefully organised works of art presenting the spiritual history of mankind in a way that made it particularly relevant to their audience. This emerged particularly in the English cycles, which made extensive use of Old Testament material, unlike the European Passion plays, which adhered mostly to the Gospels. It was suddenly realised, for instance, that the playwrights who composed these cycles were extremely selective about which episodes from the Bible they chose to dramatise: some stories appear with great frequency, whilst others – including the extremely popular story of Joseph – are not treated at all. This led to a scholarly analysis of the English plays which revealed methods of organisation that were equally applicable to all cycles, particularly when they incorporated Old Testament material.

Examination of the four complete cycles that have come down to us in England – those of Chester, York, Wakefield and 'N-Town' – together with the full list of pageants relating to the lost cycle at Beverley, show us which stories were used most frequently. Ten plays occur in all of the cycles: namely, *The Fall of Lucifer, The Creation and Fall of Man, Cain and Abel, Noah and the Flood, Abraham and Isaac, The Nativity* (usually from the Annunciation to the point where the young Jesus amazes the doctors with his knowledge), *The Raising of Lazarus, The Passion* (from the conspiracy of Judas up to the Harrowing of Hell and the release of the righteous pagans), *The Resurrection* (from Pilate's setting guards over the tomb to the Ascension of Christ into Heaven), and finally *The Doomsday* (or *Last Judgement*). Another five plays appear in four of the five cycles: these are *The Play of Moses*, dealing either with the Jews' escape from Egypt or the receiving of the Ten Commandments – (Beverley did not have this), *The Procession of the Prophets* (Beverley did not have this either), *The Baptism of Christ by John the Baptist* (it was Chester that lacked this one), *Christ's Temptation by the Devil in the*

*Wilderness* (missing at Wakefield) and *The Assumption and Coronation of the Virgin Mary* (also missing at Wakefield).

Faced with this severe selectivity, a little probing sufficed to show that two main lines of Biblical interpretation underpinned the choice made by the dramatists. The first, which detected repeated 'figures', or 'analogies', in sacred history between some aspect of Christ's life and an event elsewhere in the Bible, was an extension of the typical medieval method of distilling significant meaning from any two things that appeared to be similar, however remotely. The second line of interpretation involved looking at history as a series of successive 'ages', each having its own related spiritual guide and teacher.

Of the two, the 'figures', or historical analogies, were easily the most important, because they served to tie all the books of the Bible together into a coherent whole, and, since the Bible was believed to be a record of all the significant events of human history, they helped in this way to give man's life on earth a shape and purpose. It has already been explained that the Jews saw the Old Testament as a progressive revelation of God's great plan for his chosen people, and for Christians the New Testament continued and, in a sense, perfected that revelation. It was only the emphasis that changed. Believing, as they did, that Christ's birth, Passion and Resurrection were God's chosen means of achieving man's salvation, Christian interpreters were sure that the events of his life must provide a pattern for all significant historical events, both before and after his coming.

Consequently, a *figura*, or 'figure', occurred when some episode in Christ's life appeared to be anticipated or re-enacted by another event occurring elsewhere in history, which thus became a 'shadow' or 'reflection' of the original event. For example, the account of the Passover in the Old Testament was seen as foreshadowing the Last Supper, and Christ was thought of as a new Moses leading his followers out of the darkness of sin and death, into the light of salvation, while later events like the deaths of the Christian martyrs were seen as a re-enactment of Christ's Passion and a reiteration of his message. Thus, in the light of *figura* the whole of sacred history was seen to be woven together into a single, seamless garment.

The notion of *figura* was mainly pursued by medieval Churchmen, because they felt a pressing need to prove the unity of the Old Testament and the New, but the larger purpose of interpreting history as a whole was certainly also present, and medieval writers constantly refer to one event in history 'prefiguring' or 'foreshadowing' another, even when alluding to completely secular events. The effect of this upon the writers of the cycle-plays is clear. Apart from one or two pieces included for strictly theological reasons, the plays in any cycle were mainly bound

94

together by *figura*, the story of Christ's life providing the core of the action and the surrounding plays picking up the analogies.

So, in a typical cycle, the inclusion of plays dealing with Christ's Nativity, Passion and Resurrection is self-explanatory – since these events are the very heart of the Christian interpretation of history. The Baptism, too, is easily explained, because it is the one essential sacrament required of all Christians, and Christ's successful resistance of Satan's temptation after his Baptism satisfactorily rounds out the sequence of events beginning with his birth. These last two plays are also very useful for picking up Old Testament prefigurations: for instance, the parallel between the forty years the Jewish people wandered with Moses in the wilderness and the forty days Christ was tempted by the devil. The inclusion of the Raising of Lazarus from Christ's ministry is also easily explained, as foreshadowing his own Resurrection.

The play of the Assumption and Coronation of the Virgin Mary, recounting her bodily ascension and installation as Queen of Heaven, is not in any way *essential* to the Christian message, but it was important to people at the time, and reflects the influence of the cult of the Virgin Mary, which was so powerful in Ireland and England and parts of France in the later Middle Ages that it was dubbed 'Mariolatry' and caused much heart-searching in the Vatican. This play contains a *retrospective* figuration of Christ's Ascension, occuring *after* the event and looking back to it – an extension of the idea of *figura* found in the deaths of the saints.

The Procession of the Prophets, of course, justifies its inclusion by *prediction* of Christ's coming, rather than prefiguration.

However, this leaves the presence of many cycle-plays still unexplained, and here the Holkham Picture Book, mentioned earlier, becomes of real value, because its three divisions reveal a general approach to the history of man, showing Christ's life, flanked on either side by what are called the First Things and the Last Things. These three areas highlight the three advents, or comings, of God to mankind: his first coming to create man, his second coming to redeem him, and his third coming when he will judge him.

It is obvious that the First Things are closely related to the Last. The Fall of Lucifer is necessary to explain the origins of evil in a universe supposed to be created by a God who is wholly good, and the Bible then shows how the evil spreads to encompass the Fall of Man and Cain's murder of Abel, thus explaining why it was necessary for God to sacrifice his only-begotten Son to redeem man from sin. The continued prevalence of sin, after that supreme act of sacrifice, is the reason for the Last Judgement at the other end of human history, when the sheep will be separated from the goats, and the good who have tried to follow Christ's teachings will win Heaven, whilst the wicked suffer the pains of Hell. It was very important for the Last Judgement to be shown in a cyclical performance, because it was the only sanction the Church could use to persuade its members to behave themselves.

The Fall of Man does not *foreshadow* any other action in the holy story, but it does provide the first and most vivid illustration of Man's disobedience to the will of God, which is what made Christ's act of sacrifice necessary.

The story of Cain and Abel involves the first murder, prefiguring the murder of the Son of God himself: it also shows the intensification of evil that had occurred since Adam's fall. Abel therefore becomes the *figura* of Christ, and in many performances of the play he was murdered on the very spot where he had offered his lamb on the altar, thus becoming identified with the Paschal Lamb, or Christ in his sacrificial aspect – a vivid way of bringing the figure out. Cain was then seen to be the Jews who were responsible for Christ's death, and his stinginess was held to typify the Jewish attachment to material possessions. From a social viewpoint, he was also typical of the tight-fisted Christian farmer who refused to give God his due – a tithe, or tenth, of all his earnings for the use of Holy Church. There is good Scriptural authority supporting the figural identification of Abel and Christ, in St Paul's Letter to the Hebrews.

The actions of Noah, Abraham and Moses were seen as a kind of counterbalancing goodness, in a world of evil, which made it worth God's while to consider the redemption of man, despite all his shortcomings. However, these three incidents all have very strong figural links to parts of the Gospel story as well.

The story of Noah and the ark was always clearly seen as a prefiguration of Jesus assuming the role of a new Noah and 'preserving the family of Christ from damnation, housed in the sacramental structure of the Church, in which they will safely journey to eternal blessedness'. This comparison had the authority of no less a person than Jesus himself – 'As in the days of Noah, so shall also be the coming of the Son of Man' – and the Second letter of Peter compares the Flood with the fire that will engulf the earth at the time of the Second Coming. There was a further implicit symbolism often expressed by medieval writers when they insisted that Noah was saved by water and wood, the wood of the ark being compared to the Cross that metaphorically keeps the good Christian's head above water, and the Flood itself being compared to the water of baptism that washes away all evil, buoys up the believer, and carries him safely over the destructive enticements of the world of sin.

There is a charming picture in the Holkham Picture Book of Noah, standing with his arms spread wide, like those of Christ on the cross, with the raven perched on his left hand and the dove on his right – obviously the appropriate hands. The coal-black raven, which did not return to the ark but found food on which to glut itself, represents the sinners who are damned; the snow-white dove, which dutifully considered the good of others before itself, represents the worthy who are saved. The two birds were also held at the time to represent the two thieves who were crucified to the left and right of Christ, the one on Christ's left rejecting him, and the one on his right accepting his promise of salvation. In some cycles there is a deliberate reminder of Noah's Flood in the play of the Last Judgement, when God expresses his dissatisfaction with the bulk of mankind in almost exactly the same words he used at the beginning of the Noah play, and, where this occurred it will greatly have strengthened the significance of the *figura*.

The story of Abraham was seen as having a number of different meanings. He was the first of the Jews to accept circumcision as a mark of dedication to God, and by that action and God's acceptance of it can be seen as having made a new covenant, or agreement, with his Creator. He also, according to the book of Genesis, received sacred bread and wine from the priest–king Melchisedek, foreshadowing the Last Supper; but, though both these incidents are often mentioned in the cycles, the central and unavoidable *figura* relates to his willingness to sacrifice his son Isaac at God's command – a command given to test Abraham's obedience, just like the order given to Adam.

The whole action could be seen as a clear prefiguration of God sacrificing his only-begotten Son for the benefit of mankind – indeed, in some versions, there is a kind of bargain implied by God: 'You do this for me now, and I'll sacrifice my Son for your sake later.' In the plays, Isaac's words just before his father is about to sacrifice him often recall those of Christ on the Cross, 'Into Thy hands, O Lord, I commend my spirit', and Abraham's words when he comments on his son's innocence often recall those of Pilate: 'I find no fault in this just man.' Isaac's last-minute reprieve, when the angel stays Abraham's hand, was seen as a figure of the Resurrection, and the ram caught in the thicket, provided to replace him, was sometimes seen as the Paschal Lamb decked out for sacrifice in his crown of thorns. Some commentators even saw Isaac carrying the wood for his own sacrifice as a figure of Christ carrying his own cross to Golgotha.

The slightly less frequent appearance of Moses in the cycles may well have been because there were so many figural interpretations of his actions the dramatist did not know which to choose. To mention some: there is the unavoidable *figura* relating to the Passover and the leading of Israel out of bondage; Moses also distributed manna in the wilderness, prefiguring Christ's feeding of the five thousand; he brought water from the rock, prefiguring the mixed blood and water that flowed from Christ's side for the good of man; he spent forty years in the wilderness, prefiguring the forty days that Christ spent in the desert being tempted by Satan, and so on.

However, the two central aspects of the story of Moses – one or the other, or both, of which were usually dramatised – were the flight from Egypt and the receiving of the Ten Commandments on Mount Sinai. Perhaps surprisingly from a dramatic viewpoint, the Ten Commandments was marginally the more common. Here the link within the cycle is that Christ gave the new law, 'You shall love the Lord your God . . . and . . . you shall love your neighbour as yourself', to replace the old Mosaic law of vengeance, 'an eye for an eye and a tooth for a tooth'. There is often in the cycles a retrospective figuration of Moses in the play of the Doctors, where the eleven-year-old Jesus is in the Temple for the first time and astounds the lawyers there with his knowledge, which appears to consist of no more than an ability to recite the Ten Commandments – though this, of course, means symbolically that Jesus completely understood all the details of the elaborate Jewish Law expounded in the Old Testament. The exodus from Egypt was a more obviously dramatic theme, and, since it was seen as prefiguring Christ, the new Moses, leading his followers out of the power of the Devil, the King of Egypt was always portrayed as the Devil incarnate.

The dramatisation of his pursuit of the Israelites into the Red Sea, where the Egyptian army was overwhelmed by the return of its waters, was a very colourful incident as well, because medieval writers and painters insisted that the sea was physically red – presumably on the grounds that one of the plagues visited on the country only shortly before had turned all the rivers to blood. As a result of this interpretation of the event, the passing through the Red Sea was seen simultaneously as an image of the need for all Christian believers to pass through the waters of baptism and of their being washed clean of their sins by the blood of Christ; and, of course, the mixed blood and water that came from Christ's side on the Cross was not forgotten. This association of the crossing of the Red Sea with baptism was originally made by St Paul in his First Letter to the Corinthians.

It should now be obvious how theological considerations reinforced by figural parallels determined the selection of the main subjects dramatised in the cycles, weaving them together into an artistic whole – but this does not explain why other obvious parts of the Bible were not dramatised, particularly the story of Joseph, which was full of vivid prefigurations regularly expounded in every other medieval form of literature; nor does it explain the inclusion of occasional plays involving King David, Jacob and Esau, and King Solomon. Were these merely added because the author liked them, and, if so, why was the story of Joseph omitted?

The answer lay in the second way of endowing Biblical history with special meaning, which tended to be subordinated to the concept of *figura*, but was nonetheless an important guiding principle and certainly explains the absence of Joseph. This was the scheme according to which sacred history was divided up into a series of 'ages', each of which had its related spiritual leader.

St Matthew was unintentionally responsible for this alternative way of looking at the Bible. While he was poring over the list of Christ's ancestors, to reassure his Jewish readers that the Master really was a member of the House of David, he detected a pattern in it that might reflect some kind of divine purpose – as he writes in the first chapter of his Gospel: 'Thus there are fourteen generations in all from Abraham to David, fourteen from David to the Babylonian captivity, and fourteen from the Babylonian captivity to the birth of Christ.' Four centuries later, this plainly set St Augustine wondering whether this same pattern could be discovered before the time of Abraham? He consequently turned back to the book of Genesis, where he found the full genealogy of Abraham dating from the creation of Adam. Doubtless he was disappointed to find that fourteen was not after all the mystical number that revealed God's purposes, since there were twenty generations between Adam and the birth of Abraham. However, looking more closely at them, he realised that there *was* a principle of equal division apparent. Adam was granted the first contract, or covenant, with God, which he shamefully flouted by eating the fruit of the Tree of Knowledge. Abraham, at the other end of the sequence, was granted a new covenant when he accepted the painful ritual of circumcision. But *precisely mid-way* between these two points was Noah, and after the Flood the rainbow marked yet another covenant between man and God, when God promised never again to destroy the world with a flood because of Noah's impeccable loyalty. Here God's purpose had clearly manifested itself again, though he sometimes preferred the number ten and sometimes the number fourteen! Confronted with this fact, it was natural for medieval man to observe that ten was the number of the Commandments, and fourteen was twice the number of the days of creation.

Certainly, the seven days of Creation sprang to Augustine's mind. He now had six historical ages, beginning respectively with Adam, Noah, Abraham, David, the Babylonian exile, and Jesus Christ. But God's plan was not yet perfected, and so there must be a seventh age yet to come, which would reiterate the pattern of Creation! And what could this last age be but the Second Coming of Christ and the Last Judgement, which would usher in an eternal sabbath, an everlasting day of rest, for God himself and all virtuous Christians. He went on record to that effect in his *City of God.*

From that time onwards, all the scholars who set out to interpret biblical history tended to do so by superimposing a system of ages, though they did not always agree completely with Augustine's system. For instance, they could not see why the Babylonian exile should mark the beginning of a new age. What great spiritual figure did it have to guide it? King Jechonias? Who ever heard of him? And why was Moses missing, a truly great spiritual leader and indisputably the greatest *figura* of Christ?

For this reason, three hundred years later the Venerable Bede was still looking for a more rational interpretation of Biblical history. He refused to be blinded by mystical numbers and generations, and asked himself the simple question, 'If there really *are* ages of history, how would God probably mark their existence?' The conclusion seemed to him obvious: each age would surely be distinguished by a new lawgiver, and a new covenant, or agreement, with God. This gave him a much more satisfactory system of five ages, based upon Adam, Noah, Abraham, Moses and Christ.

This new proposal somewhat confused the issue. Most writers were not willing to follow Bede and become divorced from the seven days of Creation, although they accepted that Augustine's original system was not ideal – so they flirted with a number of Biblical figures in their search for an extended system. What about David, the builder of the Temple, or Solomon, who was surely an exceptionally talented lawgiver?

Eventually, so far as England was concerned, the system settled down to seven ages again, six of them distinguished by the leadership of Adam, Noah, Abraham, Moses, David and Christ respectively, whilst the last was to be heralded by the coming of the Day of Judgement. This system was very successful: it was incorporated into a number of popular works on theology, including *The Golden Legend*, an immensely influential collection of saints' lives, and helped to shape Higden's important fourteenth-century history the *Polychronicon*, or *Multitude of Ages*.

So far as the cycles were concerned, the idea of the seven ages was very important as a secondary structuring influence, although, in practice they were usually reduced to six because King David tended to slip back into the Procession of the Prophets and lose his independent status.

Where there was a clash between two possible interpretations, the figural version would almost always override that of the seven ages. A clear example of this is the case of Abraham: though he was strictly the maker of a new covenant with God by virtue of undertaking circumcision, this was always passed over in favour of his much more figurally important – and dramatically practical – willingness to sacrifice his son Isaac.

On the other hand, there is the case of Moses, whose story is figurally very powerful, but who is almost always shown receiving the Ten Commandments from God. This is doubtless explained by the importance of the Ten Commandments to traditional Christians, and by Christ's insi tence that he was bringing a New Law to replace that of Moses, but it is perhaps also important to remember that Moses only entered the cycle structure quite late and did so as a representative of the seven ages system, where he was more important as a lawgiver than as the *figura* of Christ.

We can see then how basic theology and figural links, backed up by the theory of the seven ages, provided the criteria for choice and organisation of material in the Corpus Christi cycles; but the structuring patterns also reached out from the historical events shown in the plays to touch the daily lives of the audience, because there was a commonly held medieval view of historical events which involves what may conveniently be called 'vertical time', as opposed to the usual linear, or 'horizontal', time.

This idea can best be described by saying that medieval man saw time not as a straight line but as a rising spiral, so that history continually repeated itself as it progressed. A man could either look forwards and backwards along the curving line of time before or behind him, in which case his point of view was essentially 'horizontal' like our own, or he could look straight up and down at the equivalent points on the many curves of the time-line directly above or below him, thus taking a 'vertical' view. To make this absolutely clear, imagine a large spiral spring, with a straight stick laid along the side of it: the stick touches each of the twists of the spiral in turn, and this is a symbolic presentation of the way the 'vertical' view of time worked, while the 'horizontal' view would be equivalent to following the wire itself along the spiral.

This 'vertical' view of time intimately linked together events of the past and the present. In its simplest application it saw each year as a single twist of the time-spiral, which meant, for instance, that every time you reached Easter you were mystically linked with the original Crucifixion and Passion of Christ. This could lead to a very crowded view of history, as is seen in a passage from *The Golden Legend*:

> This blessed Annunciation happened the 25th day of the month of March, on which day happened also, as well tofore as after, these things that hereafter be named. On that same day Adam, the first man, was created and fell into original sin by inobedience, and was put out of paradise terrestrial. After, the angel showed the conception of our Lord to the glorious Virgin Mary. Also that same day of the month Cain slew Abel his brother. Also Melchisedek made offering to God of bread and wine in the presence of Abraham. Also on the same day Abraham offered Isaac his son. That same day Saint John Baptist was beheaded, and Saint Peter was that day delivered out of prison, and Saint James the more [was] that day beheaded of Herod. And our Lord Jesu Christ was on that day crucified, wherefore that is a day of great reverence.

If you accepted this point of view, nothing could ever be really distant in time – every day drew the threads of past and present closely together and was full of spiritual meaning. Each day became sanctified, and casual

again in 1304. The principles of organisation seem not dissimilar to those of the vernacular cycles, but while the Riga cycle had a substantial Old Testament component, which extended as far as the stories of David and of Gideon, the Cividale cycle was composed almost entirely of New Testament material from the Annunciation to the Ascension, with the Creation and the Fall of Man as a preface and the Last Judgement as an epilogue. We have no evidence of any liturgical cycle in England.

It must always have been difficult for cycle-makers to decide how much they should include, and where they should call a halt. There were four logical endings to a cycle – the Resurrection and Christ's appearances to his disciples; the Ascension, the descent of the Holy Spirit at Pentecost; and the Last Judgement. If the Redemption of man was the subject of the cycle, then it could be strictly held to end at the Resurrection; but if the intention was to remind Christians of God's plan for mankind as a whole, then the Last Judgement was essential, preceded by the Creation and Fall of Man. Cycles in different parts of Europe provide examples of all these endings.

The situation regarding the Old Testament was less clear. The Creation and Fall of Man could hardly be omitted, but did you precede it with a Fall of Lucifer, and where did you draw the line in the mass of history and prophecy that followed? (And remember that all the books now relegated to the Apocrypha were still considered relevant.) Faced with such a wealth of material, the cycle-makers must have eagerly embraced the ideas of *figura* and the seven ages as some kind of guideline.

Not that all the material of the Old Testament lends itself to dramatic treatment. Genesis and Exodus certainly provide a continuous narrative, but the next three books of the Bible contain a detailed exposition of the Jewish Law and have nothing narrative in them but the story of Balak and Balaam and the death of Moses. The historical account is then picked up again in the nine books reaching from Joshua to the Second Book of Chronicles, which contain the stories of Joshua, Gideon, Samson, Ruth, Samuel, David and Solomon, amongst many others. After this come only the prophetic books and books of wisdom, though, scattered amongst them are the stories of Queen Esther, Job, Daniel, Jonah, and Tobias and the angel.

Where a writer was not pressurised by practical considerations, this narrative pattern is faithfully mirrored. For instance, the most ambitious and comprehensive treatment of this part of the Bible is the fifteenth-century French *Mystery of the Old Testament*, which runs to 49,386 lines, more than twelve times the length of the full text of *Hamlet* – which means it would run for roughly forty hours if it was played briskly: not surprisingly, it was only ever presented in extracts.

Nor was there much time for self-indulgence: though the plays were occasionally allowed to extend over several days, they usually lasted for only one, two or, at most, three. This meant that a radical selection of Old Testament episodes was required. Under these circumstances there were natural stopping-places, just as there were in the New Testament. You could include only the very First Things, the Creation and the Fall of Man; or you could extend the action to the end of the Book of Genesis, which gave you the stories of Cain and Abel, Noah's ark and Abraham; or you could go on to the first break in the historical record, at the end of the Book of Exodus, which took you as far as Moses; or you could go for the whole lot.

Of these alternatives, the end of the Book of Genesis was favoured, probably because by that time the evil effects of the Fall are fully displayed, and Abraham's willingness to sacrifice Isaac provides a powerful figure of the coming Redemption.

On the continent, however, the Old Testament material is usually only of marginal importance, because the Passion is so strongly focused that it towers above any surrounding episodes. This tendency culminated in France in the fifteenth century in a number of plays where the sweep of historical time is almost forgotten. The vast Passion play of Arnoul Greban, for instance, begins with some introductory Old Testament material covering the Creation, the Fall, and the murder of Abel, but this comprises only 5 per cent of a play more than 30,000 lines long – with a running time of about 25 hours. In the slightly later three-part version of Greban's play, made by Jean Michel, there are no Old Testament scenes at all, and the Passion is longer than all the other plays put together. Indeed, these late French plays really mark the emergence of a completely new form, which is no longer a history of the Redemption, or a Passion play of the traditional kind, but a biographical play based on the life of Christ and probably inspired by the popular meditative lives of Christ that were just coming into fashion. Indeed, it must be realised that the English play-cycle, bound together by theological intention, *figura* and the seven ages theory of sacred history, was merely the favoured form in the British Isles, and by no means the only way in which a cycle of Biblical plays could be constructed.

# 10

# STAGING THE CYCLES ON SCAFFOLDS

Despite the subtle use of contrasted images and powerfully evocative symbolism in the medieval cycle plays, the notions of character and motivation are very simple. The Bible usually labels its characters firmly as either good or bad, and though the writers seek for elementary motivation of an explanatory kind, such as fear, caution, greed or envy, they are rarely inclined to explore any moral dilemmas the characters may be facing, preferring to lay bare their feelings, as in the case of Abraham and Isaac, rather than analyse them. As a result, a cycle-play is like a tale told by a professional storyteller, where the interest springs from the development of the story itself. The characters become distanced, and it is difficult to set up the concentrated tension on which drama thrives. The writers naturally emphasise conflict where it occurs, in stories like those of Cain and Abel, Abraham and Isaac, and the Harrowing of Hell, but there are many subjects that provide little dramatic tension, like the Creation, the Procession of Prophets or the Baptism of Christ.

To compensate for this lack of tension, the plays present the viewers with extremely strong visual images that they can remember and take home with them; and, if the cycle-plays indeed sprang from the pictures and tableaux carried in the Corpus Christi procession, this was a continuous tradition. Each play tends to be dominated by a powerful emblematic image, the same images as appear so often in early Renaissance paintings – Eve offering the apple to Adam, Noah steering his ark, Christ on the Cross with Mary and John at its foot, Christ rising from the sepulchre with the red-cross banner in his hand and the soldiers sleeping round him, Lazarus being raised from his tomb, or Christ breaking the bread at Emmaus – vivid moments of frozen action which impress themselves strongly on the memory.

Indeed, the visual images probably had to compensate not only for lack of dramatic tension, but also, to some extent, for the inaudibility of the actors. In the open air, surrounded by all the noise and bustle of a public holiday, there was little scope for elaborate language and sensitive vocalisation – indeed, the performers must often have found it difficult even to make themselves heard. True, Herod occasionally 'raged' on the pageant and in the street as well, to gain attention, and thus probably managed to make his point, but it was by no means certain that the quieter-voiced characters, like God or Christ, would be audible, so the speeches are kept simple and uncomplicated, and consist of clear, often vivid, everyday phrases that can be belted out with a minimum of subtlety, in addition to which they are rhymed, to make them both easier to remember and easier to follow. All this means that the strong theatrical images created in the cycle-plays mattered a great deal, and we find the visual qualities of the plays being emphasised in whichever of the two customary methods was used to present them – the pageant-wagons moving from station to station on the one hand, or the scaffolds and mansions of the big static set-pieces on the other.

These two different traditions sprang from clearly defined geographical areas. The static place-and-scaffold performance is associated with France and Germany, and the mobile processional performance on pageant-wagons mainly with Spain. At one time, theatrical historians tended to assume that the English cycles were all performed on pageant-wagons, but it is now known that this was by no means the case. The use of pageants seems to have been restricted to a few large, independent cities in the diocese of York, while staging, using a central place and scaffolds, seems to have been widely spread all over the south, west and east of the country.

Since place-and-scaffold presentations were the more common, they will be the first kind of staging to be considered in detail here, and, when we survey the history of these big static displays, we find that, granted the inevitable use of 'simultaneous decor', which involves dressing the stage from the very beginning with everything necessary to tell the story, the medieval producers seem to have explored most of the possible relationships between stage and audience. They presented shows on end-stages, on various kinds of thrust stages with the audience on three sides, and, most frequently of all, in the round with the audience on all sides. Of these various forms, presentation in the round would seem to be the most natural because, whenever anything of interest is going on, people have a natural instinct to gather round it, in positions where they can see clearly without actually getting involved. Chronologically, though, it seems that medieval performances started with the thrust rather than the round, because, as was demonstrated by *The Play of Adam*, the early vernacular drama tended to cling to the walls of the church. This gives some force to the idea that vernacular drama was a missionary effort on the part of the clergy to reach the eyes and ears of the man in the street, as it certainly was later when it was used to supplement the efforts of the friars preachers. If so, the reason for the closeness of these early vernacular plays to the church building may well have been that the actors in them were priests –

107

though official attitudes varied on this matter: for instance, in about 1260, Alfonso the Wise of Spain encouraged the clergy to perform in plays outside the church building, while his contemporary, Robert Grosseteste, Bishop of Lincoln and first Chancellor of Oxford University, was strongly opposed to the idea.

However, the new religious drama soon gained confidence and freed itself from the church, moving into the courtyards of religious foundations, local market-places and, occasionally, quarries, recreation grounds or open fields. There it adopted different formats, depending on the nature of the venue, often, it would seem, employing a kind of interactive performance where the audience intermingled with the actors and scenic units, probably following the action round from station to station. It is only at a comparatively late date that cycle-plays seem to have adopted end-stage presentation.

This is a development which seems to be general to all drama of the time: the booth stage, for instance, which is the high thrust platform with a curtained area at the back for the actors to enter from and costume themselves in, is neither illustrated nor referred to much before the middle of the fifteenth century, and then it suddenly becomes widespread. Booth stages had certainly existed in Imperial Rome, but they seem to have vanished in the Dark Ages following the fall of the Empire, and the travelling players of those times seem to have acted and tumbled mostly on ground level. So the fact that the booth stage suddenly reappears and grows popular in the 1400s, together with other forms of end-staging, and, it may be added, the re-employment of old Roman theatres in many places for their original purpose, seems to point to a change of artistic attitudes in society, a change probably fostered by the rediscovery of descriptions of staging in late Roman times and the attempt to copy them – a typical Renaissance preoccupation.

National languages were also gaining a new importance all over Europe and stimulating interest in the power of the word, in vivid self-expression and persuasive rhetoric. This, combined with the booth stage, was bound to produce a form of theatre where attention was focused on the individual performer and what he was saying, rather than on group effort and simultaneous decor as was the case in earlier medieval pieces, and such a focus was best achieved by shutting off any distractions that existed behind the actor with a curtain. Such a policy also gave him a better chance of dominating his hearers, because he did not have to keep constantly turning to address quite so many different parts of the audience to make them all feel involved. This was obviously how and why the curtained area at the back of the booth stage arose.

So, although the booth stage never seems to have been used by the miracle and morality play producers, the period when it comes so much into prominence is significantly also the period when end-staging

*Figure 1* A booth stage in Holland, *c.* 1550

invades the mysteries and miracles, producing either large, enclosed, box-like settings of various kinds, as happened with the *Mystery of the Three Masters* at Romans in 1509 and the *Play of Saint Laurence* at Cologne in 1581, or rows of elaborate mansions along the back of an extended stage, as happened at Valenciennes in 1547.

Going back, then, to early performances, there is first the thrust presentation of the Anglo-Norman *Play of Adam*, described earlier, with its Place at the foot of the western steps, its Paradise and Hell on appropriate sides, and at appropriate heights, and God's entrance from 'Heaven' through the church doors at the back.

Matching this is an account of a play of *The Lord's Resurrection* performed at Beverley in about 1220, which was 'presented in words and gestures by the usual masked players', who were obviously professionals. It took place, 'between the buttresses on the north side of the Church of the Blessed John', namely Beverley Minster, and

> A great crowd, both of men and women, flocked together there, drawn by a variety of motives, for example pleasure, or curiosity, or the pious intention of arousing themselves to devotion. However, when many people, especially those short in stature, failed to obtain a satisfactory view because of the closely packed audience standing round in a circle, most of them went into the church.

There one young spectator fell from the triforium, which he had climbed to get a better view through the windows, and was killed; but he was restored to life again by the spirit of St John of Beverley, which appeared to him and wrought an immediate cure.

This performance may have been either in the round or backed up against the church wall, depending on what the commentator means by 'in a circle'. It should perhaps be pointed out that because of the alleged miracle, the theatrical evidence here is likely to be particularly sound, since, to persuade his readers of St John's appearance, the writer will be trying, above all things, to convince them with the truth of the other details he supplies.

When the vernacular plays left the shelter of the church walls, the logical place for them to go, since they were crusading, propagandist theatre, was into the market-place, amongst the people whose souls needed to be saved, and that is where they are most often found, particularly on the continent. Indeed, throughout Europe, the practice of performing in the market-place seems to have become almost universal by the fifteenth century. To take only a few widely scattered instances, we have records of such performances at Metz in south Germany from 1409, at Wismar on the Baltic from 1464, at Rouen in France from 1474, and so on. Sometimes, as at Mons in 1501, the houses overlooking the market were incorporated into the action and became 'mansions' for the performers, but even when they were not used directly they invariably served as grandstands for their rich owners and their friends, while the general public gathered in the street or climbed up on to the roofs and ruined the thatch or tiling.

The most fully documented case of such a performance relates to the wine-market in Lucerne in 1583, where there are detailed contemporary ground-plans covering the mansions and stations used on the two days of the cycle, some of the mansions being changed overnight, between the two parts of the play.

The plan distinguishes a rather elaborate, turretted house at one end of the square as the 'House to the East' while the opposite end of the plan is simply marked 'Sunset'. The 'House to the East', which looks as if it had a convenient balcony, and a ladder leading to it, is, not surprisingly, Heaven. At the opposite end of the market-place the designer has sketched an elaborate Hell Mouth with a note 'Lucifer and eight devils' beside it, so it looks at first as if we have here the usual confrontation of Heaven and Hell. However, the Hell Mouth is not directly opposite to Heaven but in the north-west corner of the market-place, and closer inspection of the stations where the various parts of the action take place reveals that the opposition reflected in the play is in fact not between Heaven and Hell, but between Heaven and the material world.

The mansions and stations are arranged around the edges of the

*Figure 2* The east end of Lucerne wine-market, set up for the play, 1583

square, and up the centre of it, and the action obviously moves to and fro. It starts in Heaven, on the balcony of the eastern house, with Paradise for Adam and Eve directly below. The locations for the sacrifices of Cain and Abel and Abraham's sacrifice of Isaac are set progressively further down the square. Then comes the story of Moses, with an image of the golden calf raised on a pillar, and the brazen serpent raised to cure the Israelites in the wilderness – though when Moses goes to get the Ten Commandments he travels eastwards to Heaven, which has now become Mount Sinai, and back again – a movement that will have given the event greater visual significance. The action as a whole then continues its movement towards the western end of the square, where the manger is placed for the Holy Birth at the end of day one. This is raised up on a large platform approached by what appears to be a most impressive flight of stairs, and there is a further visual emphasis on Joseph and Mary's journey to Bethlehem, because the house of the Annunciation is at the eastern end of the square, just beneath Heaven, and they must subsequently have made the long trek across the square from east to west. This is echoed almost immediately by the shepherds, who hear the angels singing on a hill beneath Heaven (the mountain again) and repeat the holy couple's journey to the manger up the full length of the market-place.

111

On the second day, the trial of Christ occurs on the raised platform, very much in the domain of the material world, but this time the action gradually moves in the other direction, and the Crucifixion takes place just beneath Heaven, at virtually the place where Adam sinned on the previous day. If there was a good sunset, the end of the play, with Christ on the Cross catching the last light, must have been most impressive. A Resurrection by torchlight would also have been very effective theatrically, even if not precisely authentic. At any rate, it is clear that the polarity of the play as a whole is between Heaven and the material world, like the staging of liturgical plays inside the church, and this explains the positioning of the Hell Mouth, because when the audience is looking towards the stage, which displays the most important events occurring in the material world, it would have Hell Mouth in the usual place on its 'sinister' side.

Although there are stands at three of the four corners of the playing-area and a very large stand built over the fountain behind the western stage, these can only have absorbed a limited number of the richer citizens, and the majority of the audience must surely have been mobile, since to get the full benefit of the important events happening on the western platform they would need to be gathered in the middle of the square, amongst the 'mansions' that had been used earlier.

When the market-place was not favoured, other civic venues were found. A popular playing-place of this kind was just outside the city walls, often using moats which had either originally been designed as dry moats or which had been drained of their water later. Such sites were obviously conveniently near the town, and the walls and moat banks could give useful support to platforms, 'mansions' and other theatrical structures. One such site was the Broadgate at Lincoln, which was the location of the former 'wardyke', or protective ditch, to the east of the city wall. Another was at Lyons in France, where in 1506 we have a document permitting the Austin Friars to have a large theatre built on the banks of the moat near the Gate of the Lantern, on condition that they do not tamper with the walls of the town and that they afterwards restore the banks of the moat to their former condition.

Some of the records are much more detailed. At Alençon, for instance, in 1520, the theatre was constructed near the Sées Gate: it was built in a right-angle made by the town walls, and some of the scaffolds were placed next to the wall and braced against it, whilst others were located on the bank of the dry moat facing the wall, which was technically known as the 'boulevard'.

Two years later, at Montaubon in 1522, the bottom of the moat was not dry, so the presenters drained it first and smoothed it over with additional soil, and then used the new foundation as the base for a platform 66 feet square which served as the main acting-area. The audience on this occasion was sitting on the banks on both sides, looking inwards, separated from the actors by a low *creneau*, or parapet, probably made of wattles or brushwood. More sizeable barriers, presumably high ones, were erected at each end of the ditch to discourage eager spectators from watching the plays without paying.

This separation of the audience from the actors is an interesting point, and arises much more clearly in the case of productions in the round in recreation grounds near the town or out in the countryside. We know that, at least in France, when plays were shown on such sites, it was customary to enclose the Place, or acting-area, with ditches, the soil from which was used to form a high sloping mound on the outer side of the ditch which could accommodate the spectators. The ditches, therefore, were used to separate the actors from the audience, just like the parapet at Montaubon, and indeed we often find a low wattle fence fulfilling the same function. The main advantage of the ditches, presumably, was that they also served to drain the Place, where the play was performed. Further, there is some question of the earth banks themselves, or an additional fence outside them, being used again to exclude non-paying spectators. On such occasions, there would probably be only a single break in the encircling bank or fence, to provide a common point of entry where all the spectators' entrance money could be collected.

These performing-areas away from the towns were usually circular in form, and the most striking examples in the British Isles were to be found in Cornwall, where earthwork amphitheatres known as 'rounds' seem to have been constructed for dramatic purposes on what had originally been prehistoric fortifications or cattle-enclosures. The only surviving example of this kind of venue is the Piran round near Perranporth, which has an 8-foot-high turf embankment with seven tiers of seats cut into it surrounding a 'plan-an-gwarry', or playing-place, which is slightly oval, with a spread of 143 feet from north to south and 135 feet from east to west. The ditch here runs round the *outside* of the whole structure, not between the actors and the audience. The round is in reasonably good condition, and plays are still sometimes performed there. The most elegant Cornish round, which is now lost, seems to have been situated near the church of St Just on the Penwith peninsula. This was described by an eighteenth-century scholar as being an exact circle, 126 feet in diameter, with an embankment 7 feet high and its outer circumference yet again traced by a ditch; there were six tiers of seats, apparently built out of stone slabs, and the top of the bank formed a circular rampart 7 feet broad. Other archaeological evidence suggests that there was also a stone wall surrounding the whole enclosure. However, both the 'rounds' described seem to have been unusually large, because a contemporary tells us that medieval rounds were usually only 40 or 50 feet in diameter.

In these two instances, the ditch plainly did not separate the actors

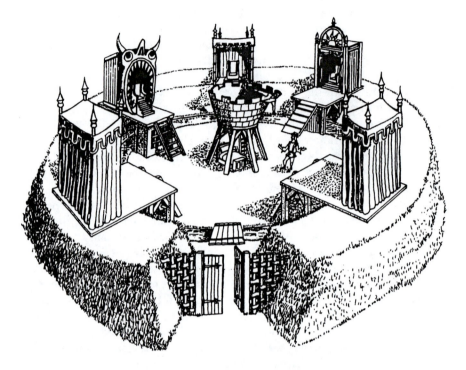

*Figure 3 The Castle of Perseverance* set up in a small round, *c.* 1450

from the audience, but served to keep non-paying spectators out. However, in the only set of instructions that exists for presenting a play in such a venue, the *Castle of Perseverance* manuscript, the ditch again seems to be serving its separating function. The instructions take the form of an annotated sketch, depicting at the centre of a circular space a large castle tower with convex walls. Beneath the castle is a bed, which is needed for the central character, Mankind. Above the castle is written: 'This is the Castle of Perseverance that standeth in the midst of the Place; but let no man sit there for letting [hindering] of sight, for there shall be the best of all.' On a first reading, this seems to imply that people sitting at that point would get the best overall view of the action, but that they should not be allowed to do so for fear of blocking other people's sight-lines. However, it might equally well mean that the best or most interesting *action* will occur in that area, and no *actor*, or prompter, should sit there for fear of spoiling the effect.

Below the castle is written: 'Mankind's bed shall be under the castle, and there shall the soul lie . . . till he shall rise and play.' The whole of this sketch and its accompanying notes are encircled by two concentric circles, narrowly spaced, between which is written: 'This is the water about the Place, if any ditch may be made where it shall be played; or else that it be strongly barred all about – and let not over many stytelers be within the place.' (A 'styteler' or 'stickler' was a marshal, who carried a white stick as a sign of his authority: the significance of this passage will be considered in a moment.)

The positions of certain scaffolds are also marked on the sketch – significantly *outside* the two concentric circles – and these seem likely to have been mansions set on platforms. At the top of the diagram is written: 'South Caro's scaffold' (Caro is a character whose name means 'the flesh', implying all the moral weaknesses that spring from self-indulgence); on the opposite side of the circles is written: 'North, Belial's scaffold' (Belial being the demon of lust and riotous living); to the east is God's scaffold, or Heaven; to the west is Mundus' scaffold (Mundus meaning 'the world'); and finally, to the north-east is the scaffold of Covetyse (or greed and envy for others' possessions). The fact that the details about the scaffolds are written *outside* the double circle representing the ditch seems clearly to imply that they were on top of the bank, facing inwards towards the playing place, with a bridge over the ditch to enable actors to reach them: several characters travel to and from them during the play. The top of the bank will have provided ample room for a small tent or mansion if it was 7 feet broad, like the round at St Just, and, in the artistically unselfconscious way of the times, the audience will have sat or stood on the bank between the various scaffolds. In that case the ditch here is performing its French function of separating the spectators from the action, and we note that, again in French fashion, if there is no ditch the Place, is to be 'strongly barred all about'. The prohibition regarding the number of 'stytelers' in the Place possibly means that marshals were placed on the inner side of the ditch to stop eager members of the public from leaping across it into the acting area; on the other hand, it may mean the production was using visible prompters, like the one shown in the miniature which is about to be described. To have too many prompters mixing amongst the actors would be confusing.

Creating a round did not by any means always involve earthworks. A much-reproduced miniature of *The Martyrdom of St Apollonia* painted by Jean Fouquet in about 1460 shows scaffolds erected on stilts around the playing-place. The picture embraces a semi-circle of scaffolds, which is usually held to represent half a circular performing area 'cut open' by the artist to show the interior. They appear to enclose a space about 65 or 66 feet in diameter, at the centre of which St Apollonia is being mocked and tortured and adjured by the Emperor to give up her wicked Christian ways. The figure is almost certainly a dummy – at least, one hopes so, because her teeth and nails are being pulled out – and that seems a little far to go even for the sake of one's art and a sound Christian morality. There is also a 'styteler' visible – his white baton proclaiming his

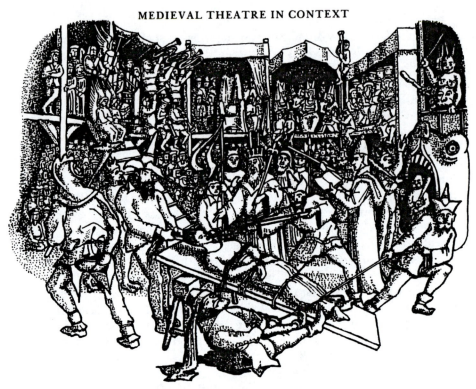

*Figure 4 The Martyrdom of St Appollonia, c.* 1460

authority – who seems to be prompting the Emperor from a large volume he is holding in his hand. He is a clergyman, and mingles quite unselfconsciously with the actors: he may even be feeding the actors their lines as they speak – as sometimes happened in country districts.

The scaffold floors stand a good 6 feet from the ground, and the scaffolds themselves rise above this base to canvas roofs about 6 feet higher. Six scaffolds are visible. On the viewer's left – the 'good' side – is Heaven, as expected, with a very precarious looking set of steps for God to descend by. God sits there on his throne, making a sign of blessing and wearing what seems to be an ecclesiastical cope. In front of him, on top of the steps, sit two young angels, duly winged, with their arms crossed and looking rather disillusioned. Beside him to his right stand two young choirboys, and to his left a fully armed older angel, who must surely be St Michael, general of the heavenly battalions.

Next round the circle, moving from left to right, is a scaffold containing the orchestra – a portative organ, three primitive trombones, three primitive woodwind and a bagpipe. The trombones stand while the others sit in front of them with their legs dangling over the edge of the platform.

Next comes the Emperor's scaffold – his throne empty, of course, since he is down in the Place, but, interestingly, a number of burghers sitting and standing on either side of the throne who are plainly not actors but important spectators. There also appears to be a curtain which could be drawn across the front of this scaffold – but, if the gentlemen gathered round the throne are indeed audience, it must have been drawn back at the beginning of the performance and then not closed again until the very end.

The next scaffold contains three *very* elegant ladies with most fashionable bonnets, two of them being amused by their lovers, together with ladies-in-waiting at the back, and one or two extremely well-to-do youths sitting on the front of the platform kicking their heels.

The fifth scaffold contains almost exclusively middle-class ladies sitting down, with gentlemen, presumably their husbands, standing behind them – although one pair, a man and a woman, are sitting on the edge of the platform chatting, quite oblivious of what is going on in the play. There are also a couple of young lads here, who are not at all well-to-do, one of whom is sitting on the front of the scaffold trying to attract the attention of a friend in the ladies' scaffold, while the other has actually climbed a flagpole, and is hanging on near the top. There is a similar intruder next to the choirboys on God's scaffold – perhaps he was a friend of theirs.

Finally to the right, or 'sinister', side, at ground level opposite Heaven, stands Hell Mouth – an impressive panther-like construction; this, and the scaffold above it, are occupied by elaborately costumed devils, the main one presumably being Satan. Currently he looks fairly relaxed and is chatting to another devil in front of the structure. A third devil, with a mask that makes him look rather like a toy bear and not at all threatening, is peering out of the Mouth, and there are more devils behind Satan up in the stand.

The main part of the audience, the less important people, can be seen squatting or kneeling under the scaffolds, leaving the Place clear, and they are there in large numbers. A wattle fence with a brushwood top is depicted at the front of the miniature, and one assumes that instead of running between spectators and actors – for it plainly does not – this must have been a barrier round the whole area, to keep out unwanted and unpaying visitors.

One thing that this miniature demonstrates very clearly is that scaffolds were kept for important people while, as an account from Vienne in 1510 puts it, producers kept 'le bas pour le commun peuple' ('the ground for the lower classes'). It also provides confirmation that at any performance a scaffold was a showing-place, like the stage boxes of the nineteenth-century or the gentlemen's boxes at the back of the stage in the Elizabethan public theatre: people went there to be seen quite as much as to see.

What might be called 'box-set' presentations seem to be more or less contemporaneous with the rounds and the market-place performances. These are productions where we have a stage area closed off from the audience on three sides and viewed from the fourth side only, allowing considerable depth of presentation. They mark a further step towards modern types of staging which is typical of the period. The earliest record of such a staging relates to a big production at Romans in France in 1509.

The production was a saints' play, specially written for the occasion, which was called *The Mystery of the Three Masters* (*Le Mystère des Trois Doms*). It was presented in the courtyard of the local Franciscan monastery, against the northern wall of the building, the playing-area being flanked by the east wing of the building to the left and the west wing to the right. The enclosed space was 180 feet broad and 120 feet deep. The seating, which was slightly curved, reached about half-way into this 'box'.

The back of the acting-area was lined with trees that grew along the monastery wall, and the stage was set in front of these and was 108 feet broad and 54 feet deep and stood 4 feet high. It was surrounded with a low trellis-work railing at the front and sides, adorned with flowers and foliage, which was mainly intended to prevent the numerous actors from stepping over the edge and doing themselves a mischief. The stage sides and front were also to be boarded below, so that the spectators could not see anything going on beneath the stage, and part of the understage area was excavated to allow for the use of trap-doors. The semi-circular auditorium was to be gently raked away from the stage, culminating in a row of boxes at the outer edge with lattice-work grilles at the back to stop small children from falling out.

Nine large scenic units were constructed for use on the stage. Heaven was in the centre of the stage's eastern side, on the viewers' left, and Hell confronted it from the middle of the western side – as usual. In the centre of the stage stood Lyons, with Rome midway to the east, towards Heaven, and Vienne midway to the west, nearer to Hell – though there is some evidence that these central mansions were shifted about during the three days of performance. At each of the four corners of the stage was a tower, painted grey. The one at the back-left corner of the stage was Africa, the one at the back-right corner Asia, at the front left was Europe, and at the front right, close to Hell, a prison (though these mansions represented other places at other times). Part of the stage inside the playing-area was covered with an awning rising from the back wall – presumably to protect the mansions against the effects of overnight rain.

At Cologne in 1581 there was another 'box-set' presentation of a play about St Laurence. It took place on a very large platform raised to a considerable height upon very large barrels. The stage must be about 45

*Figure 5* The St Lawrence play (*Laurentius*) at Cologne, 1581

feet long from side to side and about 20 feet deep, and will have posed some pretty problems of support because it carries a large number of mansions and other items. First, there are two trees equally spaced inside the right and left sides of the stage; these are not labelled at all and seem to be two real trees around which the stage has been built. The back and both sides of the stage are enclosed with canvas walls, and the audience views the piece from the front and looks as if it may have been raked for better viewing. Around the walls are various curtained entrances, carrying labels on the picture and possibly also during the performance. Structures are built out from the sides at different places – two thrones raised on steps with baldaquins, one more impressive than the other, a prison, and a canvas flat showing a path leading up into the mountains.

On the main stage and to the audience's left are an impressive mock-Roman monument and a very Roman altar, with an oil jug and ladle available to make the customary offering – the thing St Lawrence refused to do. To the audience's right, on the main body of the stage, stand an elaborate whipping-post and the gridiron on which the saint is eventually roasted, when he will not yield to persuasion. It is typical 'décor simultané', but only loosely obeys the 'good' and 'sinister' divisions of the stage, although the items implying the saint's earlier happy life are certainly on the 'good' side, and the whipping-post,

*Figure 6* The Valenciennes mystery play, 1547

gridiron and prison, which relate to his time of tribulation, are all on the 'sinister' side – the material of the play probably did not lend itself to any more precise division than this.

There is a noticeable shift here towards the enclosed picture-frame stage, as compared with *The Mystery of the Three Masters*, since the edges of the stage are no longer left open at the back and sides, but closed in with canvas, further concentrating the audience's attention. There also seem to be concessions to realism in the detailed nature of the items displayed on stage. Similar trends towards concentration of the action are to be found in some of the later pageant-wagon presentations, as will be shown later.

Lastly, it would be foolish to ignore what is perhaps the most outstanding example of this increasing interest in end-on presentation – the panoramic setting of the Valenciennes mystery play of 1547, which falls about midway between the last two examples.

In this case the mansions, which, in themselves are very impressive, are set out in a straight line facing the audience, along a stage about 100 feet long and 4 or 5 feet high. The symbolic positions are the same as usual. On the extreme audience left stands Heaven. This is elaborate. At stage level there is a large empty hall which stands about 8 feet high, and on top of this is a flat, circular Heaven, rising vertically to form a frame, with what must surely be modelled and painted angels round it (since otherwise some of them would have had to hang over God's head throughout the whole performance). Set back within this circular frame is God in full papal vestments (a typical costume for the time), with a triple crown representing his control of Heaven, earth and Hell. He is flanked by one lady on his left carrying a sword and scales who obviously represents Justice, and another lady on his right who probably represents Mercy. Two further ladies sit at the feet of the standing figures, but it is unclear what emblems they are carrying: they could well represent Faith and Hope – but the four of them together could just as easily represent the four cardinal virtues – Justice, Wisdom, Moderation and Courage. Presumably the hall below this tableau would be a useful place from which ascents to Heaven could be made, by means of a rope and pulley.

The next mansion, moving to the right, is a garden enclosed with wattle fencing with a door behind it, marked, in the picture, 'Nazareth'. Then comes a very elaborate temple, containing an impressive altar and topped by a cupola with the inevitable Muslim crescent that signified the presence of infidels – even though in this case they happened to be Jewish. Next comes a doorway with miniature towers and buildings behind it which represents Jerusalem, next a very neo-classical judgement hall for Pilate, with a Greek triangular pediment crowning its pillars and a magnificent throne inside, standing on a high-raised floor which allows space for the windows of a prison beneath. Next is a small door, again backed by miniature buildings, entitled 'the bishops' house' which will belong to Annas and Caiaphas, who are frequently called bishops in medieval texts.

By now, the eye is tending noticeably towards the right-hand side of the stage, which is definitely crowded. Next to the bishops' house is a large and elaborate gate called 'The Golden Gate', which was where Christ performed some of his healing miracles, while in front of these last two structures is a practicable reservoir about 12 feet from side to side, and about 8 feet from front to back, with a real boat on it, plainly representing the Sea of Galilee. Next, almost wholly to the sinister side, is a gaol entitled 'The Limbo of the Patriarchs', from which Christ releases the souls of the righteous pagans when he harrows Hell, with a practicable window through which the souls can be seen before they are released; and finally, at the right end of the stage, a magnificent Hell Mouth at stage level, with windows beside it with an ugly masked devil peering out and a balcony above where male and female souls (presumably models) are suffering torture on two giant wheels, topped by fire-breathing dragons and a high pole carrying a horrid devil mounted on yet another fire-breathing dragon. Inside Hell Mouth, which is open, can be seen two or three naked souls being boiled in a cauldron and appealing for aid (probably models again, though not necessarily so). The whole set-up is very impressive. It seems to be the first panoramic end-on presentation of a mystery cycle, and is indicative of a much more modern trend in staging, which is on the whole less cluttered and structurally much more neatly organised.

So this survey of the main types of static presentation used by medieval cycle and Passion plays reveals the gradual concentration of scenic units and action into an end-stage presentation, a trend given additional impetus by the regular use of the booth stage by troupes of professional players touring moral interludes. Italian experimenters influenced by these trends went on to develop an outer 'frame' standing in front of the stage, thus creating the picture-frame stage which dominated Europe from the seventeenth to the nineteenth century and is still in general use.

A brief account of the organisation and presentation of *The Mystery of the Three Masters* at Romans will serve to people these static settings with living figures. The idea for the production was first mooted on 4 July 1508, at a meeting called to consider the best way of celebrating the city's miraculous ten years' deliverance from the Plague. Representatives of St Bernard's Monastery and the town council were present, and it was agreed that it would be appropriate to present a play about the town's three patron saints, the martyrs Séverin, Exupère and Félicien, at Whitsuntide the following year, and that the costs of labour and production would be shared between the town and the monastery.

To help the complicated arrangements to run smoothly, a body of nine commissioners was appointed to supervise the production, three on behalf of the Monastery of St Bernard, two on behalf of the smaller Chapel of St Maurice, which had been drawn into the celebrations, and four representing the town. At this point, the Franciscan brotherhood from the monastery offered a sum of ready cash to act as a capital fund to finance the day-to-day expenses of production, and also offered their courtyard as a suitable venue for the performance – a practical approach which serves to remind us of the order's later dramatic activities in the New World. A number of smaller groups and individuals also made contributions to the capital fund, and the commissioners promptly set to work.

Their first move was to find an author, and eventually this heavy burden was laid on the shoulders of Canon Pra of Grenoble, who enjoyed a considerable reputation as a writer of texts for street pageants. He was provided with a secretary, and it was agreed that they should both be paid for their labours. By mid-August, the canon had something ready, probably no more than a plot-outline, which he read to the committee. A day later, the commissioners invited Monsieur Chevallet, a poet from nearby Vienne, to become co-author, but he refused, on the grounds that he did not want to work with Canon Pra. What exactly happened is not clear. Either the committee was not happy with what it had heard and wanted Chevallet to supervise and improve the work, or perhaps the

canon himself had called for extra assistance. In either case, Chevallet
may have felt that he would be reduced to playing second fiddle, and
refused for that reason – or he may, of course, have worked with Pra
before and found him impossible. So Pra laboured on alone and managed
to complete the full script by February 1509, reading sections of it to the
committee from time to time and revising his draft in the light of their
critical comments. As soon as the script was ready, three notaries were
engaged to make copies; but, though Pra was unaware of the fact, his
troubles were not yet over!

Meanwhile, in December, a good six months before the proposed date
of production, the committee had turned its attention to the physical
requirements of the play, and appointed Monsieur Sanche of Dijon as
their producer ('meneur' or 'maître du jeu') and Monsieur François
Trévenot from nearby Annonay as their designer. Under the guidance of
these two men, work began on building the stage and auditorium at St
Bernard's monastery early in the new year. By this time it was becoming
necessary to dip deeply into the capital fund that had been provided by
public subscription: for example, the carpenters demanded an advance of
412 florins for their labours in the courtyard; Trévenot, the designer, was
being paid 4 florins a month to supervise construction; and, to assist him
with the stage machinery required for the play, he had engaged two
associates from his home town: Amien Grégoire, a blacksmith, and Jean
Rozier, a clocksmith, both of whom had to be paid.

Before the stage-set was finished, rehearsals began – a situation familiar
to most amateur actors. The first rehearsal was arranged for 18 March,
barely a month after Canon Pra had finished the script, and the notaries
who were employed to copy the parts must have found themselves hard-
pressed, because there were 86 characters in the play and the performance
stretched over three days. In this production, it is interesting to note, no
parts were doubled and all ranks of society were called upon to act.
Between 18 March and 29 April, at least seven rehearsals were held –
approximately one a week. They took place in the town hall, and
refreshments were provided. The actors all seem to have been expected to
provide their own costumes, except for those playing some of the more
elaborately dressed and unusual characters, like Lucifer and Proserpine,
Queen of Hell, but we may imagine that the producer and the designer
will have provided guidelines as to what they wanted.

So far as we can tell from the accounts, there was little emphasis upon
music: only trumpets, tambourines and an organ are mentioned, but the
organ was a sizeable one, and had to be installed above the ground level,
in Heaven – a task that fell to Trevenot and his helpers; and the very
presence of an organ suggests the existence of a choir, so we can imagine
a larger musical element in the performance than is apparent from the
text.

In the meantime the industrious designer had been collecting pigments of every imaginable colour – not an easy task in those days – together with olive and nut oil to mix them, pig-bristle brushes, earthenware and wooden mixing-bowls, coloured paper, tinfoil, pins, cloth, saltpetre, wood and canvas. Where he could not find what he wanted locally, he sent messengers to acquire them from neighbouring towns, and his accounts show that he was singularly careless about costs – or perhaps all the tradesmen he patronised were friends of his and received a cut of the available funds.

At long last, on 7 May, ten months after the project had been mooted, arrangements were made for the *monstre,* or 'showing'. This was the public parade of the cast in costume which preceded almost all French mystery plays and which approximated to the 'riding of the banns' in England. On this occasion, the procession took place three weeks before the performance, providing good advance publicity, and also ensuring that all the costumes were ready for the play.

At this late stage, the commissioners decided that the text was not satisfactory and that something must be done to improve it, so a week later one of the actors was sent to Vienne to tackle Chevallet again. In particular he carried with him an important central passage of the text relating to the Four Tyrants which was to be amended at all costs, and eventually, for the price of a substantial bribe and several good meals, the actor managed to get Chevallet to undertake the task – at the same time getting his own part completely rewritten! All this took four days.

Whitsun of 1509 fell at the end of May, and the performance duly took place, more or less as planned, with a dress-rehearsal and some unforeseen last-minute hitches, the most predictable of which was the discovery that the piece ran much longer than had been anticipated. It was cut, and the production was artistically a great success, although, like most civic plays, it lost money.

This production is only one of a number in France and Germany which we can reconstruct in detail – for instance, Paris, Metz, Mons, and Valenciennes all provide detailed accounts – but in most respects it can be considered typical. Unfortunately, there is no English production that can be constructed in nearly as much detail, and all that can be achieved instead is a general impression woven out of many small pieces of information.

# 11

# STAGING THE CYCLES ON WAGONS

Pageants, however elaborately contrived, were probably cheaper to use for cycle-plays than large static structures. The wagons were constantly available, being used regularly for royal entries and other civic occasions, and they were cared for individually by the city guilds, which 'dressed' them with the appropriate pageantry and also provided the actors and the plays. By contrast, building elaborate staging and seating for a performance at a single site was likely to involve much more planning and far more expense, as we have seen at Romans, and England was not as rich as her continental neighbours.

Sir William Dugdale describes the Coventry pageants briefly in his *Antiquities of Warwickshire* in 1656:

> Before the suppression of the monasteries this city was very famous for the pageants that were played therein upon Corpus Christi day; which, occasioning great confluence of people thither from far and near, was of no small benefit thereto; which pageants being acted with mighty state and reverence by the friars of this house, had theatres for the several scenes, very large and high, placed upon wheels, and drawn to all the eminent parts of the city, for the better advantage of spectators.

So the plays were considered big business by the city because they drew the crowds, and innkeepers and others benefited from the sale of food and drink and the provision of lodgings, particularly when the show lasted for several days. Presumably 'the better advantage' accruing to spectators from the wagons being drawn 'to all the eminent parts of the city' was that if the performances had all been on one site, crowding would have been severe and made it difficult for everybody to see the plays, despite the fact that the wagons were so high – which reminds us of the dense crowds round the players at Beverley Minster when the boy fell to his death. The statement that the friars acted the plays has been questioned and even discounted by many scholars, but nothing else Sir William says in his

125

account has been proved untrue, and the friars may indeed have been involved, as they certainly were sometimes on the continent.

More informative is an account of the Chester plays by Archdeacon Robert Rogers, which was edited by his son after his death in 1595. He writes:

> They were divided into 24 pageants or parts, according to the number of the companies [guilds] of the city, and every company brought forth their pageant, which was the carriage or place which they played in: And yearly, before these were played, there was a man fitted for the purpose which did ride, as I take it, upon St George's Day [23 April] through the city and there published the time and matter of the plays in brief, which was called the reading of the banns. They were played upon the Monday, Tuesday and Wednesday of Whitsun week and they first began at the Abbey gates: then it was wheeled from thence to the Penthouse at the High Cross before the Mayor, and before it was done the second came, and the first went into the Watergate Street, and from thence unto the Bridge Street, and so all, one after another, till all the pageants were played appointed for the first day – and so, likewise, for the second and the third day: these pageants, or carriage was a high place, made like a house with two rooms, being open on the top: the lower room they apparelled and dressed themselves and in the higher room they played, and they stood upon six wheels. And when they had done with one carriage in one place they wheeled the same from one street to another, first from the Abbey gates to the Penthouse, then to the Watergate Street, then to the Bridge Street, through the lanes and so to the Eastgate Street. And thus they came from one street to another, keeping a direct order in every street, for before the first carriage was gone the second came, and so the third, and so orderly till the last was done, all in order, without any staying in any place; for word being brought how every place was near done, they came, and made no place to tarry till the last was played.

It is interesting to note that the plays 'first began at the Abbey gates', as they did at the gates of the Holy Trinity Abbey in York, again suggesting the possible involvement of the clergy. It is also interesting to find that the forward movement of the wagons was co-ordinated to some extent, at least between any two stations on the route, and that the performance was hurried along as much as possible, while the word 'wheeled' seems to imply that in this case the wagons were pushed by hand rather than horse-drawn, a practice which some scholars think was usual in England on days of performance.

In 1565 the Grocers' Company at Norwich, who presented the play of the Fall, possessed

A pageant, that is to say, a house of wainscot, painted, and builded on a cart with four wheels. A square top to set over the said house. A gryphon, gilt, with a fane [pennant] to set on the said top. A bigger iron fane to set on the end of the pageant. Three painted cloths to hang about the pageant. Six horse cloths, stained, with knobs and tassels.

In 1433 an agreement between the York Mercers and the Masters responsible for the play of Doomsday, mentions another pageant with four wheels which is carrying a Hell Mouth, and also

a great coaster [hanging] of red damask painted, for the back side of the pageant; two other less coasters for two sides of the pageant; three other coasters of an eleventh's breadth for the sides of the pageant; a little coaster four-squared to hang at the back of God: four irons to bear up Heaven . . . a brandreth [gridiron] that God shall sit upon when he shall fly up to Heaven, with four ropes at four corners . . . [and] two short rolls of tree to put forth the pageant.

Note these two 'rolls of tree', or wooden rollers, which are to be used to 'put forth the pageant', despite the fact that the wagon already has four wheels: their importance will emerge later.

The final piece of evidence is the only remaining visual record of pageant-wagons being used out of doors. It dates from 1615, not too long after the last performance of the cycles, and comes from the Spanish Netherlands, which are likely to have been fairly conservative in their presentation of religious tableaux. It is a painting of *The Triumph of Isabella* given in Brussels, which shows several pageants, both sacred and profane, one of which, representing the Nativity, is of particular interest.

The pageant in question is a cart on two pairs of wheels, both large, the front pair being about 4½ feet in diameter and the back pair about 6 feet. It is drawn by four horses, with a driver sitting on the back of one of the hindmost pair. The lower part of the cart is about 5 or 6 feet deep, and clears the ground by about 2 feet, which means the stage floor of the pageant is about 8 feet above the ground. It is hung round with elaborate painted cloths carrying frond-like decorations. The top of the cart appears to be about 15 feet long and about 11 feet broad. On it stands a practicable house, representing the stable, about 10 feet long and 11 feet wide, filling the whole width of the pageant but not the whole length. There is a narrow ledge at the front behind the horses and a broader ledge, about 3 feet deep, at the back. On the back ledge are disposed a shepherdess with what looks like a cider jug and three shepherds, one playing a bagpipe. Behind them is the manger, with the model heads of an ox and ass munching hay. Everything inside the house is clearly

*Figure 7* Side elevation of a pageant-wagon, 1615

visible, because each side has two large arches to look through and both
the ends are open. The sides of the house up to the thatched eaves are
about 7 feet high, and the roof-beam of the house is about 5 feet higher,
say 12 feet above the platform and 20 feet above the ground, and perched
on its very corner, above the manger, is either an actor in angel's clothes
or a model angel. Inside the house, but clearly to be seen through the
arches, are the Virgin Mary with the baby in an extemporised cradle, her
husband Joseph and another angel. Near the front of the pageant there is
a shadowy figure apparently hammering vigorously at the floor with a
mallet – probably the stage-manager dealing with some last-minute
hitch. The Mary and Joseph scene inside clearly faces towards the front of
the wagon, where the carter is sitting, so presumably the horses were
unhitched at some point so that the actors could come forward to
perform, or so, at least, they could be more clearly seen. The pageant
must have been extremely heavy, whatever the house was made of, and it
has nine people on it besides!

The proportions of the wagon depicted here also seem to conform to
probability. Scholars have observed that medieval streets rarely exceeded
25 to 30 feet in width, so the wagons could hardly have been larger than
20 feet by 10 feet if they were to negotiate the corners: 15 feet by 11 feet
therefore seems about right, though it must be remembered that these
particular pageants in Brussels were involved in a very special celebration
and may have been larger and more magnificent than usual.

Though many of these pieces of evidence are late, and they are rather
widely spread in place and time, they fortunately tend to confirm one
another. If the picture of the Brussels pageant is anything to go by, then

there is no reason for doubting that the pageant-wagons at Coventry were very large and high, or that at Chester the acting occurred on a high place, since the Brussels pageant is massive and its stage floor is a good 8 feet above the ground. However, Rogers's description of them as being 'made like a house with two rooms' seems to suggest something simpler, a kind of 'one up, one down' cottage on wheels, with corner-posts ascending directly from the bottom of the cart to the roof. The existence of a roof is confirmed by the square top mentioned in the Norwich account, and, indeed, this would be wise considering the vagaries of the English weather. When Rogers says the pageant was 'open on the top' he presumably means that nothing interfered with the people's view of the actors from any side – another feature present in the Brussels pageant, by virtue of the arches that pierce the sides of the house; and the Chester pageants may very easily have had six wheels to support them, even if other places made do with four.

There is obviously no visible evidence that the actors' dressing-room was in the lower part of the wagon, but in the Brussels pageant there is plenty of space for it below the stage floor, and it would have been extremely useful. The stage-manager could have stored the costumes and hand props there when they were not needed, and occasionally plays required a trap-door for an entrance or exit, which would have been very difficult to arrange without some kind of 'basement'.

The mobile 'house' in the Norwich inventory is described as being made of wainscot, and this should not be passed over, because wainscot was an expensive and very fine-grained variety of oak, specially imported from Russia – implying that no expense was spared to make the pageants impressive. It also suggests that the sides of the lower wagon in this case may have been panelled. The fact that the roof of the pageant is listed separately probably implies that it could be taken off in the pageant-house for easier storage. The horse-cloths need no explanation, since decorating horses was an old-established pastime for tournaments and other special occasions, but it is interesting to note that the Brussels horses are not caparisoned in any way, which suggests that the English pageants may have been decoratively even more elaborate and impressive than the Flemish ones.

The description of the York pageant shows that some wagons carried stage machinery, and the itemisation involved suggests again that the upper part could be removed for easier storage. The four iron posts to 'bear up Heaven' were presumably needed because of the extra strain of hoisting and lowering God on his gridiron, and perhaps to support the weight of angels standing above. The 'two rolls of tree' used to 'put forth the pageant' are particularly interesting. They have never been explained, but clearly suggest that something was intended to be rolled off the top of the structure – but surely not on to the ground 8 feet below, when there

129

would have been so much difficulty getting it back again. This point will be clarified in due course. The other interesting thing about the description, particularly in view of its early date, is the virtual certainty that three sides of the upper pageant were screened off with hangings, meaning that what occurred could only be seen from the front; this arrangement demonstrates the same trend towards concentrating the attention of the audience as was detectable in the later static settings. In fact, it is possible that *all* the York pageants were intended to be seen only from the front, since all the stations that have been identified prove to be located on the left-hand side of the processional route.

So far the picture that emerges suggests considerable similarity in the structure of pageant-wagons wherever they were used, but this does not imply that they were identical in design, or that they were used everywhere in the same way.

For instance, at Chester different guilds shared the same pageant-wagon. This was quite possible in a three-day festival, always providing the actual scenic unit on the wagon was suitable for more than one play. For example, there was one pageant that had a 'hill' on it. This was used for three plays: on the first day the Painters used it for their *Shepherds* play, where it was the hill on which the shepherds were pasturing their sheep; towards the end of the second day, the Coopers used the same pageant for their play of the *Flagellation*, which ended with Christ's Crucifixion, and the hill became Calvary, where the Cross stood; and at the start of the third day, the pageant was used again by the Skinners for their play of the *Resurrection*, and here the 'hill' represented the holy sepulchre – so it was presumably big enough to have a 'cave' in it.

However, the action of the *Shepherds* play demands not only a Heaven in which the angels and the star appear – presumably on an upper level – but also a stable for the manger to stand in, and with a large hill already on the wagon, this must have left very little acting-space. A similar situation arose, in different ways, on quite a number of the pageants, and it led to the discovery of an interesting feature of pageant production that had not been suspected – the probable extension of the acting-area on the pageant wagons by pre-erected stages. Evidence for this is to be found in a part of Rogers's account of the Chester pageants which has not yet been quoted, where he mentions 'scaffolds and stages made in the streets in those places where they determined to play their pageants'. Nobody seems to have read this passage with sufficient care, because historically, however the words are interpreted, Rogers definitely means that two different kinds of structure were erected at the sites where the Chester cycles were played – something to hold the crowd, and also an acting-platform. The players, in short, were not confined to the top of the pageant-wagon, but could move freely on to an adjacent stage, presumably of about the same height as the floor of the pageant. In fact, with the pageant drawn up behind the platform, and the actors performing mostly in front of it, you have an arrangement that begins to look like a rudimentary booth stage, without curtains.

Coventry provides evidence of a similar arrangement, though it differs in detail. There are many entries in the guild accounts coupling pageants with scaffolds as a common cause of expense. In 1584, for instance, the Cappers paid two shillings and sixpence for 'the setting and driving of the pageant and scaffolds', and there are many other similar instances.

Like the pageants, these scaffolds were on wheels. For instance, the Smiths' Company pays a man eightpence 'for making a wheel to the scaffold' and another man fourpence for 'an iron pin and a cotter for the scaffold wheel'. They are guild property, and they are driven out and set up at the same time as the pageants, so there seems little doubt that they are mobile equivalents of the scaffolds that Rogers mentions at Chester, movable apron-stages that can be used to extend the action beyond the limits of the pageant and give the players room to work in. In that case they would presumably be driven out before the pageants and left at all the playing-stations. They would also be very easy to clear away once the festival was over.

The two wooden rollers in the description of the pageant from York suggest the same technique. They are surely intended to roll the Hell Mouth off the top of the pageant-wagon on to the adjoining platform, so that God can have free passage to Heaven and back on his gridiron. A Hell Mouth is a substantial item, as is revealed in all the illustrations of the time, and would have taken up a great deal of room on top of the pageant, seriously hampering God's movements. If the platform was the same height as the acting-level on the wagon, the Mouth could easily be rolled back again at the end of the play, and so away to the next station. With the pageant curtained off on three sides, because the presenters wanted it viewed from a particular direction, the arrangement would again have been like a booth stage without a concealing curtain.

Indeed, if, as seems possible, the apron-stage was customarily used to extend the acting area at the various stations, as we know it certainly was in Spain, that fact gives added importance to the rare occasions when the actors actually descend from the stage to the street. The direction 'Here Herod rages in the pageant and in the street also' in the Coventry plays probably exists because it is extremely *unusual* for an actor to come down off his high platform, and such directions are rare because, with the additional stage-space provided, there is no need for such an action, except as a special effect.

Not surprisingly, the stations chosen for showing the plays were often in front of the houses of local dignitaries - for example, 'the Penthouse at the High Cross before the Mayor' - and doubtless most of the civic officers and well-to-do people watched the plays from the rooms of private houses overlooking the stations. This certainly happened at Coventry, York and Chester, and presumably the practice was general. The middling rich are likely to have had sitting- or standing-room provided – the 'stages' mentioned in Rogers's report – while the 'common people' will no doubt have milled about at ground level.

It would be interesting to know if people paid to enter the stands at Chester; they certainly did so at York, where the corporation leased 'performing rights' for each station to the highest bidder, the money taken going towards the cost of production. The fact that the cost of such leases amounted to more than a month's wages for a skilled workman, and that they were acquired by bidding, means that this is unlikely to have been simply a way of raising extra money to support the plays: on the contrary, it implies that there was a good profit to be made by erecting stands to seat the spectators who could afford it – though it has also been suggested that the intention may have been to reserve seats (still at a price) for the members of particular guilds and their families.

The number of plays performed at some of the festivals has caused doubts, particularly at York. If, as at Chester, you have 24 plays given over three days at only four, or perhaps five, stations, the proposition seems feasible, but if, as at York, you have between 48 and 57 plays given at twelve stations in 1417, and sixteen stations in 1554, all in a single day, the bounds of possibility become rather strained! There were only about two dozen plays in the Coventry cycle, yet in 1457 Queen Margaret saw 'all the pageants played save Doomsday, which might not be played for lack of day', and *she* was sitting at the *first* station, so the shortfall of plays must have been severe at stations further along the route. A similar conclusion can probably be drawn from the fact that at York people favoured the first four stations and tried to avoid buying seats for the last one.

Many scholars are drawn to the idea that the plays were not actually *performed* at the various stations during the day, but simply shown there as *tableaux vivants*, or dumb-shows, and later presented as parts of a single unified performance somewhere in the city, but there is no evidence to support a total presentation of this kind, while there are constant references to performances at the stations. Other scholars have suggested that perhaps only a selection of plays was given in any particular year, but this contradicts the guild accounts. More recently it has been proposed that full performances occurred only at one or two stations on the route, a particularly ingenious suggestion being that the first four plays were played in sequence at stations 1-4, that these then moved on over the bridge to stations 5-8, while the next four plays took over the earlier stations, and so on, so that only three performances occurred; but while this neatly explains the years when there were twelve or sixteen stations, it does not explain the occasions when the number of stations was not divisible by four, as sometimes happened. So the problem remains unresolved.

The town of Wakefield also had a large number of plays: 32 have been preserved, and several are missing. As at York, all these plays are presumed to have been performed on a single day, which has led to similar suggestions with regard to their presentation: namely, that the pageants passed in procession through the town and were then gathered together in the market-place or the cathedral close, or at some other convenient venue, where they were drawn into a circle and became the scaffolds for an in-the-round performance of the plays, wagons being taken out of the circle when their part was done and others being introduced as necessary. In this case, the theory has a tiny fragment of evidence to support it, since there is a reference to the plays being staged in the local quarry on at least one occasion.

A final possibility that has been canvassed in the case of these large cycles is that each pageant-wagon may have moved to a specific location and given its play there at a different time of day, while the audience moved from pageant to pageant to follow the story, but this implies a tremendous crush of people at the showing-places, and at York three or four plays would still have had to be given in sequence at each station. These considerations, coupled with all the evidence about driving and moving wagons, make the proposal inherently unlikely.

In the nineteenth century it used to be believed that the performances of the miracle cycles must have been 'amateur' in the worst sense of the word, but it is now agreed that this cannot possibly have been the case. For instance, the workmen employed to build and mend the pageants were paid at a very high rate, and the materials used are of very high quality. This would apply to all aspects of the production, because it was a big civic occasion, at which the prosperity of each guild was displayed nakedly to the eyes of not only the townspeople but also important visitors from other cities, who were often trade rivals. Each guild would want its pageant to be the most magnificent, its plays the best-written, its actors the most outstanding. For this reason it would turn to specialists in the appropriate guilds to do its building, decorating and prop-making, and would pay them the highest rates for their work – and the workmen employed would certainly do their best, for the honour of their guild and the city. So the Painters would do all the painting, the Whitawers, or fine-leather-workers, would provide the skin-tight leotards used by Adam and Eve, the Drapers would supply the cloth, the Tailors and Cutters would make the costumes, the Glovers provide the gloves, the Smiths the stage-machinery, the Armourers weapons and armour, and so on. All the best skills of the city would be mobilised for the production, and the workmanship would be of the very finest – better than any single company could ever have hoped to achieve.

Doubtless it was to keep costs down and to make sure that the best wares of the guild were displayed that various plays were allotted to what were felt to be suitable companies, even though there may also have been a symbolic affinity. Thus the Goldsmiths and Goldbeaters would tend to produce the play of *The Magi*, where the kings' gifts could be turned to advantage; the Armourers, Cutlers, Bladesmiths, Sheathers, Bowyers and Fletchers undertook plays involving armed men, like *The Betrayal of Christ* and *The Scourging*, though not surprisingly the Ropers sometimes presented the latter piece; the Skinners or Whitawers did *Adam and Eve*; the Nailmakers and Ironmongers presented *The Crucifixion*, because of the nails; the Bakers or Vintners *The Last Supper*, because of the bread and wine; while the Litsters or Dyers often took on *The Play of Pharaoh* because they could show their skill in the dyeing of the purple cloth representing the Red Sea that was gradually raised to show the drowning of the Egyptians – purple always was, and still is, a notoriously difficult colour to dye evenly! Sometimes the symbolism was more important than the craft. For instance, it seems a bit odd for the Plasterers to do *The Creation* and the Waterleaders and Drawers *Noah's Flood* – the Flood was a much more natural choice for the Shipwrights if the city had them, as in Hull or Newcastle. Other forced associations occurred when the Cooks and Innkeepers presented *The Harrowing of Hell*, because of the fire, and when the Parchmenters and Bookbinders undertook *Abraham and Isaac*, because the ram caught in the thicket, which was substituted for Isaac, was the source of parchment; but however the plays were distributed, the 'foreigners' from other municipalities who visited for the festival will certainly have seen the city's produce at its very best.

Most of the financial responsibilities relating to the cycles fell on the shoulders of the pageant-masters or 'keepers' appointed by the wardens of the guilds to undertake the organisation of the festival. It was they who paid the ground-rent for the pageant-houses in which the wagons were kept when they were not in use; they paid for the mending and readying of the pageants and scaffolds, when necessary; they received money, where appropriate, from the leasing of performing rights at the various stations; they paid the craftsmen who built new scenic elements on the wagons when these were required; they paid the dramatists who occasionally revised or edited old plays, or wrote new ones; they paid the actors and directors, the musicians, the stage-managers, drivers, guards and workmen involved; they paid for, or provided, all the special costumes and props; they paid for food during rehearsals and during performance; and so on; and they seem to have been expected to meet any extraordinary expenses out of their own pocket and reclaim the money from the guild later.

Expenses were considerable, and the strong-box dedicated to the production sometimes held large sums. In some places, like Coventry, care was taken to ensure that those who controlled the cash were appointed from different guilds, and each held a separate key to one of the multiple locks on a single communal treasure-chest, so that no money could be expended without the presence and agreement of all those involved.

In York many of the pageant-masters held office for several years, thus acquiring valuable experience of the problems that were likely to arise. Their appointment was confirmed annually sometime in Lent, and they started by drawing up an inventory of all the properties remaining from the previous year's production and lists of necessary replacements and repairs. They probably also assessed the likely cost of the exercise at this point, since it was they, and not the wardens of the companies, who levied the tax on the guilds, known as 'pageant silver', which raised the bulk of the funds required. They would then appoint subordinates to hold auditions and, seemingly, at that point wholly withdrew from the artistic aspects of the production, leaving it in more experienced hands – though doubtless they kept a beady eye on expenses.

It was presumably also the pageant-masters who arranged for the banns to be ridden, as soon as the Mayor and Corporation had confirmed that the performance would take place. This involved members of the guilds, usually actors in costume, travelling in procession through the main streets of the city and stopping at important places to proclaim the date and details of the plays' performance while others rode round the local countryside, crying the proclamation aloud. This was done for any play, not just the cycles, and the texts of one or two banns have been preserved, for instance:

Oyez, oyez, oyez! We command on the King's behalf and the Mayor and Sheriffs of this city that no man go armed in the city . . . in disturbance of the King's peace and the play . . . and that they leave their harness in their inns, saving knights and squires of worship . . . on pain of forfeiture of their weapons and imprisonment of their bodies . . .

– and so on.

An account of the plays to be performed would follow – in the case of the cycles, usually pageant by pageant – together with the actors' authority to play them. The calls for good order and the relinquishment of weapons were doubtless a necessary precaution when dealing with a rowdy, holiday-making and quite possibly drunken crowd.

It will also have been the pageant-masters who imposed the fines authorised by the city authorities for various shortcomings that might be observed in the production. These fines were sometimes very high for the times and were doubtless met by the guild concerned rather than the individual. Their purpose was certainly to ensure that standards remained high. Examples of the fines levied are: for playing anywhere but at the pre-arranged stations, 40 shillings (about a month's wages); for an actor taking more than two parts, also 40 shillings; for not having 'good players, well arrayed and openly speaking', 100 shillings; for an actor not knowing his lines, half a mark (about five days' wages); for his being late when the pageants assembled in the dawn light at 4.30 in the morning, 1 mark; and so on. Such sanctions encouraged the long sequence of plays to run smoothly and, if possible, be over by nightfall.

The acting will have been no more 'amateur' than the rest of the presentation. There is no evidence that professional actors were hired from outside the guilds at first, but, as always happens with 'amateur dramatics', there are some people who are better actors than others, and who are likely for that reason to be much in demand, particularly when the honour of the guild and the city are at stake.

For instance, consider the fact that at York an actor was forbidden from playing in more than two pageants. If an actor was playing in two pageants, he was playing in one that did not belong to his own guild, and the only reason for that must be that he was a good actor. Since he will also have been paid for his work by both guilds, this is a form of professionalism. Probably the restriction on playing more than twice was to ensure that the few really good actors didn't hog all the good parts and totally undermine the sense of guild responsibility for individual plays. It may also have been to avoid hitches in the movement of the pageant-wagons which might be caused by an actor having to rush from one to another: even where only two roles were concerned, if the plays were presented in a single day, a doubling actor's first part would need to be in one of the pageants near the beginning of the sequence and his other part near the end.

There also seems to have been a kind of 'quality control' of the performances. For example, at York the pageant-masters appointed four of the 'most cunning, discreet and able players' within the city to audition all applicants for parts in the plays. These seem to have been essentially a group of artistic supervisors or commissioners ensuring the general level of performance, not in any sense directors.

The arrangements for directing each play were made by the guild presenting it, but the business of providing and rehearsing the actors was often farmed out to a specialist 'producer' or a group of specialists. For instance, individuals sometimes took over the presentation of one of the plays for a set number of years, or even for the rest of their working life.

One such man was Thomas Colclow, a skinner at Coventry. In 1454 the Smiths – not his own guild – agreed to give him the 'rule' of their pageant 'unto the end of the 12 years next following'. A number of things are plain from this agreement. First, he had no responsibility for 'dressing' the wagon or supplying the 'rushes' for the actors to perform upon (which probably already meant, as in Elizabethan times, a stage-cloth of rush matting). Nor did he have direct responsibility for the costumes or the play-book, although he was to return them to the master of the guild, in the condition in which he received them, on the Sunday after Corpus Christi. This really only leaves him with the acting to supervise, and for this he gets paid handsomely in Whitsun week each year and is invited to dine with the Keepers of the Smiths' guild. This man is certainly a professional director, though a local one, and his case is by no means unique in the history of the cycles.

To take a few more examples, there was a man called John of Arras who undertook the presentation of 'a play called Paradise' at Beverley on much the same terms as Colclow. At Coventry, Thomas Massye went further and provided both the play and the players for the Drapers in 1591, and in earlier years he had been employed variously by the Smiths, the Cappers and the Mercers for the same purpose. In this case he received for his pains 40 shillings, which is about a month's wages. It is not known what guild he belonged to, but he was apparently a professional director who had put together his own company.

Robert Croo, or Crow, is another professional from the same city, who not only revised pageants for the Weavers and the Shearmen-and-Taylors at various times, and provided the Drapers with the whole 'book' for their *Doomsday* pageant, but also played God in it for them later on, and at different times received money for 'mending the devils' coats', 'making three worlds', and making 'a hat for the Pharisee'. As usual, his guild is not specified, but, from the provenance of his work, it must surely have been one of those dealing with cloth. He seems to have been a professional playwright rather than anything else, because he also wrote a completely secular play for the Cappers called *The Golden Fleece*. In most respects his involvement is paralleled by another all-rounder, William Jordan, accredited as the 'author' and 'conveyor' of the Cornish *Creation of the World* in which he, too, seems to have taken the part of God – perhaps it was felt to be the most appropriate role for the play-maker, or perhaps nobody else felt inclined to risk their immortal souls by delivering his words.

By the early 1500s corporations seem to have been going further afield. A man called Gover Martyn was apparently brought down from London to New Romney in Kent in 1560 to take charge of the arrangements for the Passion play there at Whitsun, and a 'player' called Burles was hired by Chelmsford in 1562, presumably from outside the town, to supervise the construction and decoration of the scaffolds and conduct the rehearsals of the pieces being presented. However, Burles seems to have proved unsatisfactory, or perhaps he fell out with the authorities or the local actors, because eventually he only supervised two of the plays involved and local men directed the other two.

Sometimes it was a group and not an individual that produced a play.

At York in 1483 an eight-year contract was given to four men by the Ostlers' Company to produce their spectacular *Coronation of the Virgin* each year. These four men may quite possibly have been a production team of 'professionals' – director, designer, mechanic and business manager, for instance.

In the light of the presence of such experienced men, the short rehearsal schedule enjoyed by the cycles is not quite so alarming as it seems. At Chester, three rehearsals and one dress-rehearsal sufficed for the Coopers' *Resurrection* in 1574; in Coventry, there could be as few as two rehearsals or as many as five, depending on the guild and, presumably, the ability of the actors. In 1490 these rehearsals were held in Easter and Whitsun weeks, and took place before the officials of the guilds concerned at breakfast-time, doubtless so that the daily labour of the guild members involved should not be disrupted.

The musical contribution to the performance was probably organised separately. Those involved, apart from actors with good singing voices, were usually the town waits – the official band – with their shawms and trumpets, for the more pompous 'worldly' music to accompany characters like King Herod and Pilate, and the choristers, choirmaster and organist from the local church to provide 'heavenly' music. There seems to have been considerable competition between guilds to acquire the services of these two bodies, not stopping short of outright bribery – for instance, the Smiths' guild at Coventry made all four of the town waits honorary members in 1481, together with their wives, to help ensure their loyalty to the guild's pageant. On another occasion, the Smiths' guild at Chester was unable to hire the group of choristers it had used in previous years because the Painters' guild had got in first with a better offer.

Presumably the pattern everywhere was the same as that at Chester, where the guilds got in touch with the Precentor ('Mr Chanter') or the Master of the Choristers at a very early stage of the proceedings to arrange terms and allocate available resources. The town waits, too, are likely to have been approached at that time, either individually or as a body. Afterwards, we may imagine, the musicians themselves will have decided what they were going to provide for the festival, and will have rehearsed it separately, only ensuring that it was ready on the day. Sometimes, as in the case of at least one angels' 'Gloria' sung to the shepherds, there is a precise indication in the text as to how much of a standard liturgical piece is to be sung; and sometimes, as at Coventry, special music was written to accompany songs in the performance, though this would need to be 'sung through' for the benefit of any musicians accompanying the piece, because in those days most musicians played wholly by ear and were quite unable to read music – only the organist and choristers would have been fully trained. In any case, we can be fairly sure that both waits and choristers would be happier drawing on their customary repertory than attempting new material, even for a special civic occasion; so, on the whole, the musical component of the plays is not likely to have been very innovative.

There was also, of course, the lower echelon of the theatrical organisation to be appointed – namely, the stage-managers on whom all producers depend – and this emerges most clearly in the Coventry accounts. There each pageant had a 'dresser of the pageant', whose duties concerned such things as tending the windlass when ascents and descents took place, dyeing costumes where necessary, and so forth – the familiar duties of a stage-manager, in fact. Doubtless he also made the actual *arrangements* for hiring rooms for rehearsals and providing food and drink for the actors and stagehands.

Interestingly, he was not considered important enough to take responsibility for the costumes, or parts of costumes, which were provided from the wardrobe belonging to the guild – that was done by the pageant-master himself, who signed for each item when it was handed over and had it checked against the official inventory, and who did not relinquish responsibility for the costumes even when a specialist producer like Thomas Colclow was in charge, as we have seen. Nevertheless, the job of actually keeping a check on where the costumes were from day to day will almost certainly have been the stage-manager's concern, although some actors who regularly played the same part kept their costumes at home, despite the fact that they were guild property.

Amongst the least considerable members of the 'backstage' staff were the effects men and dressers. A versatile technician called Fawston at Coventry only got eightpence for cock-crowing and hanging Judas, and dressers got even less; the man who carried the costumes for the actor who was doubling the roles of Herod and Pilate at Chester in 1572 received only sixpence.

The actors who performed in the cycles were paid well for their trouble, wages of tenpence for playing God and a shilling for playing Noah at Hull in the early days rising with inflation to half a mark (or five days' wages) towards the end of the fourteenth century for actors playing important roles, like God at Coventry, or Simeon at Chester – the latter not a demanding part, but one that involved singing. This was double the amount earned by one of the king's own players in those days.

It is virtually impossible to assess the quality of acting in the plays, but we can be sure that the professionalism of the production, reinforced by the system of fines, will have produced quite a polished performance – and probably a very serious one. In Oberammergau in Bavaria, where there is a long tradition of presenting a Passion play every ten years, the actors have always taken their roles very seriously indeed, even the comic ones. The preparation of the piece stretches over the whole period between productions; the girl playing the Virgin Mary must have no slur against her morals, all the good characters must refrain from smoking and drinking; and on several occasions, when the play has been revised, the whole community has been split into bitter factions for years at a time. Similarly, in many places the person playing Christ was considered to need to feel real pain during the performance, and was treated quite brutally: one performer in Greece nearly died in the process. It may well have been the same in England in the late Middle Ages, because in those days the plays were not just a trap for tourists, but also a statement of faith, which taught how Everyman could escape to salvation out of the very jaws of death and damnation.

# 12

# PRODUCING THE CYCLES

The producers of the cycles enlivened the simple but effective techniques developed for early vernacular drama with a degree of extra sensationalism, particularly on the continent.

For instance, they favoured spectacular ascents and descents, using techniques pioneered in Italy to raise and lower clouds with winches and ropes. The clouds could be single or double, could open up their 'leaves' to reveal God inside them, and could carry more than one actor. Eventually it became possible to fly in as many as six angels on a single cloud – belts with catches being provided, as at Romans in 1509, to ensure they did not fall off. Clouds were also used to mask characters at important moments: for instance, when they were changing their costume. This happens in *The Transfiguration* at Valenciennes, where a cloud comes down and hides Christ while he dons the golden mask and gloves he needs for his miraculous meeting with Moses and Isaiah.

The theatrical technicians also used harnesses to fly individual actors. For instance, when he ascends to Heaven at Chester and Wakefield, Christ goes to the place of the Ascension in good time and stays there long enough for somebody to attach a line to him before he rises bodily into the skies.

Sometimes more sensational effects were sought. At Mons in 1501, Christ mounted himself on the Devil's shoulders and they were both hoisted to the pinnacle of the Temple 'in a trice . . . by means of a sudden counterweight'. This technique could also be used to achieve even more startling effects, as at Valenciennes, where the whole prison tower in which Joseph of Arimathea had been incarcerated was miraculously lifted into the air to help him escape.

Turning from the space above the stage to the space below it, there is evidence that trap-doors and tunnels were often used in French plays, and were dug under the earthen rounds with all the expertise to be expected of sappers who regularly dug mines and countermines under the walls of besieged cities.

The traps and tunnels were used for a number of different purposes:

some were for actors to escape from coffins or houses that were about to be burnt on stage, others were to provide startling and unexpected entrances, while a number were simply for the convenience of actors who would otherwise have been stuck for hours in a given spot without any way of answering the calls of nature or obtaining food or refreshments. They also allowed actors to get away early: at Mons there is a note reading 'those who do not have further lines to speak that day should depart by the underground devices'. At Valenciennes there must have been several traps in the stage, because in *The Last Judgement* the dead are required to rise from their graves in considerable numbers.

To preserve the element of surprise, the traps at Mons and Romans, were hidden with foliage which was strewn over the whole playing-area, and some similar method was probably used wherever such secret entrances were employed. An example of their use is to be found in the Mons *Passion*, where the devil Fergalus is instructed to proceed to a trap, above which stands a girl possessed by a demon, and, when the demon is cast out by exorcism, to leap from under her skirts, accompanied by smoke and the firing of a cannon from below. Rather tricky for the girl, perhaps, but an element of danger often attached to the devils' performances, owing to the predilection of medieval audiences for seeing the 'father of lies' go down to Hell 'apparelled foul with fire without'. Strangely the only recorded casualty was at Seurre in France in 1496, when Satan's costume caught fire and he got badly burnt. He was speedily dragged away and stripped by eager stagehands, rapidly reclothed in another devil's costume, and apparently proceeded with his part 'without the least show of disturbance'.

The network of tunnels under the more frequently used theatrical sites could be quite extensive. At Doué-la-Fontaine underground corridors 4 feet wide and 5½ feet high formed an irregular cross under the whole arena, giving access to at least three different traps. Under the Cornish round at Perranporth there is a tunnel which was used for the same purpose, now known as the Devil's Spoon, but it is not nearly so ample in its proportions. Similar passages must also have been present at Bourges in 1536, because at the Resurrection 'Jesus dressed in white, accompanied by three angels . . . should suddenly . . . spring forth from below the ground beside his tomb, by means of a little wooden trap, covered with earth, that closes again without anyone perceiving it'. The idea of Jesus suddenly leaping into sight at such an important moment seems rather comic, but in those days the audience's sincerity may have counterbalanced the humour.

Water posed another problem for producers – the River Jordan for the Baptism, the Sea of Galilee for Christ and Peter to walk on, the Red Sea, where the waters parted for Moses and returned to drown the Egyptians and, of course, Noah's Flood. Not all producers went as far as the one at

Bourges, where the whole arena was given a watertight parapet, and water was pumped into it through underground pipes to simulate the Deluge. It was more usual simply to provide a large wooden tank or reservoir, lined with sheepskins to render it watertight, and this was frequently done - there is one on stage in the play at Valenciennes. On this the ark was floated, Peter and Christ walked on the water by means of a plank cunningly concealed below the surface, and Christ preached to the people from a boat on the Sea of Galilee, to avoid the press, and travelled over it when the text demanded, with the help of a concealed stagehand hauling on a rope. At Mons the boat was borrowed from a fisherman on the river. These reservoirs could be the scene of impressive theatrical effects: at Mons the Deluge must have been most spectacular, because the producer had arranged for large wine barrels filled with water to be set in the upper part of a nearby building and these were upended by a tug on a rope when 'the fountains of heaven were opened'.

Where water was not used to simulate the Flood, the producers probably used lengths of cloth, painted with waves and fishes, which were rippled by performers waving them at both ends. This is suggested in the French *Mystery of the Old Testament*, which needed to use 'water' twice: once for the Deluge, when the instructions read, 'Here the waters shall rise over the entire area where the mystery is performed, and there may be several men and women who shall pretend to drown, but let them not speak'; and once when the Egyptians are overwhelmed by the Red Sea, where the instructions read, 'Then something resembling a sea should be shown, which had been covered over before, and some fish in this same sea' ('covered over' here possibly means 'folded up').

Obviously, when the waters were unreal Noah's ark would be either a stationary structure, swiftly erected on the spot, possibly by unfolding canvas-and-frame screens which were jointed together, or simply a decorated pageant on wheels which was dragged or pushed across the arena. The fact that it was fully built from the beginning of the play did not prevent a symbolic 'building' being presented to the spectators - as at Chester, where 'Noah with all his family shall make a sign as though they wrought upon the ship with divers instruments'.

Noah's ark logically leads us to the question of how the animals were displayed in the Noah plays. In Chester the problem was handled by having the ark 'boarded round about. And on the boards all the beasts and fowls painted.' The actors then pointed to them as they were named; but later on, the method seems to have changed - in 1607 the animals were on painted cards, and these were held up in turn for the edification of the audience before being handed to Noah to be stowed away on board.

On other occasions actors dressed up as animals - particularly as lions for *The Play of Daniel* - but occasionally the plays went all out for special effects, and full-scale models had to be used. *The Acts of the Apostles* at

Bourges was a case in point: this incorporated not only lions, but tigers, a leopard, a camel, a dromedary, a wild boar, serpents, a dragon and a two-headed monster – all apparently in the form of carnival structures. The dromedary could move its head, open its mouth and stick its tongue out, and the 12-foot dragon could move its head, eyes, tail and tongue. Compared with this, the more usual problem of presenting Balaam's talking ass seems trivial: sometimes, as in the Chester Cappers' play, it was played by a disguised actor – presumably half of a 'pantomime' donkey – but elsewhere it was often a model on wheels with a small boy hidden inside to provide the voice. The other fairly persistent artificial animal, or bird, displayed was the dove that returns to Noah after the Flood: he usually despatched a real dove, but it invariably returned to him as a model sliding down a fishing line, or lowered from the mast.

Live animals also appeared in the mysteries – mostly horses and donkeys fulfilling their usual functions; but in 1536 the ever-sensational Bourges production contained a dog that sang at the command of Simon Magus – possibly it just howled on command, or perhaps it was one half of a ventriloquist act. The same production employed an owl which had been trained by a falconer to fly down and perch on the shoulder of Herod Agrippa just before he was dragged off to Hell: there was probably a certain amount of nail-biting while its trainer waited to see if it obeyed command – but it did. Live ravens and doves were often despatched from the ark, and real doves were sometimes prevailed upon to flutter down from above to represent the Holy Spirit descending. Birds were also used symbolically to represent departing souls: at Lasfeld, for example, a white dove was released when Christ died on the Cross, and at Donaues-chingen a black bird of some kind flew up to represent the wretched soul of Judas when he hanged himself.

The mention of Judas' suicide opens up the question of violent death and torture in the plays. Beheadings were frequent, particularly in saints' plays, and 'frames for the beheading', which are illustrated in various books on Elizabethan stagecraft, were already in use in medieval times. Here the actor went up to the scaffold and as he laid his head on the block the executioner pushed it down into a hole, which instantly brought up a mock head in its place: it was this that was severed and displayed to the audience dripping with blood – a cunningly concealed bladder in the neck having been severed by the axe. Similarly, at the beginning of various scenes of torture, the actor was secured to a frame and then, whilst the audience's attention was distracted, the frame was swiftly revolved on its axis, substituting a dummy for the live actor, who crawled away through a trap-door.

When an actor was beaten or scourged, he could be protected by the use of dummy weapons, such as soft truncheons, or by wearing a protective leather leotard, as Christ seems to have done at Coventry. Whips and

144

scourges could be laid on lightly, and could be dipped in animal blood or paint so they marked the victim's back. On other occasions when weapons were required to draw blood, specially prepared props could be used, as happened at Lucerne, where Cain's axe secreted a container of blood which split open when he hit Abel, and the head of Longinus' spear was similarly full of blood, which ran down over the hands of the actor when Christ's side was pierced.

In saints' plays, the action often grew too rough for simple acting. The medieval audience loved its tortures. Saints were continually being decapitated, roasted on gridirons, burnt in ovens, torn limb from limb, or otherwise carved up. St Denis, in the long French play devoted to him, was progressively whipped, racked, tormented on a red-hot grill, savaged by wild animals, steeped in a furnace, crucified, beheaded and disembow-eled, with his bowels shown bursting out of his slit belly. St Barbara, in another play, was stripped naked, bound to a stake, beaten and burnt, had her breasts cut off, was rolled in a nail-studded barrel and dragged over a mountain by her hair, before being executed. Presumably in these cases dummies were substituted at some point for the actors.

Violence was also often reflected by the use of fire. In addition to flaming swords for angels and burning bushes for Moses, there are many instances of the destruction of houses, shrines and idols by lightning, fire or explosion, like the three worlds, made by Robert Croo, that were consumed with fire in the Coventry Drapers' play just before the Day of Judgement. In one of the French miracles, the gates of Burgos are consumed by fire, and in the lively Digby play about Mary Magdalen the devils set light to a house and reduce it to ashes, and later a cloud from Heaven strikes a heathen temple with lightning and sets it on fire - an effect probably achieved, as at Valenciennes, by rockets travelling down a wire attached to the top of the structure - an old Italian trick.

Sound effects will certainly have accompanied the fire from Heaven, because late medieval directors already had thunder-sheets and thunder-rolls in their possession. At Mons a brass-worker was paid to provide two large copper sheets to make thunder with, while two large casks full of stones were rotated with handles to supplement the noise of the sheeting. These devices were to be located in Hell, and their operators were strictly warned to follow their cue sheets - and stop when God bid the thunder cease.

The question of sound effects raises that of music. To judge by the texts, music does not seem to have been nearly as important in the vernacular plays as it was in the liturgical ones, but this may be an illusion, since the music seems to have been separately rehearsed and very much the province of specialists, receiving scant mention in the script. The instruments used seem to fall into two categories: those that accompanied the choristers and other singers who provided 'heavenly' music – for the most part portative organs, but sometimes members of the string family, or a full-sized organ, as at Romans; and those that provided 'earthly' music – assertive instruments like bagpipes, shawms, sackbuts, trumpets and drums – which were used mostly to accompany battles or sound fanfares when important characters like Herod appeared. There will doubtless also have been a discordant charivari of pots and pans employed by the devils in Hell. In addition, the plays contain many vocal renderings of hymns and songs, some of which may have been unaccompanied part-songs, like those of the three shepherds in the *Second Shepherds' Play* at Wakefield. The shepherds are particularly noted for their singing in these plays, and they hardly ever appear without at least *talking* about music. Vocal contributions are also provided by Noah's family, Simeon, the Apostles, and even the Virgin Mary, amongst the blessed, while Mak the deceiver in the *Second Shepherds' Play* sings completely out of tune, to show his wicked nature – harmonious music implying heavenly order ('the music of the spheres') while diabolical discords, like bad language, come straight from Hell.

The other main use of the musicians in these secular pieces seems to have been to play music to cover possible 'gaps' in the action, such as entrances and exits, longish ascents or descents, and extended processional movements – the points in the play where the audience might become restless – largely, it seems, to ensure continued silence from the spectators: the French called these bursts of incidental music *silêtes*, and an instruction in the Mons play well illustrates their function – God is instructed to descend from Paradise and the rubric adds, 'if he takes too long, play a *silête*'; so presumably they were mostly impromptu, and their use depended on whoever was leading the band.

Turning next to the actors' costumes, it is clear that costume in medieval drama was designed to assist in the immediate recognition of the characters rather than being strictly realistic, but it was also chosen to delight the eye with the colours and textures of the material used, and to harmonise with the surrounding decor, which would consist mostly of tapestries, curtains and other hangings, for it was an age in which cloth predominated.

Colour was important, and where the cloth was not vivid enough to satisfy the audience's taste it was often painted. Medieval people were very fond of bright colours, which no doubt provided a pleasant contrast to the general drabness of life around them, and there is little doubt that colour had symbolic associations for them, although these were not by any means systematised. White and black were perhaps the most clearly defined. White was a good colour associated with purity, untroubled faith, mercy and liberality of spirit: black, by contrast, usually implied the presence of evil, envy, sin, death or misfortune. Violet and purple were always colours of nobility or royalty, and gold and yellow usually implied the presence of wealth. Blue was the colour of good reputation, and of heaven, and the Virgin is frequently depicted with a blue mantle and a white gown, showing her good fame and purity. Green was widely used to signify 'what exists' like truth, or nature, or sensual delight – indeed, it was the colour of Venus, and green sleeves were worn by women of pleasure who wanted to encourage sexual advances. Red was a very ambivalent colour: on its good side it was associated with energy, both mental and physical, strength, power and militant righteousness, but on its bad side it could also represent pride, ambition, blood and violence: which is why it is both Adam's and Cain's colour in *The Play of Adam*. The catalogue is almost endless, but it is perhaps useful to mention one less obvious colour, carnation pink, which was popular in both medieval and Tudor times as a symbol of good health and cheerfulness.

There were three basic categories of character which needed to be costumed in medieval drama: simple mortals, supernatural beings like God and his angels, or Satan and his devils, and finally intellectual abstractions like Death and the various virtues and vices that affected the spiritual state of man.

When the actors were playing simple mortals, the costume was contemporary, and they were usually expected to provide it for themselves, though it has justly been pointed out that this does not mean that they used their everyday clothing: what they wore was expected to be theatrical and showy. The guilds had their own wardrobes covering the more unusual and decorative items, and kept a careful inventory of what they contained, and, in the smaller towns churches often maintained extensive wardrobes from which costumes could be hired. The producers provided any really unusual costumes: for instance, those for the Prophets dressed 'in ancient fashion' in the London pageants of 1501 – though whether this implied some attempt at antiquarian costuming, or merely an outdated version of the usual ecclesiatical vestments, is not known. The costumes of virgins, in particular, tended to come out of the budget, because the parts were usually played by boys, who did not own suitable clothes, and because in any case they expressed an artistic ideal, consisting of very simply cut surplices or gowns, girt in at the waist with girdles – though these were often made of richly decorated fabrics. The boys also wore wigs made of flax, which were sometimes dyed yellow with saffron, and various beads and brooches.

Amongst the supernatural characters, angels were dressed very much like the virgins, although they naturally wore no jewellery. They did, however, have wings which were 'golden and glistering' with 'feathers of many and sundry colours', sometimes peacocks' feathers, and occasionally they seem to have worn what one scholar describes as 'feathered catsuits'. Otherwise the costumes of the 'good' supernatural characters owed much to the drama's ecclesiastical origins. Christ in majesty wore rich episcopal dress, and God the father was frequently dressed to resemble the Pope, with an impressive triple crown, and sometimes a golden mask.

Devils were much more elaborate: there are many illustrations of them in contemporary manuscripts, showing grotesque dragon-like masks and sometimes bat-like wings, and a lot of hair and even feathers were purchased to decorate their costumes. By contrast, some devils, used to satirise contemporary fashions, are very elegant: one called Enguignart in a French *Day of Judgement* is dressed like a young dandy of the time, in a blue surcoat with long ermine sleeves falling almost to the floor, and a red hood – though his attendant devils were more traditional, and he will himself probably have worn some kind of grotesque mask. The cynical Tuttivillus in the Wakefield *Last Judgement* was probably similarly dressed, in view of his suave manner and his criticism of the latest fashions.

Saints and the more abstract characters, like virtues and vices, were distinguished by emblems they carried, just as they were in contemporary paintings. St Peter would carry the keys to Heaven and Hell, St John a lamb or an eagle, St Christopher a child on his shoulder, St George his red-cross shield, St Catherine a model of the wheel she was tortured on, and so forth. Similarly, if the character represented some abstract vice or virtue, they would carry an appropriate symbol – Liberality a horn of plenty, Justice a sword and a pair of scales, Love a bow with gold-tipped arrows, and so on. This convention also applied to kings, who always wore a crown, even if they were asleep in bed – and sported a crimson-purple robe. In addition, if they represented a particular nation, they would carry the heraldic animal of their country emblazoned on their costume: the English leopards, the French hart, the Imperial eagle, or the red dragon of Wales.

Facial masks were used not only for God and the devils, and sometimes for Jesus, but usually for Herod as well, as is shown by many accounts for making and mending his 'head'. It seems that his mask could be either red if the dramatist saw him as proud and choleric, or black if he saw him as primarily melancholic, or mad. There were also specific masks for particular occasions, like the one in the Cornish *Life of St Meriasek*, which is slipped onto the Emperor Constantine's face when he contracts leprosy. Masks will also probably have been used by Death and the more colourful vices when they made their rare appearances.

Other wicked characters who were likely to be dressed at the production's expense were Annas and Caiaphas and those rulers who represented the glory and pride of the world, like Herod and Nero. Traditionally Annas and Caiaphas were dressed as bishops, but in an unusual fashion – 'in a scarlet gown and over that a blue tabard furred with white and a mitre on his head after the old law'. According to some scholars, the last phrase means that the mitre was worn the 'wrong way round' with the division of the crown running from front to back, not from side to side, a practice clearly shown in contemporary paintings of Annas and Caiaphas; according to others, it means that they wore an approximation to the Jewish high priest's tiara, which will have been a sort of phylactery, or jewelled headdress.

The rulers of the world were much more magnificent. At Lucerne, Herod's costume was to be the 'most costly and splendid' that could be obtained, and was to have 'a Jewish, heathen feeling about it', while Pilate was to be dressed in an equally impressive costume, but one that stressed quality rather than show, 'like a provincial governor, rich, rough, with a . . . pointed hat, heathen and imposing . . . a burgher's coat with sleeves reaching below the knee, a sabre and high boots – a sceptre or staff in his hand', which, as one scholar observes, will have made him look more like a Turkish pasha than a Roman governor. Some of the female figures, too, could be gorgeously dressed, such as Pilate's wife, and Mary Magdalen in her early, unrepentant days.

Occasionally the producer had enough money to dress the whole play. In the Bourges *Acts of the Apostles* he almost bankrupted the town by dressing the whole cast, which was very large, with inappropriate magnificence: in that production even the beggars were costumed in rich silks, and the apostles, instead of wearing their traditional working clothes, were all clad in velvet and satin, with damask robes. Nothing could have been more inappropriate artistically – but then Bourges was the heart of a prosperous textile industry, and there were thousands of visitors to be shown the products of the region.

On most occasions, though, the quality of the materials, at least in England, was closer to that found in civic livery than to that found in court masques. Some garments were loaned from members of the public year after year, often showy cloaks or rich mantles which were theatrically impressive in their own right, or dresses belonging to the ampler women of the community which could be used by the men playing Mrs Noah. Costumes were also made of richer people's cast-off clothing, the usable pieces being cunningly worked together into 'slashed' garments, in the time-honoured manner of wardrobe masters and mistresses. Sometimes there were unexpected windfalls. For instance in Henry VIII's reign, when the monasteries were dissolved, there was a sudden upgrading of the costumes in most civic performances, when second-hand popish vestments became available in large numbers.

On the matter of the actors' performances there is really very little to add to the general comments made earlier, except to touch again upon the participation of the clergy and to consider the occasional involvement of women as performers.

In England, there is very little evidence that the clergy ever took part in vernacular plays, with the possible exception of priests who were attached to the religious guilds which presented some of them, and occasional sympathetic friars, but the case was very different on the continent, where priests assumed the role of Christ at both Mons and Lucerne, took many lesser roles in other towns, wrote plays, like Canon Pra at Romans, and were widely in demand as producers.

Women, by contrast, rarely appeared on stage, even on the continent, perhaps because it was thought immodest, but more probably because the organisations responsible for presenting the plays were male. However, it would not be true to say that women never acted in the mysteries. In 1468, for example, the daughter of Dediet the glazier at Metz delighted everyone with her performance as St Catherine – a part that involved her committing some 2,300 lines to memory: she accomplished this feat perfectly, speaking 'with such feeling and so piteously that she provoked several people to tears', and was rewarded with the hand of a rich nobleman, who had been overwhelmed by her stage presence. However, this did not prevent the citizens of Metz from choosing a barber's son to play St Barbara in 1485, and he was equally successful, being very good-looking, 'like a beautiful young girl', and playing the role 'so discreetly and devoutly that several people cried with compassion'.

In France and Italy the practice varied: at Mons in 1501 the parts of Eve, Noah's wife, Queen Herodias (who demanded the head of John the Baptist) and Mary Magdalen were all played by men, despite the fact that various girls appeared in minor roles. The most prominent female performer in that production was Wandru, daughter of Jorge de Nerle, who was 14 years old and played the Virgin Mary, Salome daughter of Herodias (who danced the dance of the seven veils), and the wife of John the Evangelist. At Romans in 1509 all the female roles in *The Mystery of the Three Masters* were taken by women; the same thing happened at Bolzano in Italy in 1514. In 1535 it seems that Grenoble witnessed the performance of a very talented amateur actress called Françoise Buatier, who won praise for 'her gestures, her voice, her articulation, her delivery'; she aroused 'universal admiration' and 'in her, grace and beauty were added to good speaking'. Having said all this, though, the fact remains that the one part most often played by a woman in France was the Virgin Mary, and a young woman would often play the Virgin even when all the other female parts in the play were performed by men. In Italy all-male casts were preferred, and even the Virgin would usually be played by a boy; nor is there evidence of any women acting in England.

When the plays were not presented by the craft guilds, the actors were drawn from all classes, and theoretically everybody had an equal chance, but the better roles were often cornered by the richest and most influential members of the community, and where the plays were performed annually they would often remain in the same families for year after year. This led to a number of plaintive notes, like the one from a hopeful burgher at Lucerne, who put in a claim to play the part of the Saviour 'in the event of the Reverend Muller not appearing in it again'.

The casts of these productions were sometimes vast: for instance, the Bourges *Acts of the Apostles* had 494 separate roles to fill and the Mons *Passion* 350. This put an enormous strain on the sheer human resources of an area. Within these large casts, there is evidence that groups of the principal actors sometimes banded together in order not to lose their identity. An amusing case occurred at Mons in 1501, where God the Father and his associates chose to sup at the Sign of the Gryphon, while Lucifer and his companions, who called themselves the 'compaignie infernale' preferred to eat at the Sign of the Key. Perhaps there was a class division here lurking beneath the humour – but, since it was France, it may merely have been an undying disagreement about the quality of the cuisine.

The number of spectators attending a performance of the vernacular plays can only be roughly estimated, but one responsible theatre historian suggests that roughly 5,000 spectators a day attended the *Three Masters* at Romans in 1509, and that similar numbers attended the mystery plays given at Vienne in the following year and at Valenciennes in 1547. No attempt has been made to assess the possible attendance at any of the English processional performances, but it was probably of about the same order of magnitude.

Such large audiences naturally posed problems of crowd-control for the organisers, and, quite apart from armed men guarding the pageants at York, strict rules were established in several towns to determine the eligibility of spectators. For instance, at Mons in 1501 no frail elderly people, pregnant women or children under 10 years old were to be admitted, which suggests that the crowding could be quite severe. Children were also forbidden at Valence in 1526 – but this was not always the case, since in 1509, as we have seen, a trellis was erected at the back of the boxes in Romans to stop children from falling out of them.

Toilets were provided for the audience on many of the bigger occasions in France: at Romans there were four *lieux d'aisance*, one at each corner of the theatre, as well as one below the stage for the convenience of the actors, and there were similar *retraits* available at Vienne in 1510. In England there is reason to think the arrangements at this time were much more primitive.

Care was given in France to other aspects of the audience's comfort as well: food and drink were often supplied free of charge, and at Romans the boxes were supplied with a lock and key so that belongings could be safely left there overnight.

Since the crowd attending the plays was large, and in a holiday mood, with intoxicating drinks available, it tended to be noisy. This is borne out by constant references in the texts to the need for silence during the performance. At Angers in 1486 the organisers decreed that the Prologue, who happened to be a priest, should celebrate Mass before the play began, 'both to make a better start and to ensure silence', and on the third day of the same festival children were to 'sing sweetly until a perfect silence is achieved'. In *The Mystery of St Etienne* the Prologue, playing St Peter, begs the audience to 'listen peacefully for a little while, without making so much noise', and it is clear that when the crowd did fall silent it came as a delightful surprise – one organiser noted at Autun in 1516 'God granted that on this occasion there was no whistling, uproar, mockery or barracking'.

In England the more violent or frightening characters were often used to terrorise the audience into silence – characters like Herod, or Pilate, or Cain's boy, or Cain himself, or maybe a couple of devils. But audience control was never by any means certain, and it seems to have been a general custom to have had five or six officials on call 'to throw out those who make a nuisance of themselves'. No doubt the men in armour accompanying the pageants in York were ready to undertake similar police duties if necessary.

There were also unforeseen and unpredictable disturbances, of course – brawls between members of the cast, or quarrels between them and the audience, or within the audience itself. At Romans in 1509 one of the devils attacked a woman in the crowd who owed him money; at Sainte-Honorine in 1516 a fight broke out between two factions of the spectators and brought the play to a halt; and at York in 1419 the Skinners were attacked by the Cordwainers and Carpenters in the middle of the Corpus Christi procession – but on the whole the crowd seems to have been very well behaved.

In France and Germany, the main moving-force behind the mystery plays was likely to be not the craft guilds but the local church or a local religious guild dedicated to their production. These religious guilds were known as 'brotherhoods'. They were middle-class associations of citizens which gathered together for various civic and charitable purposes, and some of them were dedicated to the production of plays – usually sacred plays, but occasionally also secular pieces. The earliest record of such an organisation is of a *confrérie* that pledged itself to produce religious plays in Nantes in 1371.

Without doubt the most famous brotherhood on the continent was the Parisian Confrérie de la Passion et Resurrection, better known simply as the Confrérie de la Passion, which was already active in 1380 and continued to be so for three hundred years. In 1402 this society received letters patent from Charles VI giving it the right, without seeking further permission, 'to play any mystery whatever, be it the said Passion and

Resurrection or any other matter, such as plays of male and female saints' anywhere in Paris and its suburbs, and to wear their theatrical costumes wherever they went without fear of molestation. This permission conti- nued until 1548, when the critical ripples arising from the Reformation reached them and they were forbidden to perform religious plays by the *parlement* of Paris, the Parisian city council.

The local 'Brotherhood of the Passion' often took over complete responsibility for presenting the mystery plays and organising the festival, but no brotherhood could possibly afford to mount such a large- scale spectacle single-handed, and they were jointly financed by the Church working through various local religious foundations and chari- table organisations, on the one hand, and the city authorities working through the guilds, on the other.

Funds were raised in a variety of ways. First gifts, loans or guarantees of money would be begged from the wealthier members of the community; then taxes would be levied, either on the community as a whole, or on the members of guilds and brotherhoods; then rents and tithes might be earmarked by the local churches for dramatic purposes; and, finally, the usual random means of fund-raising were resorted to – the collection of money in the street and by house-to-house visitation, bring-and-buy sales, 'church-ales', which were drinking-festivals held for charitable purposes, and many other devices. Occasionally a production might have an unexpected windfall, if a local lord or a member of the royal family attended the plays. In 1456, for example, René of Anjou paid 18 gold écus for a command performance of the Resurrection play at Metz, and no doubt when his daughter, Queen Margaret, the wife of Henry VI, visited Coventry to see the plays in the next year an appropriate sum of money will have found its way into the city coffers.

The town itself also usually contributed a sum from the civic purse, but it mainly seems to have acted as a kind of guarantor in the event of takings from the performance not covering the costs of production – which was almost always the case. The Romans *Mystery of the Three Masters*, for instance, cost 1,737 florins, and, taking into account all sources of revenue, including the purchase of seats by the audience and the selling of all the costumes and structural materials after the show, it left a debt of over 1,000 florins to be accounted for by the town and the play's ecclesiastical sponsors. The great production at Mons in 1501 fell just as badly short: it cost 2,281 livres to stage and produced a shortfall of 943 livres. At Lucerne the city always bore the main cost of the Wine Market production, which in 1571 amounted to over 1,233 gulden excluding the cost of erecting the stands for the spectators and the mansions for the play; there is no indication of the shortfall in this instance, but the Brotherhood of the Crown of Thorns and a number of private individuals regularly contributed to the cost. In any case, city

153

councils were always ready to meet any losses because of the extra business attracted to the area, and this motive was often explicitly recognised: for example, at Issoudun, where 'the play in its entirety lasted a month, and almost all the citizens . . . put up visitors, exactly as they do for the fairs at Frankfurt'.

The elaborate Valenciennes mystery of 1547 seems to have been unique amongst the large-scale mysteries, in that it made money. It was a corporate financial venture on the part of all those involved, including the actors. Each of them entered into a contract to pay a gold écu, with which he purchased a share in any financial profit, or loss, resulting from the production, with the proviso that any fines he incurred should be deducted from his profits or added to his losses. At the time, this must have seemed a highly speculative undertaking, but though the expenses totalled over 4,179 livres, which must have given some of the shareholders sleepless nights, the receipts were more than 4,680 livres, and when the proceeds from the sale of costumes and materials after the show were added the backers found they had cleared over 1,230 livres profit, to be equally divided amongst them. Quite a triumph for private enterprise.

# 13

# THE MORAL DIMENSION

In about AD 400 a Christian writer, Prudentius, wrote an epic poem called the *Psychomachia*, or *Battle for the Soul*, in which the vices and virtues of his time appeared as warriors waging a heroic struggle to gain control of the human mind. The idea was quite new, and Prudentius explained that his intention was to create an exciting poem which was more instructive and less dangerous for Christians to read than Virgil's popular *Aeneid*. In this he succeeded, because the piece achieved wide circulation, and the new technique he had introduced, of representing inner desires and motives as 'characters' in a 'drama', was regularly used by later writers to analyse the processes of the human mind and eventually led to modern theories of personality.

Seneca had already provided a vision of life as a moral pilgrimage through an enchanted and dangerous land, which led to allegorical adventure stories like *The Pilgrim's Progress*, but Prudentius was the first writer to produce allegory with dramatic potential. The central image of the *Psychomachia* was *conflict*, and that pointed directly towards a new kind of allegorical drama.

The further story of that drama is really the story of how effective patterns of dramatic action were developed to exploit the technique of self-analysis-through-personification that Prudentius had introduced. For instance, it was not long before the inner struggle for man's soul was reflected far more aptly by the image of a court intrigue, where the Vices all indulged in hypocrisy, cunning, honey-tongued persuasion and constant back-stabbing – a much more valid image in psychological terms, since people are very ready to persuade themselves that their own worst instincts are really nothing but good. This new development went hand in hand with the appearance of political allegory.

The only way to tackle the subject is to look briefly at the content of a few key works.

The *Psychomachia* itself is obviously the first of these. The action of the piece is very simple. The Seven Deadly Sins of Prudentius' time – Idolatry, Lust, Anger, Pride, Extravagance, Avarice and Discord – decide to attack the rich town of Psyche, or Man-Soul, in order to plunder it. They are opposed individually by the seven champions of the town – Faith, Chastity, Patience, Humility, Temperance, Reason and Concord. However, because all the vices and virtues mentioned are feminine nouns in Latin, the champions all become warrior maidens, and the association of female figures with graphically described scenes of horror and carnage is sometimes rather grotesque.

The action splits up into seven contests between pairs of adversaries, with pauses for breath in between. These pauses have some vivid and lifelike details, probably drawn from the author's own experience of military service. For instance, when the generals mount the tribunal platform in the middle of the camp to harangue the troops, word is passed through the ranks, and as the troops assemble, the doors of all the tents are thrown wide to make sure nobody is taking a nap and likely to miss the briefing.

After each of the contests there is first a shout of triumph from the victors and then a peaceful passage where swords are laid aside and a blessed quiet descends – though, needless to say, after the final defeat of the sins, there is a grand Roman triumph to end the piece. 'Realistic' details of this kind already point in the direction that allegory was later to follow.

The details of the battle are rather less convincing, and in places it becomes unintentionally amusing. For instance, Patience, having provided herself with an excellent suit of armour, simply stands still and allows her enemy Anger, who is naturally in a furious temper, to bounce darts off her breastplate and break a sword over her helmet, which is funny enough; but when Anger, having lost all her weapons, goes on to commit suicide in a fit of frustration, the image becomes hilarious. The encounter between Pride and Humility is equally amusing: Pride, mounted on a magnificent warhorse, wearing armour which is ornamented with mighty walled cities, and a lion's skin thrown Hercules-wise over her shoulder, charges down on her opponent after taunting her in vain for nearly fifty lines, and promptly falls into a pit dug by her own ally Deceit just before the battle started. The moment has now arrived when Humility must triumph over her enemy – yet she must obviously remain humble. The unhappy Prudentius can only explain that she triumphs modestly, 'lifting her face to heaven with moderated pleasure, with civil looks tempering her joy'.

However, though the psychology of the 'characters' involved may seem inappropriate in places and generally over-simplified, the poem's strength is that it deals extensively with the idea of self-deception, which is hardly ever touched upon in classical literature, and, though Prudentius himself was lacking in psychological insight, the method he originated was later used by many writers whose understanding of the mind was very acute, and some of them extended it beyond simple morality into a whole body of literature dealing with the psychology of sexual relations, beginning with *Le Roman de la Rose*.

The next development in the history of moral allegory is of particular interest to us, because it is a play. It is called *Antichristus* (*The Antichrist*), and was presented at Tegernsee in Austria some time in the twelfth century. It was the first of a long line of pieces which carried the allegorical method of moral analysis into politics. It contains several characters representing earthly power, such as the Emperor, the Pope and three European Kings, together with the personification of three religious forces, Non-Jewry, Jewry and the Church, and two virtues, Mercy and Justice. The action anticipates much of what we find in English moralities when their authors have an eye on contemporary social evils but want to pretend they are dealing with general issues. Consequently, the hypocrites in the play – who use propaganda to prepare the ground for the victory of Antichrist over the Kings of Greece, France and Germany, and manage to persuade Synagogue that he is the Messiah – stand for the contemporary supporters of the Pope in his struggle against the Emperor Barbarossa. The French King, too, is shown as bribed with gifts and is branded by Antichrist as his follower because, though Louis VII supported Pope Alexander III, the German imperial party thought that he did so only 'for gain'.

Apart from this contemporary comment, the piece is really little more than an elaborate military pageant, demanding considerable resources in terms of space and performers. Psychologically it can be seen as an elementary study of two opposing senses of duty in the individual, one to the Church and the other to the State, and also as an inner struggle between honesty, which is politically risky, and deception, which is more successful. Here, too, for the first time in drama, the 'body' of the State is treated as an analogue of the human body, and this later became a very popular image.

However, despite this early venture into allegory, moral plays remained few and far between until the outburst of religious drama in the late fourteenth century, when the urgent need to be cleansed of sin, reinforced by the presence of the Black Death, gave the same impetus to the moral drama as it did to the cycle-plays.

One of the earliest moral plays to spring up at that time was *The Play of the Paternoster* (*The Play of the Lord's Prayer*) at York. Unfortunately there is no existing text of the piece, and only a few references to it here and there, but these show us that it was indeed a morality play. It was certainly in existence by 1389, because that was the year when a Guild of the Paternoster was established to perpetuate it, and the document instituting the guild explains that the play had been first written and performed in the city some time before.

It should be explained here that, in the new system of personal confession, repetitions of the Paternoster were often prescribed as a penance, because theologians maintained that it could be used to fortify oneself against all the Deadly Sins. They saw it as containing seven distinct petitions: 'Hallowed be thy name' is a reminder to resist pride, which led Lucifer to try to usurp the throne of God; 'Thy kingdom come' warns us against envy, which will be no part of the Heavenly kingdom; 'Thy will be done' counsels us to control our anger and humbly accept whatever fortune God sends us; 'Give us this day our daily bread' is a warning against idleness, because since Adam's fall we have had to work for it; 'Forgive us our trespasses as we forgive those that trespass against us' warns us against avarice, which might lead us to be uncharitable to those who have wronged us; 'Lead us not into temptation' is a reminder to avoid gluttony and other indulgences of the sensual body; and 'Deliver us from Evil' is a specific warning against lechery, the easiest and most disruptive of sins.

The relevance of the petitions is rather strained, but, because the Lord's Prayer was so well known, this proved a popular system of recall, and it became a keystone in the campaign to implement the new sacrament of Penance. Strings of Paternoster beads, looking rather like rosaries, began to be produced to help count the number of times the prayer had been repeated, and French records show that there were guilds of Paternosterers specifically founded to manufacture them. Such a string of beads is given to Mankind in the play of that name when he is converted to Christianity, lost when the Devil persuades him to wickedness, and given back to him again when he is reclaimed.

The guild's documents at York provide only a very general idea of what the Paternoster play was about – its subject was the benefit of the Lord's Prayer, and in it 'many vices [were] denounced and virtues commended'. In addition, records of the guild which are now lost contained an entry of 'various expenses with regard to the play of Accidie', which is apparently the same play. 'Accidie' is the usual medieval word for sloth or idleness, which was seen as the cause of many sins, so it is generally assumed that the York Paternoster play was a dramatisation of the Seven Deadly Sins in the order in which they were recalled in the Lord's Prayer. Yet the reference to it as 'the play of Accidie' surely implies that this character had some special importance.

Reinforcement of this assumption is to be found in the records of Beverley, where, on 1 August 1469, they performed 'different pageants of Paternoster'. Eight pageants are listed in this instance, together with the guild responsible for each of them, showing that the arrangements were the same as those for the cycles. We can also fairly safely assume that the presentation of the plays was processional, because only seven stations in the town are provided for eight pageants.

The first pageant was 'the pageant of Vicious', and the remaining seven are listed as the pageants of the usual Deadly Sins. Interestingly, though, in a list of the *characters* involved, 'Vicious' comes *last*, so he may well have been a kind of infernal master of ceremonies who introduced the various sins and indulged in some kind of commentary at the beginning and the end. If so, it is possible that Accidie fulfilled a similar function at York.

The possible form of the Beverley Paternoster play has aroused much speculation, and theories have ranged from Vicious being the actual leader of the sins to his being an Everyman figure representing the frailty of man and the destructive effects of vice. In the York play, too, Accidie could be either an active vice or a typical human backslider; but unless more evidence emerges, it will never be known which of these assumptions is correct. In view of the existence of rascally Vice figures in many popular moralities, the 'leader of the sins' seems more likely – but it is easy to see why many scholars would prefer an Everyman character, because a 'morality play' is commonly supposed to deal with the fortunes of such a figure.

The Paternoster play at York continued to be presented until late in the sixteenth century, receiving its last performance in 1572, when Shakespeare was eight years old. At that time it attracted the attention of Archbishop Edmund Grindal, who had been appointed by Elizabeth to suppress Catholic propaganda after the Earls' Rebellion of 1569. He called in the playbook for examination, and though the council, who could see what was coming, offered to provide him with a 'true copy' for his perusal, he insisted on seeing the original, and that was the last that was ever heard of the York Paternoster play.

The earliest moral play in England that conforms to the 'expected' pattern is a piece called *The King of Life* from the early fourteenth century; and, although the text is fragmentary, it contains a prologue summarising the action, so it is possible to reconstruct the play's general shape.

It begins with the entry of the King of Life, boasting of his power and majesty. He is accompanied by two bodyguards, Strength and Health, who are sworn to defend him against all enemies. First his queen, and then a bishop, warn him that he is mortal, but he ignores their warnings and instructs his messenger to proclaim Life's dominion over all the world and to challenge anyone, even Death, to fight if they deny it. When the Messenger has made his announcement, the King of Life dreams that he will be killed by Death, and Death indeed comes to challenge him. They meet in battle, and Death first overcomes the King's two bodyguards and then Life himself. As Life dies, his soul is seized by fiends, and the Body and the Soul dispute over where the blame should be laid, the Soul all the while bewailing its fate. However, finally, through the intercession of the Virgin Mary, the Soul of Life is freed from the fiends' clutches and allowed to ascend to Heaven, and all ends happily.

There are interesting similarities between this play and the King of the Year ritual. The King of Life brags, like St George in the play; he fights, dies and undergoes a spiritual resurrection, parallel to the Doctor's magical revival of the fallen hero. This suggests that the writer chose to drive home his message by using a well-known popular story – a typical missionary device. On the other hand, this pattern of life-death-and-resurrection, is also parallel to the Passion of Christ, and it certainly pervades all the moralities, appearing as a moral progression from innocence, or ignorance, to sin and then repentance or, in some plays which deal with education, from study to idleness and later reformation; so the author could have drawn on a number of sources.

In the later fourteenth century, 'moral plays', as they were called then, become so abundant that it becomes convenient to consider the different categories into which they fall and select only a few of the most typical examples. In terms of physical presentation, to take that first, the plays can be clearly divided into two groups: large-scale plays mounted by the community, in the same way as the mysteries; and small-scale plays, known as 'interludes', usually intended for production by companies of professional travelling players, often at a dinner or banquet. These two groups can be sub-divided again according to their main subject, into what are called by modern critics 'general moralities' and 'specific moralities.' The general morality casts its net very wide and embraces the whole life-journey of man, often pursuing it through a series of 'ages', each of which has its associated vices, while the specific morality deals either with the sins of one particular 'age', usually youth, or a particular problem of Christian life.

The general morality's technique of subdividing man's life into separate 'moral ages' was a very common medieval approach: for instance, at the opening of *The Divine Comedy* Dante finds himself lost in the midst of the forest of life, and as he points himself towards the star of hope, his path is crossed by three wild beasts who try to drive him back: first a leopard, with a very beautiful skin and lithe movements, which represents the sins of youth, idleness, lust, and self-indulgence; then a lion, which is very powerful and majestical, and represents the sins of middle age, intolerance and pride; and lastly a lean and withered wolf, which is very vicious, and represents the sins of old age, envy and avarice. Needless to say, the poet manages to escape all three.

Like the *Psychomachia*, the general morality involves a prolonged struggle, and sometimes even a pitched battle, between the vices and the virtues, and, like *Antichristus*, it sometimes contains a lively allegorical comment on the contemporary political scene. *The Castle of Perseverance* is a good large-scale example of a general morality, and the popular interlude *Mankind* is a good small-scale example of the form.

The specific moralities, of their nature, are almost all small-cast plays. *Everyman* is the most famous example, but it is not typical of the genre, having too large a cast and lacking the typical bawdy humour. Usually these pieces, for sound commercial reasons, placed more stress upon entertainment than morals. Two good examples of the genre are *The Marriage of Wit and Wisdom* and *Hick Scorner*.

The large-scale public moralities were very popular and were produced, like most cycle-plays, on an essentially non-commercial basis by groups of citizens – often quite large groups. Sometimes the audience had to pay to see them, but the intention was usually not to make a profit but simply to defray expenses, as happened with the large-scale continental mysteries and saints' plays – after all, scenic units and costumes must have made considerable demands on the pockets of the producers in the case of plays like *The Castle of Perseverance*, and such costly pieces cannot possibly have been intended for professional production. In an age when it was difficult to keep even a six-man troupe together, it would have been economic suicide for travelling players to risk mounting anything so enormous: if it had failed, they would have spent the rest of their lives in gaol for debt.

The moral interludes, by contrast, were usually presented by small troupes of between four and six players, who travelled the countryside earning their keep. They would be attached to the household of some lord, and wear his livery – which meant they must take care not to disgrace him by bad behaviour, bad performances or unacceptable material. However, the livery was mainly used to prevent them being whipped as rogues and vagabonds or forced into labour as 'masterless men'. When their lord required them to provide entertainment for himself and his guests, they would be expected to turn up at the ancestral hall – particularly at Christmas time – but the demands made on them seem to have been few and far between, and they spent most of their time simply earning enough to live on.

The commercial nature of the interlude explains the difference between itself and the large-scale morality. The large-scale play aims to be vivid and instructive, but is always serious and restrained, whereas the interlude aims to amuse and is lively and often bawdy, particularly where the vices are concerned, because the audience needs to be entertained if it is going to pay; it also has many references to the spectators, to involve them in the action or, alternatively, to stop them crowding the entrances to the hall that the actors are using; it contains quite a lot of comment on contemporary abuses, to amuse them and gain their sympathy; and it contains a considerable amount of doubling of parts, so the play is contantly interesting, but does not involve sharing out the profits between too many actors.

In Tudor times, when interludes had become popular and well established, they began to be used for other purposes too: we find them being produced for 'amateur' performances at schools, universities and the Inns of Court, and elsewhere as propaganda exercises for politicians like Wolsey and Thomas Cromwell.

A brief summary follows of the action of one or two moral plays which are typical of their respective genres. For this purpose, four will suffice: *The Castle of Perseverance* as a large-scale general morality; *Mankind* as a typical commercial interlude; *Kynge Johan* as a typical political piece; and *Wit and Science* as an example not only of the plays about youth, but of the humanist interludes dealing with education.

*The Castle of Perseverance* is a massive play encompassing several moral plots: the struggle between the vices and virtues for Mankind's soul, the coming of Death to Mankind, the debate of the Body and the Soul (as in *The King of Life*), and the debate of the Four Daughters of God over the fitness of Mankind's soul for Heaven.

The play begins with Mankind in a state of infancy, newly born and weak in a sinful world, but already accompanied by his Good and Bad Angels. He wants to be rich and enjoy displaying his wealth, but he also wants to save his soul. The Bad Angel suggests he should wait until old age to repent, and become rich in the meantime. Mankind agrees to this scheme and joins the service of the World, soon falling into the hands of the Seven Deadly Sins, but his Good Angel sends Conscience, Confession and Penance to recall him to an honest way of life. He repents, and a bevy of beautiful Virtues – Meekness, Patience, Charity, Soberness, Busyness, Chastity and Generosity – bring him to refuge in the Castle of Perseverance.

The Bad Angel now rallies his forces, in particular Covetousness, the envious desire to enjoy others' pleasures, who urges Mankind to pursue Gluttony, Lechery and Idleness in place of Soberness, Chastity and Busyness. The Good Angel struggles to keep him in the castle, where he will be safe, while the Bad Angel tries to lure him out and eventually, by getting Covetousness to offer him material goods, persuades him to leave the castle and spend his declining years in wealth.

As Mankind grows older, Covetousness gains more and more power over him and he revels in his greed, but Death comes unannounced, and when Mankind shows concern about who shall inherit his huge wealth he is told it will be a new, young lad, called 'I-wot-not-who'. Mankind's soul is then carried away to Hell, begging mercy for his sins. His Body and Soul debate over where the blame should be laid, and the Soul is brought before the Four Daughters of God for his case to be reviewed. Mercy speaks in his favour, but Justice and Truth say he should get what he deserves. Peace finally suggests that they should lay the case before God the Father, and there Mercy answers all the charges brought against Mankind and God is moved to forgive his Soul and send it to Heaven, though he ends the piece with a stern warning to all men to take thought of their own last day. The play is very uneven, but has great variety – containing comedy, exhortation, action and debate – and in places it works very well.

By contrast to *The Castle of Perseverance*, *Mankind* is an excellent example of a popular moral interlude. First a friar called Mercy appears, and delivers a deliberately boring sermon exhorting the audience to shun temptation so they can be saved on the Day of Judgement. After a few minutes he is interrupted by Mischief, who mocks him outrageously. The three vices of the piece, New Guise, Naught and Nowadays, now burst in, force Mercy to join in a wild dance and rough him up thoroughly before leaving. Mercy thanks God and resumes his sermon, dwelling on the way in which the bestiality of man far exceeds that of animals, because man is a rational being and should know better.

Mankind, a simple, innocent labourer, now appears, and is lectured by Mercy on the avoidance of sin and given a set of Paternoster beads to help him recall the Seven Deadly Sins. This lesson is interrupted by the re-entry of the vices, first New Guise, and then the rest, and when Mercy has gone and Mankind has started to dig the ground with his spade they try to distract him from his work. At this point they get the audience to sing a little song, which is innocent enough at first but later proves to be full of lavatory humour. They then pester Mankind until he strikes out at them with his spade in frustration, apparently wounding them all, and they flee from the stage.

Mischief soon reappears to say all his plans have gone astray because Mercy has too much influence over Mankind. He calls back the vices, who come in moaning and bewailing their bruises. He suggests they need the aid of the devil Tittivillus, the demon of slipshod work, if they are to overcome Mankind, so they call him up. Tittivillus roars offstage and says 'I come', but he doesn't come until the vices have taken up a collection from the audience, egging them on by describing the devil's costume and threatening to stop the play if they don't get enough money. Tittivillus then enters with his net. He agrees to revenge the vices on Mankind but sends them off in the meantime to visit hopeful converts to vice who live nearby, and each of them lists by name one or two local worthies and the vices for which they are particularly noted.

When they are gone, Tittivillus buries a board in the ground for Mankind's spade to strike upon; Mankind finds he can get no further and is easily persuaded the ground is too hard to till, so, in order not to be idle, he takes himself to his prayers. Tittivillus then creeps up behind him and convinces him that he urgently needs to relieve himself, thus breaking the mood of prayer. As he bolts off to open his bowels, Mankind leaves his Paternoster beads behind, and Tittivillus scornfully throws them away. When Mankind returns, Tittivillus sends him to sleep when he ought to be attending Evensong, and while he is sleeping whispers in his ear that it was wrong to hurt the vices and he should make it up to them. The devil then retires.

When Mankind wakes, the vices return and he begs their pardon. At first they don't believe him, and then Mischief says they must put him on trial. The mock trial that follows is an elaborate parodic reversal of the sacrament of Penance, during the course of which Mankind is instructed in the way of practising six of the Deadly Sins – the seventh, lechery, being taken for granted – and he is admonished to practise robbery and self-indulgence. In token of his changed state, his sensible working-gown is progressively trimmed down to the fashionable guise of the gallant's trivial little short jacket, which cannot even serve to keep him warm, and off they all run to seek their pleasures before Mercy can catch them. Mercy appears just in time to intercept Mankind, but Mankind will not listen to him any longer, and this development worries Mercy, who discusses it with the audience.

Soon, the vices reappear with Mankind, now far gone in wickedness; they mock Mercy, and offer Mankind a gibbet and a rope with which to hang himself, after which they run away again. Mankind is confused and ashamed, and almost despairing, but Mercy gradually wins him round by assuring him of God's indulgence, and eventually he repents and Mercy gives him back his Paternoster beads.

A point worth noting about this play is the importance of Mischief as a kind of leader of the vices. This was a tendency that grew steadily stronger in the interludes, until this dominating character, who became known simply as 'the Vice', completely overshadowed the actors playing the lesser sins. 'Vicious' in the Beverley Paternoster play seems likely to have been such a figure.

There were many interludes which depicted aspects of contemporary politics, and not a few of them were polemical – which means devoted to arguing a case. Such interludes supported either the Catholics or the Protestants. *Kynge Johan*, written by John Bale, a skilled propagandist, is a good example of such a piece, because it combines political themes with religious ones.

The aim of the play is to turn King John into a Protestant Christian hero who stoutly rejected any unwarranted interference by the Pope in his secular rule. He is shown as being victimised by a papal interdiction which makes the common people submit to Cardinal Pandulphus, after Nobility, Clergy and Civil Order (all characters) have been undermined by Sedition (another character) disguised as Religion. Thus John is forced to yield his crown, and all England's troubles are proved to have been the fault of Usurped Power (the Pope) and Sedition, who declares that popes may depose kings. John denies this doctrine and advances that of the divine right and divine appointment of kings – proving from Scripture that he who condemns a king tacitly condemns God – and he claims that a Bible in English is essential so men can learn obedience to God's laws without interference from the priesthood.

The play thoroughly explores the possiblity of satirically identifying actual individuals with the abstract political forces in the State, and this has led many scholars to miscalculate the number of actors it needs. They reckon that there are nineteen parts because they insist on treating the named individuals like Stephen Langton, the Pope, Pandulphus, Raymundus and Simon of Swynsett as separate characters, when they are, in fact, only temporary incarnations of the political vices which are introduced elsewhere in the play – Langton is identical with Sedition, Pandulphus with Private Wealth, Raymundus and Simon of Swynsett with Dissimulation at different times, and the Pope with Usurped Power. Once you look at the play in this way you find that, far from needing nineteen actors, it can easily be performed by six.

The last moral genre to be considered, the humanist interlude, was often written by schoolmasters, and was particularly apt for universities and schools, so, as the trend towards amateur dramatics intensified, these plays became more common. They are very educational and, being humanist, their virtues are usually Moderation and Reason and their vices Excess and Foolishness.

*Wit and Science*, by John Redford, is a good example of such a play. It is an allegory of undergraduate life, in which Wit, a young scholar, woos Miss Science, the daughter of Doctor Reason and his wife Experience, and sets out to conquer Giant Tediousness and win his way to the peak of Mount Parnassus (in other words he sets out to make good use of his university course and gain a degree).

At first he is too keen and goes to Study and Diligence before seeking help from Instruction. As a consequence he contracts a shocking headache, and in his first bout with Giant Tediousness (his first exams) the giant has an easy victory. Here Wit falls down and dies, but he is resurrected by a chorus consisting of Honest Recreation, Comfort, Quickness and Strength, who sing a song about the need for a little relaxation and recreation from time to time. Wit now falls into the opposite extreme: he throws off his gown, cuts a caper, and collapses exhausted into the arms of a strumpet, Idleness. While he sleeps in her arms, his face is blackened and he is dressed up in a fool's cap and motley.

Meanwhile Miss Science, whom he has jilted, is approached by many other respectable suitors, such as Worship, Favour, Riches and Fame, who all sing her love-ditties, only to be turned away. Wit then comes back to her, but she snubs him, thinking he is Ignorance. He does not understand what has happened until he sees himself in Reason's looking-glass, but then, after he has submitted to chastisement from Shame, and a lecture from the other academic virtues, and has been cleaned up and made to look respectable, he succeeds in slaying Giant Tediousness by cunning (serious application to his finals) and gains the peak of Parnassus and his lady's hand, and all ends happily.

The influence of the moral drama on later playwrights was strong but variable, and did not stem from the larger-scale pieces: general moralities had little influence because they were too expensive to be professionally viable, and were unlikely to be toured beyond their local area, and the appeal of the specific moralities, brilliant and viable though some of them were, was soon undermined by printed pamphlets dealing with the same moral problems, because people apparently felt that the printed word was far more meaningful than simple plays.

On the other hand, the moral interludes were of incalculable importance to the Elizabethan drama. Moral interludes that dealt with specific sins, especially those of middle age, began to be used by playwrights as a means of 'patterning' real historical incidents, the central Mankind figure becoming the King, and his inner conflict being externalised into counsellors offering him conflicting advice, or into a single external figure opposing his natural inclinations, often a Vice-like character. This led not only to the typically Elizabethan history play, with some title like 'The Troublesome Reign and Lamentable Death of King X', but also to the closely related tragedies of Elizabethan and Jacobean times – either moral tragedies like *Hamlet, Lear* or *Macbeth*, all of which are 'historically' based, or domestic tragedies founded upon real events, like *Othello* or *The Duchess of Malfi*, where the characters of Iago and Bosola relate directly to the old Vice. These dramatic forms drew plainly upon the early Tudor interest in real history as an instructive moral example, which we find best expressed in the ever-popular *Mirror for Magistrates*, which was full of examples of good and bad rulers of the past.

Moral interludes dealing more argumentatively with political matters, like *Kynge Johan*, were important in a different way. They contained abstractions representing different social *forces* in the kingdom – the King himself, Papal Power, Nobility, Commonalty, Clergy, and so on, and this provided a framework for serious political analysis and led on to more complex, moral history plays, like those of Shakespeare, where the characters are simultaneously abstractions of forces in the State and also individuals.

Finally, the moral interludes dealing with the sins of youth – the most popular 'age' so far as sins were concerned – produced plays like *Lusty Iuventus* and *Hick Scorner*, which were full of ill-behaved and intemperate young men and became increasingly realistic in their depiction of

London low life. These plays became the direct inspiration of the city comedies of Ben Jonson and others.

In this way the moral interludes provided a nucleus from which most of the later Elizabethan drama sprang, the only exception being the romantic comedies that derived from the Italian pastoral plays and picaresque romances, which were fashionable with the more intellectual aristocrats and were mostly disseminated by troupes of Italian players in the form of lively improvisations.

# 14

# MORAL INTERLUDES IN ACTION

The cycle-plays may have helped Elizabethan writers to take a more cosmic view of life, but the traditions of staging and acting they employed sprang immediately from the interludes, and so did the way they handled their material.

The early companies of travelling players had established a technique of doubling which enabled them to use their limited numbers to the greatest advantage. This is seen best in the early moral interludes, where the pattern is clear. They focus on a Mankind or Everyman figure who is constantly being worked on by good and evil forces - the evil forces trying to lure him away from God, and the good forces trying to win him back again - a movement that may be repeated several times. However, usually, the good and evil forces will not need to be on stage at the same time, so, by a change of costume, the actors playing the evil forces can easily become the good forces for the next scene, and vice versa - all they need is time to change, which can easily be provided by having Mankind soliloquise or put some argument to the audience. Such a pattern of role-change is found in many early interludes, and some acknowledge the fact on their title-pages, first indicating the number of actors involved and then listing those characters that should be assigned to each actor.

This technique of progressively suppressing characters in order to free the actors for new parts was very useful when the Elizabethan writers turned to chronicle-history and picaresque romance, where exactly the same thing happened as in the interludes - many characters made fleeting appearances and were never heard of again, or, at best, only reappeared briefly at widely scattered points in the story. By careful doubling it became possible to tackle such large, rambling subjects with quite a small company, and this had a liberating effect on the early Tudor theatre, when companies were, indeed, very small - consisting usually of four or five men and a boy.

Later on, as the drama flourished and companies became larger, the technique of progressive suppression became less important. In a company of perhaps twenty actors, like Shakespeare's, which was rich enough to hire extras, the principal players did not expect to have to double; indeed, very much the contrary: they expected parts that fitted their particular 'line' of performance – but that was much later. At first the additional freedom given to the playwrights by the convention of doubling was very important, and encouraged an adventurous approach to new material.

A review of all the moral plays preserved between the late fourteenth century and 1576 – the year when James Burbage built the first theatre in London intended as a permanent base for an acting-company – reveals a three-stage development. First there are the large-scale civic pieces, which demand big casts; then a period dominated by small-cast interludes, covering the years when drama was not yet popular enough to support large companies; and, finally, a period when the size of the companies was increasing as they gained access to the new popular audience.

The first period contains the fourteenth-century *King of Life*, which certainly needs a large cast, though how large is unclear because of the fragmentary text, and the early fifteenth-century Croxton *Play of the Sacrament*, which needs nine players, together with *The Castle of Perseverance*, from the same period, which needs more than twenty. Then in about 1460 comes *Wisdom*, which needs seven men and seven boys and probably also employed six female dancers. These were all, plainly, community plays.

The second period begins in about 1465 with *Mankind*, which is the first obviously commercial interlude, and here, for the first time, the piece needs only six players, and interestingly provides for Mercy, the principal 'goodie', to change his costume and play his opposite, the devil Tittivillus, and then change back again for the end. Possibly *Everyman*, in 1495, was also in this category – though it needs seven actors, an unusually high number for a professional interlude, and may have been a community piece.

The other plays that fall into this second period are all clearly commercial and include *Mundus et Infans* (*The World and its Child*), which is a full-length general morality from 1508 which can be played by just two players; *Hick Scorner* in 1513, which needs either five or six, depending on how you double; *Youth* (a simplified version of *Hick Scorner*) from 1520, which also needs five or six, and two plays by John Heywood, *The Four PPs*, which needs four players and *Johan, Johan*, which needs three.

The years between 1538 and 1559 saw the production of six further interludes, one of which needs five actors, while the rest need only four – it would be tedious to detail them here.

In late 1559 there is a change. John Phillip's *Patient and Meek Grissel* demands eight actors, and from that point until as late as 1610, interludes were clearly being written for large companies of performers as well as small ones, despite the fact that from 1572 the use of public theatres in London was growing steadily, and from 1578 really major plays were being presented in them by big permanent companies, which ought to have undermined the finances of the travelling companies completely.

Of sixteen interludes written between 1559 and 1610, exactly half are designed for a company of six players or less, the rest demanding between seven and ten. However, plays that give a breakdown of the casting on their title-page virtually disappear after the foundation of the Theatre in 1576, and the implication is that small companies did indeed die out when they were faced with the competition of the big new permanent theatres. In fact, it is believed that after 1576 large-cast interludes only continued to be published because amateur dramatic performances had emerged between 1559 and 1610 in schools and universities and the Inns of Court, where large unpaid casts were available, and money was collected either to help maintain the institution or simply to defray the costs of production.

In early Tudor times, this amateur activity gave birth to companies of professional boy players in the choirschools, and it was these companies, with their entrée to the court, that did much to raise the literary level of the early Elizabethan drama and open the way for the first wave of important dramatists, like Marlowe and the University Wits.

The professional companies that produced the early interludes were a new phenomenon. They were not descendants of the minstrel troupes, because they looked on them as rivals. However, they clearly organised their companies in the same way, presumably because economic and social considerations dictated the same pattern. They travelled extensively, had a lord as their patron, and carried letters of recommendation from him to prevent themselves being whipped as rogues and vagabonds; the size of the company was small, for financial reasons; and they were essentially all-round entertainers with musical and tumbling skills to match their powers of delivery.

Their main difference from the minstrel troupes lay in their repertory. The jongleurs were general entertainers - their show might include acrobatics, sleight of hand, conjuring, puppets, animal imitations, performing dogs and monkeys, dancing bears, sword-fights, farces, and the recitation of heroic poems or popular tales in rhyme, but their staple fare was music and dance, and they usually seem to have performed in masks.

The interluders, by contrast, were much more dependent upon the written word, and though they were all-rounders who could tumble, present sword-fights and wrestling-matches, and sing and dance, they were not specialists in these areas - for instance, they would often hire local musicians to play for them rather than do it themselves; nor did they use masks.

The first record of native interluders in England is in 1472, when they appear before Henry VI. This is very late compared with the continent, but their numbers soon begin to grow, and the companies begin to take the names of the noblemen who protect them: 'The Duke of Gloucester's Men,' for instance. The Earls of Essex, Oxford, Derby and Shrewsbury, and Lord Arundel were also amongst those who began to sponsor players – all rich and powerful nobles, whose name and livery could help to get their retainers received throughout the kingdom. Even Henry VII, who had little time for courtly entertainments, was fond of interludes and had his own company. Henry VIII later increased its size, and appointed the actors for life, which meant they received a pension when they could no longer perform.

By the early sixteenth century, troupes of 'players of interludes', or by now simply 'players', had become a familiar sight on the roads and an important means of public entertainment throughout the nation. They began to develop touring circuits around the country, some of which continued to be used up to the nineteenth century. Taking London as a starting-point, they would travel out to Canterbury and then round selected places on the south coast till they turned north again towards Bath and Bristol; or they could go straight to Bath and Bristol by way of Oxford and Reading. From the Bristol area the route was invariably up to Shrewsbury. Then there was another choice. Most companies swung east and passed through Stratford and Leicester, but it was possible to make a long loop northwards to York and then back to Leicester by way of Lincoln or Derby, or both. From Leicester, if they wanted, they could make a further diversion through Cambridge, Ely and Norwich, before going on to St Albans and returning to London. These were all well-established circuits.

Nor were their wanderings limited to England. Troupes were soon travelling on the continent, particularly in the Low Countries, West Germany and Denmark, where the reputation of the 'English actors' stood very high, despite competition from similar German, French, Dutch and Italian troupes. Presumably they used more mime and tumbling overseas than they did in England to get their message across, but it is plain from the accounts that they were still presenting plays, not general entertainment. The evidence shows they were very successful. By contrast, continental troupes visited England rarely before late Elizabethan times – probably because it was still too much of a cultural backwater.

At first the players travelled in groups of four or less, on foot, with packs or packhorses, and perhaps a wagon for the more prosperous. Later, the more successful troupes could afford riding-horses, and by the late fifteenth century the more successful players were sufficiently well-to-do to provoke comment on the splendour of their dress. When touring they played in all sorts of venues - the village green, the inn yard, the 'great chamber' of the inn when it was wet, the dining-halls of nobles and gentlemen, and often municipal buildings at the request of the mayor.

A writer called Robert Willis vividly recalls such a performance, which he had seen as a boy in the 1570s. He recounts his memories in a book called *Mount Tabor*, written in 1639, when he was over seventy - which shows what a strong impression the occasion had made on him. He writes:

In the City of Gloucester the manner is (as I think it is in other like corporations) that when players of Interludes come to town, they first attend the Mayor to inform him what nobleman's servants they are, and so to get licence for their public playing; and if the Mayor like the actors, or would show respect to their Lord and Master, he appoints them to play their first play before himself and the Aldermen and Common Council of the city; and that is called the Mayor's play, where everyone that will comes in without money, the Mayor giving the players a reward as he thinks fit to shew respect unto them. At such a play, my father took me with him and made me stand between his legs, as he sat upon one of the benches, where we saw and heard very well. The play was called *The Cradle of Security* wherein was personated a King or some great Prince with his Courtiers of several kinds, amongst which three Ladies were in special grace with him; and they keeping him in delights and pleasures, drew him from his graver counsellors, hearing of sermons, and listening to good counsel and admonitions, that in the end they got him to lie down in a cradle upon the stage, where these three Ladies, joining in sweet song, rocked him asleep, that he snorted again, and in the meantime closely conveyed under the clothes wherewith he was covered, a vizard like a swine's snout upon his face, with three wire chains fastened thereunto, the other end whereof being holden severally by those three Ladies, who fall to singing again, and then discovered his face, that the spectators might see how they had transformed him, going on with their singing; whilst all this was acting, there came forth of another door at the farthest end of the stage, two old men - the one in blue with a Serjeant of Arms's mace on his shoulder - the other in red with a drawn sword in his hand and leaning with the other hand upon the other's shoulder, and so they two went along in a soft pace round about by the skirt of the stage, till at last they came to the Cradle; whereat all the Courtiers, with the three Ladies and the vizard, all vanished; and the desolate Prince, starting up bare faced, and finding himself thus sent for to judgement, made a lamentable complaint of his miserable case, and so was carried away by wicked spirits. This Prince did personate, in the Moral, the wicked of the world; the three Ladies, Pride, Covetousness and Luxury [Lechery]; the two old men, the end of the world and the last judgement. This sight took such impression in me, that when I came towards man's estate, it was as fresh in my memory, as if I had seen it newly acted.

Willis's account amply illustrates the reasons for the interludes' popular success – in this instance a clear simple plot, a lot of singing, unusual surprise effects like the pig's mask, bright, colourful costumes, and, no doubt, memorable devil-masks. The courtiers must have doubled as devils, and there must have been at least two of them – they probably also played the two old men: to this add the prince and three boys to play the ladies – making a minimum of three men and three boys, six in all.

Another important piece of more-or-less contemporary evidence about interludes is to be found in the anonymous play called *The Book of Sir Thomas More*, presented in about 1590. It is a late play, of course, but not written before all memory had passed away of the interlude players about seventy-five years earlier, and the conditions under which they performed, and the overall impression is of a playwright of the 1590s looking back on his professional ancestors with a certain amount of humorous condescension.

The piece contains a play-within-the-play acted before More and his family on the occasion of a state supper given for the Mayor of London and some aldermen and their wives. The actors who are to provide entertainment before the banquet announce themselves as 'My Lord Cardinal's Players'. More questions them: 'How many are ye?' – 'Four men and a boy, Sir' – 'But one boy,' says More, obviously expecting two at least, 'Then I see there's but few women in the play.' 'Three, my Lord,' says the player, 'Dame Science, Lady Vanity and Wisdom she herself.' 'And one boy play them all,' declares More, amazed, 'By'r Lady, he's loaden!'

If this is a typical troupe of interlude players, they are few in number (and perhaps short of a boy or so), they are itinerant, they have an important patron, and they depend upon doubling (in the boy's case, tripling) to get them through the performance. It proves later that they also manage their simple costume-changes mostly by means of exchangeable beards. In fact, the loss of one beard precipitates a crisis which brings the witty More himself into the play as an impromptu performer.

The play also gives us a notion of the players' usual repertory. More asks, 'I prithee tell me, what plays have ye?' 'Divers my Lord', says the player, '*The Cradle of Security, Hit the Nayl o' the Head, Impatient*

*Poverty, The Play of the Four PPs, Dives and Lazarus, Lusty Iuventus* and *The Marriage of Wit and Wisdom*.'

Judging from Willis's account of *The Cradle of Security*, they must have re-allotted the parts, and probably lost one of the ladies, to fit it for the company. *Hit the Nayl o' the Head* is lost, but sounds like one of William Wager's pieces, in which case it will have been a shortened general morality. *Dives and Lazarus* is also lost, but is mentioned by several writers, and was presumably based on the story of the rich man and the poor man in the Gospel and the reversal of roles they experienced after death.

*The Four PPs* is an entertaining piece by John Heywood, a member of More's own family, where the four PPs of the title, a Pedlar, a Pothecary (or quack doctor), a Pardoner and a Palmer (or Pilgrim) have a competition to see which is the best at their speciality – lying. It is thoroughly humanist, needs virtually no props at all, and can obviously be played by four actors, who should have good singing voices. It stands up well to modern performance.

*Impatient Poverty* needs only a playing-space with somewhere for Misrule to sing where he cannot be seen. Costume-changes take place on stage, showing how simple the arrangements were, and the division of eight roles between four actors suggested on the title-page is eminently practicable. It is a general morality, in which Impatient Poverty is the Mankind figure. It is an extremely lively comic piece which runs the whole gamut of burlesque – profanity, abuse, scurrility, threats, fights on stage, constant references to cards, women, taverns, usury, bribery and the French; and, needless to say, it contains a lot of song and dance.

*Lusty Iuventus* (*Lusty Youth*) is a very similar piece, in which nine roles are divided between four actors. The humour here is not quite so broad, but, on the other hand, all the characters have a much greater tendency to involve the audience, like Lusty Iuventus in his first speech, when he asks, 'Is there any man here who will go to game?' and, 'Who knoweth where there is e'er a minstrel?' Staging and costuming are elementary, but all four actors have to be able to sing part-music, and the songs, which are delightful, must have been a very important feature.

The last play in the list, *The Marriage of Wit and Wisdom*, is a re-working by Francis Merbury of *Wit and Science*. It has a comical central vice character called Idleness, who keeps changing his disguises and dominates the show, a lot of London low-life, some fairly cruel clowning, and a number of excellent songs. It performs extremely well for a modern audience, and, though it has 19 roles, the breakdown the author suggests for just six actors works like a charm. A company with 'four men and a boy', though, would find it rather difficult to stage.

A word or two here on the by-products of this practice of doubling by professional actors. First, since doubling made it possible to present a larger number of characters, there was an increasing tendency as time went on, particularly in low-life plays, to bring in additional characters simply to add 'local colour', and this will have stretched the actors to the utmost. Some critics believe that this led to 'profuse characterisation', which ruins the plays, but these later interludes certainly give a strong impression of the London streets, seething with all kinds of humanity.

Again, the increase in the number of characters presented led to a reinforcement of the medieval tendency to use costume symbolically. Each character needed to be 'typed' on entry to make it easier for the actor to show that he was playing somebody different, and this was most conveniently done by using emblematic costumes or hand-props which instantly revealed who he was – Anger or Justice carrying a sword, Treachery a cloak and dagger, Vanity a mirror, and so on – but there was also another tendency from quite early on in the moral drama to use a change of clothes to symbolise the character's change of heart. So a convention developed where a costume-shift showing a change of *character* took place *off* stage, while one showing a change of *heart* took place *on* stage in full sight of the audience – like the trimming-down of Mankind's practical country gown to a tiny fashionable coat, which shows his moral decline.

A final effect of doubling arose because of the increasingly popular nature of the interludes. For characters to change off stage you needed somebody to provide cover-speeches. This was fine as long as the attitude remained serious and Mankind or one of the virtues could lecture the audience. But by the early sixteenth century a change had set in. John Rastell notes on the title-page of his *Four Elements* that the play takes an hour and a half, but adds: 'if ye list, ye may leave out much of the sad matter . . . and then it will not be past three-quarters of an hour in length'. This says something about both the change in style of the pieces by Tudor times and the average length they were expected to run.

The consequence of this change of mood was that the audience could no longer simply be lectured but had to be entertained, and this was why the Vice character developed. As a stand-up comic and master of ceremonies he was able to provide the intervals needed for off-stage changes by filling in with slapstick and foolery.

So much doubling meant, of course, that there was no chance of the interlude players specialising in particular 'lines' of business as actors did later in the large permanent companies, although the Vice, who is often too busy to be doubled, comes near to it, and will have needed to be a very strong comic performer.

There is little to say about the staging of the pieces except that when it was professional it was kept to a minimum, as were the costumes and props. Out of doors, on the village green or in the market-place or the inn-yard, the interlude players were very attached to their booth stage,

*Figure 8* Preparing a small hall stage at any time between 1550 and 1700

while indoors they kept things as simple as possible, and in both places they relied strongly on the imagination of their audience.

The indoor performances were usually in halls. The average medieval hall had a high table across one end, on a raised dais, for the lord and important guests, and one or more large doors at the other end, known as the 'screen' doors, through which waiters served food from the kitchens. In between, tables and benches for the commoners ran the length of the hall. Above the large doors was usually a gallery where musicians would play during the meal. There is little evidence that raised platforms were set up for acting in such halls before the second half of the sixteenth century. Before that, the tables tended to be cleared to either side of the hall, and possibly some of the benches were set on top of the tables to provide a bank of seating for the spectators. The players then performed in the centre of the hall, in good view of the high table.

Later they shifted back towards the screen doors, thus avoiding the long entries needed to reach the acting-area, and in due course often built a simple lath-and-canvas 'house' at that end, if they needed one, or used the balcony above the doors as an upper level. There they would find themselves amongst their audience, for the important folk had now moved into the gallery from the high table, to get a good view of the action from above. Sometimes a central curtained space is reserved there for the actors, but it is likely that they usually simply intruded on to the balcony amongst the audience when they needed to.

The last development at the screen end of the hall was a raised stage, thrusting forward from the doors, which were now left open and covered over with tapestry hangings, through the slits of which the players could make their entrances and exits, thus recreating most of the features of a booth stage within the hall.

Playing conditions under these circumstances were very intimate. not to say cramped. It is plain that, before the players used platforms, people tended to form the usual circle and get between the actors and the doors where they needed to make their entrances and exits, and one of the most characteristic features of early interludes is the players calling for room as they make their way in. The intimacy, though, made possible a number of techniques which are usually considered quite modern, like the entrance of characters from amongst the audience or the planting of actors there to respond to certain lines – in one play the Vice sells firewood to a confederate amongst the spectators.

It was also in halls that special performances occurred, either at the request of a wealthy patron, or before the members of a school or college. In these cases, financial considerations were usually not important, and the producers of the piece would lash out on rich costuming and additional scenery and props. Many of the political interludes were produced in this way for important guests, and they obviously set out to impress. In some cases, the author designed a most elaborate setting, which took up the whole of the hall: one instance is Garter's *Vertuous and Godly Susanna*, which required a walled garden area with a pool, two flats representing bushes to left and right, a practicable orchard 'door' and a complete legal tribunal, with chairs, tables, witness box, and everything appropriate.

Where boys are the actors, as in school performances, other features become obvious, as well as the showy presentation. For instance, the plays written for them have many women's parts, whereas professional adult companies tried to keep these to a minimum. They do not use doubling much either, because they have ample resources of boypower and the educational objective is to give as many pupils experience of public speaking as possible and show them off to their parents. Since most schools had choirs associated with the nearest church, there is also quite a lot of complex part-singing in these interludes which would have been quite beyond the abilities of any adult company, and if the boys are from an actual choirschool, where they were taught the organ and other instruments, the author often calls on their instrumental skills, particularly if he is their master – for instance, in *Wit and Science*, Redford has four of his actors demonstrate their versatility by performing as a consort of viols.

There is also a tendency in interludes written for boys to play on the actors' natural high spirits. The pieces are full of witty young pages and servant lasses, and a lot of coincidental humour is obtained by getting youngsters playing old men to seriously lecture those playing young people on the error of their ways.

To conclude, many moral plays have proved their worth in modern performances. *Everyman* proved its holding-power when it was first rediscovered, early in the twentieth century, and continues to do so every time it is revived; *The Castle of Perseverance* has been well received once or twice in edited versions; and *The Satire of the Three Estates* was highly acclaimed when it was revived for the Edinburgh Festival by Tyrone Guthrie in 1948, and has reappeared there several times since with equal success. So the large-scale community plays are still viable.

The smaller-scale interludes, too, are receiving more and more attention from both amateur and professional actors – including specialist medieval troupes, both in England and Canada – and they deserve such attention. They are very vital pieces, particularly when they have a central Vice character who is played by a strong comic actor.

Moral interludes differ interestingly in their style and effect from the cycle-plays and the large-scale moralities. Whereas the larger, open-air pieces are planned with the aim of getting over the situation in simple, basic words and actions to a noisy holiday crowd, and leaving strong, static images lodged in the viewer's memory as a moral example or a spiritual inspiration, the interlude has no interest in static tableaux, and favours comedy of situation, particularly when the situations are lively and continually changing. In the intimate conditions of a booth-stage or hall performance the audience can naturally pick up far more detail of movement, so these pieces leave the audience with a kaleidoscopic impression of many active pictures being thrust quickly at them one after another, without there being any single 'key' piece of display. Because of the intimacy, the language too can be detailed, and there is a far greater emphasis not only upon wit and word-play, but also upon quite detailed argument and debate – usually involving a good and a bad character who each put their case to the audience, drawing forcible examples from the community they see around them, and who not infrequently get into a heated argument, ending up in a brawl.

So, ironically, the biblical cycle-plays, which in origin seem to be more tightly tied to reality, or at least to history, end up by presenting powerful emblematic and symbolic pictures; while the moral plays, which seem to begin in abstractions, are the pieces that leave the strongest impression of the dash and vitality of everyday life.

# 15

# NEWS FROM THE COURT

While the mystery cycles and the moral plays were developing in the cities of Europe, courtly entertainments had not been standing still. The mummery, and mumming in general, had been replaced at court by a new amusement, called the 'disguising'.

This was because mumming had unfortunate associations. The Christian clergy did not like it because it was a heathen institution, and it was distrusted by the State because it allowed people to enter the houses of the great in masks, without ever revealing who they were. To governments who were pathologically worried about plots, conspiracies and assassinations, and particularly the supposed machinations of the Lollards, or Christian communists, such a procedure seemed at best foolhardy. Nor did they hesitate to circulate alarmist rumours to strengthen their case, like the one in 1414 to the effect that 'Lollards had cast to have made a mumming at Eltham, and under colour of the mumming to have destroyed the King and Holy Church!'

Their response to the danger they perceived was decisive, as can be seen in the phrasing of an English decree in 1418:

No manner person, of what estate, degree or condition that ever he be, during this holy time of Christmas be so hardy in any wise to walk by night in any manner of mumming, plays, interludes, or any other disguisings with any feigned beards, painted visors, or deformed or coloured visages in any wise.

France was even earlier in the field, here: for instance, in 1395 Lille declared categorically: 'It is forbidden to indulge in mumming in the night time, either wearing false faces, or with the face covered with make-up or anything else.' So, although mumming continued to be enthusiastically pursued in the countryside, causing prohibitions like these to be constantly repeated, it was superseded at court by the 'disguising', a new theatrical form, which shared the idea of personal concealment with the mummery before it and the masque after it, but had the advantage, from an official point of view, of not actually containing the Germanic root *mommen*.

One of the earliest examples we have of a disguising, although it is still called a 'momerie' by the observer, occurred at a very famous feast given by Philip, Duke of Burgundy, in 1454. It is worth describing the occasion as a whole, because it gives us some idea of how the various strands of the Theatre of Social Recreation were woven together on special occasions.

The feast in question was the Feast of the Pheasant, and it was apparently held as part of a recruiting drive to find crusaders who would recapture Constantinople, which had just been taken by the Turks – a motif which, as we shall see, gave some shape on this occasion to the random elements which usually went to make up such an entertainment.

The day began with a *pas d'armes*, in which Adolf of Cleves appeared as the Knight of the Swan, taking on all comers. This was followed by a banquet, set out on three high, cloth-covered tables in the great hall decorated with elaborate scenic constructions, the chief of which was a large church with four musicians inside it, who were to sing and play the organ. There was also, on another table, a huge pie containing twenty-eight people, each of whom was capable of playing a different musical instrument.

In the middle of the hall was the statue of a naked woman, draped in a veil embroidered with Greek characters; this was set up on a pillar which also served as a fountain, pouring out hippocras, wine flavoured with spices, for as long as the supper lasted. Near to the statue was another pillar, to which was attached a living lion, who was clearly the statue's defender and guardian, for on its pillar was the inscription 'Touch not my lady!' Emblematically, the statue represented Constantinople and the lion the spirit of Christianity which would reclaim her.

A great multitude of noble visitors was present at the banquet, who had come from far and wide to take part. As soon as they were all seated, a bell sounded in the church on the table, and three little choirboys and a tenor inside it sang a very sweet song, which appears to have been a kind of grace before meat. When that was done, a shepherd played on a *musette*, or rural bagpipe, from inside the pie, and this format of a song from the church answered by a virtuoso performance from the pie was repeated before each entertainment that accompanied the meal.

There were twenty-eight entertainments in all, one for each person in the pie, and most of them made their entry through the great central door of the hall, accompanied by fifteen or sixteen knights clothed in the duke's livery. The two that particularly impressed our observer were a fiery dragon, which swooped down from the roof, flew the length of the hall, and disappeared with a loud explosion, and a mimed dance based on the story of Jason and his quest for the Golden Fleece – a piece in three acts, which was performed on a platform placed at the end of the hall and covered with a curtain. The dragon was plainly an emblem of knightly adventure and its destruction a symbolic driving-out of evil, while the dance about Jason's quest once again stressed the theme of daring undertaking, particularly in the area near Constantinople, where the Golden Fleece was found. The dance brought the entertainments which accompanied the meal to an end.

The build-up to the central event of the evening now began. A gigantic man came in, disguised as a Saracen from Granada and leading an elephant with a castle on its back, in which rode a lady dressed as a nun. As soon as this strange cortège made its appearance, the lady looked round the hall and exclaimed, 'Giant, I desire to stop here, for I see noble company.' Then, after the giant had obediently led her before the duke, she recited a long lament, the substance of which was that she, Holy Church, after making a round of all the European courts, had finally come to appeal to him for help against the Saracens. The duke's king-of-arms then brought in a living pheasant, and upon this bird the duke and the other nobles present made their vows to take up the Cross against the infidels in Constantinople – a vow never to be fulfilled, because the days of crusading were long past.

After this ceremony, the tables were cleared and a 'momerie' followed. First came torch-bearers and musicians; then another lady dressed as a nun, with the name 'God's Grace' ('Grace Dieu') inscribed on her shoulder in letters of gold; and finally twelve masked knights, each of whom held a torch and ushered in a lady. The ladies had their faces covered with transparent veils, and each of them had the name of a virtue clearly inscribed on a scroll fastened to her left shoulder.

The company advanced to the duke, stopping before him, and God's Grace recited verses declaring that she had come to introduce the twelve virtues and bring him a letter. The letter was accepted by the duke and handed to the Seigneur de Créquy, who read it aloud, its substance being that God, having heard the pious vows of the duke and the other Christians present, had sent his ambassadress God's Grace to present them with the twelve virtues who would be most helpful to them in their enterprise.

When the letter had been read, God's Grace announced that each of the ladies would now deliver her name to the duke in writing, which they did, at the same time handing verses to God's Grace which she read aloud, describing that lady's particular virtue. When all twelve of the virtues had been introduced in this way, God's Grace bade the duke farewell and withdrew, and the ladies took the scrolls off their shoulders and danced a set dance with their twelve gentlemen companions.

Whilst this dance was going on, the kings-of-arms and heralds consulted with all the ladies present to determine who, in their opinion, had performed most dashingly at the Tournament of the Swan in the morning. This was determined to be the Count of Charolais, and two princesses duly presented him with a prize, the festivities ending between 2 and 3 o'clock in the morning.

From this description you can see the loose relationship between the various kinds of social recreation current at the time, and also how they could all be subordinated to a grand design. The 'momerie' is of particular interest, bearing, as we shall see in a moment, the germ of the new 'disguising'. The dice-game had by this time obviously developed into the visitation of a 'divine' figure presenting the host with gifts of any kind, even emblematic ones, but the dancing remained, and was still performed only by the visitors.

The disguising usually retains this pattern of a processional entry and the presentation of a gift or blessing, followed by first 'formation' dancing and then ordinary social dances. Some confusion has been caused by the fact that such an entertainment was known as a 'morisco' in Italy rather than a 'momerie', because the morris dance had made such an impact upon the courts of that country. In fact, in the fifteenth century, the morris dance suddenly became a craze in *all* the courts of Europe, the simple black faces that marked the participants and gave the dance its 'Moorish' name having been replaced with more complex disguises. The dancers were now costumed as 'wild men', or jesters, or even characters from the Robin Hood ballads in England, all figures which clearly related to the original fertility ritual danced out by the morris men.

In Italy, this craze coincided with a period of vigorous dramatic activity on the part of the 'academies', which were literary societies founded by rich amateurs to investigate the newly rediscovered arts of ancient Greece and Rome. These academies gave us modern opera and ballet as a result of their attempted reconstruction of Greek drama, and they had a wide-ranging antiquarian interest in anything, like the morris dance,which seemed ancient and which they could use creatively to provide their members with entertainment.

These gentlemen took the *morisco* further and turned it into a variety of different entertainments ranging from a rather less serious form of disguising to a form of narrative dance. Some of these entertainments were used as *intermezzi*, or 'inserts', between the acts of more serious dramatic works, while others served as the main entertainment of the evening in their own right. In fact, the term became so general that it virtually came to mean any piece which contained figures in theatrical costume, and, had they been present at the Feast of the Pheasant, the members of the academies would not have hesitated to call both the 'momerie' and the dance on the subject of Jason a 'morisco'.

What the Italians seem to have added to the *morisco*, as they did to the tournament, was a strengthened visual aspect, the presence of some impressive scenic element, to fulfil the kind of introductory role taken by

Holy Church with her giant and elephant in the Duke of Burgundy's mummery. A single example will be enough to make the point. It is taken from the account of a ball held in Sienna in 1465: here the chief attraction was a construction in the form of a great, gilded wolf, out of which issued a *morisco* of twelve persons, each of them dressed as a nun, who danced to the sound of singing and then re-entered the wolf. This entry from, and return to, a decorative structure in the hall is reminiscent of the Italian use of triumphal chariots for the entries at tournaments, and, indeed, static units of this kind were later replaced by elaborate pageants which were wheeled in and could be wheeled out again to make way for the general dancing.

It is easiest to look at the disguising in its later, developed state, which occurs, from an English point of view, at the time of Henry VII. This is ironical because, despite his period of exile in France, Henry disliked elaborate and essentially mindless entertainments and preferred to watch moral interludes presented by his players. He was also by disposition a thrifty man, and, coming to the throne as he did directly after the Wars of the Roses, he had very little money in the coffers to indulge in expensive revels. However, as the country's financial circumstances improved, he became aware of a spirit of nationalism growing up around him in Europe which made it expedient to encourage 'goodly disguisings' at court, especially at times when foreign ambassadors were present – if only to demonstrate that England was not artistically backward as a nation.

This explains the very elaborate celebrations that accompanied his eldest son Arthur's marriage to Catherine of Aragon in 1501, an occasion which provides us with an excellent account of a series of fully developed disguisings.

The presence of so many French and Spanish guests was no doubt a great stimulus to the devisers of these entertainments and they were by far the most elaborate undertaken in the English court up to that time. To provide them with a suitable background, the king also caused the whole of Westminster Hall to be adorned with rich hangings, and turned out a huge supply of gold and silver plate to impress the visitors.

The disguisings were spread over several days. The first was on Friday evening, when a wonderfully devised castle was drawn into the hall by four great artificial animals. Eight disguised ladies were looking out of the windows of the castle, and on each of the four turrets sat a little choirboy, dressed like a maiden, who sang sweetly as the pageant advanced into the hall. Next came a ship, which appeared to be sailing on the sea, with its captain and crew all busy about their tasks. This cast anchor near the castle, and two emissaries, called Hope and Desire, descended by a ladder, approached the castle, and informed the ladies that they were ambassadors from the knights of the Mount of Love, who desired to come and court them. The ladies gave them a curt refusal and, while the ambassadors were warning them of the grave consequences of their stubbornness, a third pageant made its entry, shaped like a mountain and containing eight goodly knights. When the newcomers were informed that negotiations had failed, they made a vigorous attack upon the castle, reduced it to submission, and induced the ladies to descend to the hall floor and dance with them. During the dancing the three pageants were removed and after a while the disguisers, half of whom were dressed in English style and half in Spanish, in honour of the marriage, also departed. The Duke of York and a few other distinguished members of the audience then descended into the hall and danced basse dances, which were a slow and dignified form of social dancing.

On Thursday evening the court again assembled in Westminster Hall and two marvellous pageants were disclosed at the lower end of the chamber. These pageants were fastened together with a golden chain and represented two great mountains, one of them green and full of all kinds of trees and herbs and flowers, the other like a dark rock, scorched with the sun, but full of metals and precious stones. On the sides of the green mountain sat twelve disguised noblemen with musical instruments, and on the dark mountain ladies with clavicords, dulcimers and other instruments – one of them, who was dressed like the Princess of Spain, being seated upon the topmost peak. As the pageants moved in unison up the hall, both companies of disguisers played sweetly upon their instruments with pleasant mirth. Then, when the pageants had come to rest, the lords first descended and danced deliberately and pleasantly, after which the ladies descended and paired off with the lords and danced 'many and divers rounds and new dances, full curiously and with most wonderful assurance'. Whilst they were doing this the two mountains departed and vanished from sight.

Another evening in the same revelries, there was another disguising which involved two pageants, the first, shaped like an arbour, containing twelve knights, who descended and danced many different dances and then stood aside. After this the trumpets sounded and a pageant entered that was round, like a giant lantern, with many windows and more than a hundred 'great lights', or separate large panes of glass, which were very rare and expensive at the time, 'and all made so transparent that the 12 ladies disguised within it could be clearly seen'. When it came to rest, the ladies descended and danced first alone and afterwards with the knights.

These descriptions make the nature of the Tudor disguising pretty clear. It was extremely decorative and theatrical, and also contained simple dramatic elements not unlike those of the *pas d'armes*. One or more groups of disguised persons made an entry; usually there were two groups, one of men and the other of women. Each group then danced alone, and finally the two groups joined forces and danced together. Often the disguisers arrived in one or more pageants, and descended to the hall floor to dance; sometimes they retired into the pageants again after their dances and were drawn out of the hall. They appear to have danced the most fashionable dances of the time, which we can be sure the audience will have been eager to learn, and the quality of the music they used seems to have been quite outstanding. We notice, though, that they did not mingle with their audience any more than the mummers did.

In fact, the disguisings just described are really quite sophisticated. Each of them is carefully constructed around a single theme, which is both symbolic of the actions of love and courtship on one level, and an allegory of the occasion it is celebrating on another – indeed, all three disguisings are reiterations of the same political theme. The 'Spain and England' motif is obvious: the fertile mountain representing England's green and pleasant land is contrasted with the dark mountain standing for Spain, scorched outwardly by the sun, but inwardly rich with the gold from her American mines; while the golden chain symbolises both political union and marriage. We can also see that the disguising has in no way abdicated the ancient responsibility of folk-ritual to bring a blessing upon the land and its people: the images it employs, like the fertile male arbour, and the great lantern representing female beauty that lures men on to procreate the race, and even more, in the first disguising, the symbolic 'conquest' of the ladies in the castle, are no more than a sophisticated form of sympathetic magic, the 'enactment' of a fertile union to ensure that it is brought about.

Within the period we are considering, the only other new form of social entertainment that appeared was the court masque, which sprang from the disguising, much as the disguising had sprung from the mummery. Again, its roots were in Italy, where, during carnival-time, which stretched from New Year to Easter, the streets were full of masked people looking for entertainment. In those months, the well-to-do young men of Ferrara and Modena in the north were in the habit of going about the streets by night wearing masks, and also disguised in a kind of heavily hooded cloak, known as a domino, in which they could conveniently hide their identity. In this guise they would penetrate unasked into supper-parties and balls and invite the most attractive young ladies present to dance with them. Romeo breaks into the Capulets' party in precisely this way on the evening when he first meets Juliet. The practice was known as masquerading, and we should note how the masked intruders asked the ladies to dance with them, because that idea was quite new.

In due course this disruption of balls by masked gate crashers was incorporated into the disguising and produced the masque, where, during the social dancing at the end, the masquers took partners from the audience to dance with – a thing that had never happened before in a masked performance.

It was a daring thing to do in an age when young men and women tended to be quite severely segregated and virginity was an essential commodity for a young girl if she wanted to sell herself profitably in the marriage-market. Indeed, unwelcome associations and unwanted pregnancies sometimes occurred as a result of masques, and the practice acquired quite a scandalous reputation.

Respectable citizens felt something should be done to curb the new pastime. One group of French husbands complain bitterly 'that when they are at pleasant social gatherings, with their wives and daughters, the gallantry arrive "en masque", choose demoiselles, take them away into a corner, make love, dance with them, and stay till midnight'. They suggest that these irritating young men should be allowed no more than half an hour for dancing and half an hour for flirting, after which they should be forced either to unmask or to retire – which implies that they usually got away without even revealing their identity.

Predictably, it was Henry VIII who introduced the Italian masque into England. Unlike his father's, his reign was marked by prodigal expenditure, though this was largely directed, it must be said, at getting the nobles to spend their wealth on magnificent clothes and elaborate banquets and entertainments rather than using it to build up private armies of retainers.

Henry was a strong and vigorous young man, and enjoyed all kinds of social amusements. He was famous for his handling of horse and spear in the tilt-yard, so the entertainments of his reign tended to be marked by a close association with the tournament; he also loved hunting, so many of them had motifs drawn from the hunt; and he flirted outrageously, so the informality of the new Italian and French diversions, particularly the masque, appealed to him strongly. He also liked to spring surprises on his companions, so he would sometimes slip away in the middle of a disguising to join the male group of dancers – an action that was in no sense *lèse majesté* since by this time the dancers were all nobles.

His introduction of the masque occurred during the Christmas of 1512, and was plainly an attempt to bring England up to date in artistic matters. Hall provides an account of the occasion in his chronicle:

On the day of Epiphany at night, the King with eleven other were disguised after the manner of Italy called a mask, a thing not seen afore in England. They were apparelled in garments long and broad, wrought all with gold, with vizards and caps of gold, and after the banquet was done, these maskers came in, with six gentlemen disguised, in silk, bearing staff torches, and desired the ladies to dance. Some were content, and some that knew the fashion of it refused, because it was a thing not commonly seen. And after they danced and commoned together, as the fashion of masks is, they took their leave and departed, and so did the Queen and all the ladies.

As we know, the essence of the Italian masque was indeed the 'commoning together' of the masquers and the most attractive members of the opposite sex, so the field was wide open for flirtation and amorous adventure; hence the doubts of the ladies. Some of them were either *complaisant* or daring or did not know about the masque's shocking reputation and simply went like lambs to the slaughter – thinking, no doubt, that this was rather an odd way for disguisers to behave – but other ladies 'that knew the fashion of it' refused 'because it was a thing not commonly seen'. In short, they were not sure how to respond to the king's challenge, and chose not to compromise themselves by engaging in this scandalous new pastime until they saw how it was received by the court. Doubtless their scruples were soon laid to rest, because it was in fact accepted with great enthusiasm, and became a regular feature of English court entertainments from that time on, giving Henry many delightful opportunities for flirtation.

The dramatic aspects of the masque were destined to develop considerably later on, as its narrative content strengthened and it came to incorporate elements which graphically represented the driving-out of evil in the antimasque which preceded the masque proper, and the blessing of the reigning monarch by the gods in the masque itself. But such developments lie beyond the scope of this chapter.

# 16

# MYSTERIES' END

A number of social trends combined to undermine the mystery-cycles and Passion plays. For instance, when towns became rich in the late fourteenth and early fifteenth centuries their corporations seem to have acquired a new sense of responsibility for the moral and religious welfare of their citizens. This was good for dramatic activities at the time, because it led councils to favour the presentation of religious plays for the instruction of the people and to encourage the guilds to mount them – but it proved a stumbling-block later, when the councils became Protestant, because it then encouraged them to oppose the presentation of all plays as sinful and corrupting – an attitude vividly displayed by the Common Council of London during the reign of Elizabeth.

This new puritanical attitude was reinforced by the economic decline of many large towns during the late fifteenth and early sixteenth centuries – a decline resulting from a steady rise in population, the progressive collapse of the old wool trade, the migration of weavers into cheaper premises in the suburbs, and the growth of a national market for goods which undermined the local monopolies of the guilds. Equally important were the fluctuations in property values which resulted from the widespread religious strife during the Reformation: the guilds had invested heavily in land and properties as a means of stabilising their assets, and they suffered severely from this volatile state of affairs. Under the circumstances, then, it is hardly surprising that they found the cost of mounting religious festivals they no longer approved of unacceptably high.

In fact, in every way it was the growth of Protestantism that undermined the religious drama. Protestants believed in the personal responsibility of each individual for the state of their own soul, so nothing must intervene between them and their Maker – certainly not saints and holy relics, which were a kind of idolatry; nor priests, who perverted the role of moral counsellor into a usurpation of God's authority. Nor must they let themselves be corrupted by any form of art, which was inevitably a human distortion of God's truth – and drama was

188

a particularly reprehensible form of art, utterly trivial in its treatment of life, a temptation to murder and fornication, and a great waster of God's good time. This particularly applied to the cycles and Passion plays, which had originally been missionary propaganda of the Catholic Church and were thus assuredly snares laid before the feet of the true Christian by the Great Satan in Rome.

In any case, a religion which accepted no interpretation of the Scriptures other than that arrived at by the individual through a process of close personal study, and which believed in 'God speaking directly to the heart of man', could hardly tolerate the traditional meanings and interpretations given to Biblical incidents in the mystery plays; while a religion which so much emphasised the need for strictness of life, and the swift vengeance of God upon the sinner, was unlikely to be interested greatly in the tenderness, humour and tolerant humanity with which the cycle-plays abounded.

In England, the movement for suppression of the plays echoed political events. In 1531, Henry VIII broke with Rome and was acknowledged supreme head of the Church in England. In 1539 came the dissolution of the monasteries, and the English Reformation dropped like a ripe fruit into the none-too-tender hands of Thomas Cromwell, who profited so extensively from the sale of church lands that he would have been the very last person to relax the pressure against the Catholics. It was therefore scarcely surprising that, from 1535 to 1575, well into Queen Elizabeth's reign, successive governments set out to undermine the Catholic stage in England, first by ridicule, censorship and threats, and later by direct suppression. It fell victim, in fact, to the same outburst of iconoclasm that 'protector' Cromwell directed against all the other visible manifestations of Catholic doctrine in the churches - statues, frescoes, stained glass, reliquaries, and so on. For instance, 'In the first year of Edward VI [namely, 1547] there were certain commissioners appointed to deface all such ornaments as were left in the parish churches at Durham undefaced in the former visitation.' There Dr Harvey called for the shrine of Corpus Christi, 'and when it was brought before him he did tread upon it with his feet and broke it all to pieces, with divers other ornaments pertaining to the church'.

Looking back on the development of Christianity, though, we can see how the Reformation was an almost inevitable backlash - resulting from the alienation of the common people from the Mass throughout the Middle Ages, with the accompanying mystification of the service, and the elevation of the priest into an exclusive mediator between God and Man. In their simple, undecorated chapels the Protestants for the most part returned to celebrations of the Mass which were closer to the original form - though it must be said that they lacked much of the joy of the early Christians. They had inherited above all else the late medieval emphasis on the painful sacrifice that Christ had made for man rather than the joy of his Resurrection, and tended to see his triumph as a triumph of the will over the flesh, like their own spiritual soul-searchings. This was so much the case that a large proportion of the Protestant sects definitely ended up as 'kill-joys'.

Some city councillors would have liked to preserve the cycle-plays in some form, because they were a source of revenue and prestige for the town, and these favoured revision of the texts; but others seem to have objected to fundamental aspects of the plays like the physical representation of God the Father, who they felt should be 'a voice only to hear, and not . . . in shape or person to appear'. They also objected to the representation of the sacraments of Baptism and the Last Supper on stage in the context of a mere 'game', and many of them felt that the description of transubstantiation – the assumed conversion of the bread and wine into the actual body and blood of Christ – that was provided in the plays of the *Last Supper* went far beyond the intention of Christ's actual words in Scripture. The Elizabethan reviser of the banns at Chester reflects all these problems and also apologises for those plays that have no Scriptural authority, making a plea for the good faith of writers who created scenes like Christ's Harrowing of Hell simply 'from their opinions'.

Eventually, though, all such shifts failed, and the mystery plays were deliberately suppressed in Protestant countries – while even in Catholic countries they began to look outdated and to cause grave doubts amongst the clergy.

Of these two parallel trends, the Protestant suppression is the more blatant. For instance, after its performance in 1523 the Freiburg Whitsun play was abandoned, and in exactly the same year the Nuremberg Good Friday play met with the same fate. In a temporarily Protestant France, in 1548, the Paris *parlement* (or city council) forbade the Confrérie de la Passion to present any sacred mysteries, and this trend soon spread to the French provinces, similar measures being passed by the *parlements* of Bordeaux and Rouen in 1556 and by that of Rennes before 1565. In fact the Parisian edict changed the nature of the Confrérie de la Passion completely; the document reads:

> [This *parlement*] restrains and forbids the said petitioners to perform the mystery play of our Saviour's Passion, or to play any other sacred mysteries, on pain of a discretionary fine, permitting them nevertheless the freedom to present other worthy and lawful secular mysteries without offending or harming anyone; and the said court forbids all others to perform on stage henceforth any plays or mysteries whatever, in the city or its suburbs as well as the

outskirts of Paris, except under the name of the said Confrérie and for the benefit of the same.

The 'secular mysteries' referred to would be things, like saints' plays, that were not directly based on the Bible, but the actual effect of this edict was that the Confrérie de la Passion rapidly turned into a monopolistic group which used its royal charter to extract money from anybody performing plays in Paris or proposing to do so, and became a positive hindrance to the development of new drama, until it was finally disestablished by Louis XIV in 1680, and its powers were transferred to the Comédie-Française.

The authorities in England pursued a similar programme of repression. In the same year as the Parisian ban was promulgated, Hereford agreed to spend the money contributed by 'divers corporations of artificers, crafts and occupations' to 'set forward divers pageants of ancient histories in the processions . . . upon the day and feast of Corpus Christi, which now is . . . omitted and deceased' on repairs to the 'ruinous and decayed' causeways, pavements, streets and walls, and on cleaning out the town ditch. This is a precedent that has unfortunately marked the artistic policy of too many city councils in England since that time – and more than one government. In the same year, 1548, at York, the plays featuring the Death, Assumption and Coronation of the Blessed Virgin, the most overtly Catholic elements of the cycle, were cut from the annual performance, and they were not restored when the plays were temporarily revived in 1561, the third year of Elizabeth's reign.

By 1568, the tide had definitely turned against the cycle-plays in England, because in that year the usual play scheduled for production at New Romney was cancelled, and at York the city corporation decided to present the less contentious *Play of the Creed* rather than the Corpus Christi cycle. However, even *The Play of the Creed* encountered opposition from the Dean of York, Matthew Hutton, who was a member of the Commission for Ecclesiastical Causes in the north. He advised the city fathers against its presentation:

as I find so many things that I much like because of the antiquities, so I see many things that I cannot allow because they be disagreeing from the sincerity of the gospel, the which things, if they should either be altogether cancelled or altered into other matters, the whole drift of the play should be altered, and therefore I dare not put my pen unto it, though in good will I assure you if I were worthy to give your lordship, and your right worshipful, counsel, surely mine advice should be that it should not be played, for though it was plausible forty years ago, and would now also of the ignorant sort be well liked, yet now in the happy time of the gospel' [i.e. the Reformation] I know the learned will mislike it – and how the state will bear it, I know not.

As a result of Hutton's advice the *Play of the Creed* was withdrawn and never heard of again, and the following year, 1569, saw the last performance of the Corpus Christi cycle at York until the twentieth century.

The dark hints which Hutton had dropped about possible reprisals against any councils that might rashly take it upon themselves to sponsor performances of the cycles, were not idle threats. This is shown by what happened at Chester, shortly afterwards. In 1571 Edmund Grindal, the Archbishop of York, banned the performance of the Chester plays, the town of Chester being within the diocese of York. As it happened, his ban reached the mayor, John Hankey, too late to prevent the performance. Hankey was summoned before the Privy Council of the queen, no less, to account for his flagrant disrespect for higher authority, but was able to clear himself. All then remained peaceful until 1575, when the mayor for that year, Sir John Savage, who can hardly have been ignorant of what had happened four years before, decided to stage the plays again. When this intention became known, he received specific bans from both the Archbishop of York and, more importantly, the Lord President of the North, but he still went ahead with the production, possibly intending to make it a test case. In due course he too was hauled before the Privy Council to give an account of himself, and appealed to his successor, Mayor Henry Hardware, for a supporting letter from the corporation to make it clear that he had not acted on his personal authority alone, but according to their wishes. Hardware duly wrote defending Savage, and gave clear reasons for the presentation of the plays on the most recent occasion, pleading their customary production in the city over many years and, more significantly, the fact that their performance redounded 'to the common wealth and benefit and profit of the same city' - in other words it was financial considerations, like the loss of the trade brought to the shops and inns of the city by visitors, that had induced the council to fly in the face of authority. The Privy Council eventually cleared Savage, but on the explicit understanding that the cycle was never to be performed again; it too only came to be revived in the twentieth century.

In the meantime, Archbishop Grindal had been pursuing his crusade at York. The city council was now reduced to producing the Paternoster play, and he was determined that this last relic of the dramatic repertory should be suppressed. In 1572, after seeing a performance, he demanded to read the play for the purposes of revision, and never returned it . . . This happened to a number of religious plays at this time; some of them reappeared in the eighteenth century, in private libraries, whilst others vanished for ever.

In 1576 the proposed staging of the Corpus Christi plays at Wakefield was also banned, this time by the Diocesan Court of High Commission, which included Matthew Hutton, who was still Dean of York, as one of its members. The court communicated its wishes in good time, on 27 May:

> This day upon intelligence given to the said Commission that it is meant and purposed that in the town of Wakefield shall be played this year at Whitsunweek next or thereabouts a play commonly called Corpus Christi play which hath been heretofore used there, wherein they are done to understand that there be many things used which tend to the derogation of the Majesty and Glory of God, the profanation of the sacraments and the maintenance of superstition and idolatry, the said Commissioners decreed a letter to be written and sent to the bailiff, burgesses and other the inhabitants of the said town of Wakefield that in the said play no pageant be used or set forth wherein the Majesty of God the Father, God the Son, or God the Holy Ghost, or the administration of either the sacraments of Baptism or of the Lord's Supper be counterfeited or represented, or anything played which tend[s] to the maintenance of superstition and idolatry or which be contrary to the laws of God or of the realm.

In short, the Wakefield plays were censored out of existence.

Even in those countries on the continent that remained staunchly Roman Catholic, the leaders of the Counter-Reformation – though they were not as hostile to the drama as their Protestant opponents – became much more cautious in their attitude and subjected the old mystery plays to a far closer control and scrutiny than they had received in the Middle Ages. The Protestant move towards self-examination and personal responsibility awoke introspection in the Catholic ranks as well, and although the Council of Trent (which convened between 1545 and 1563) did not openly mention religious drama, its concern for purification and uniformity in liturgical matters, and clarification and definition in doctrinal ones, alerted the Church to possible abuses and excesses in religious plays, even those performed within church buildings as part of the liturgy.

The Council of Trent in turn prompted other ecclesiastical councils to review their procedures. The one that met at Salamanca in Spain in 1565 was gravely concerned by the unsuitability of much material employed in the Spanish Nativity plays and decreed they should be submitted to the local bishop or his deputy for approval, adding that anything that might divert the congregations from their devotions was to be set aside. The Council of Toledo in 1582 went further, totally forbidding the performance of plays and dances at times of divine service. The examples are taken from Spain, but similar things were going on throughout the whole of Europe, and the fact that the Church of Rome felt that some regulation of previous practice was necessary suggests that the attitude towards religious drama in Catholic countries had become much more defensive.

The year when the last major English cycle at Wakefield was suppressed, 1576, was also the year in which James Burbage, Dick Burbage's father, built the first public theatre in England intended to house a permanent company. So the question naturally arises as to whether the coming of an active professional theatre also contributed to the collapse of the cycles, and the answer is that it certainly did – not by overt competition, but by altering public taste.

The Renaissance interest in imitating ancient Greek and Roman plays encouraged a new elaboration of plot and characterisation which was very popular with the theatre-going public: people began to demand a new type of play, involving a shift away from medieval symbolic narrative towards psychological realism, and this trend was perhaps the last nail in the coffin of the religious drama. The change can be demonstrated by describing various treatments of the story of Jephtha's daughter, before and after the Reformation.

The original story comes from chapter 11 of the Book of Judges, where we read that, when he joined battle with the Ammonites, who greatly outnumbered him, Jephtha rashly vowed to God that, if he was granted victory, he would offer up the first living creature that met him on his return home as a burnt offering. The battle was duly won – but when Jephtha returned home the first living creature to meet him was his only child, his daughter, who came out to welcome him with music and dance. He tore his garments and cursed himself at the sight, but his daughter, when she learnt about his vow, insisted that he kept his word, begging only two months with her fellow-maidens in the hills in order to prepare herself for the ordeal – and so, when the two months were up, he sacrificed her, according to his word.

When this story was treated by medieval writers, it was always presented, like Abraham's sacrifice of Isaac, as a figure foreshadowing God's sacrifice of his only begotten Son, and also as a moral parable showing the danger of making rash vows, often accompanied by an argument that bad vows should not be kept.

As the Renaissance approached, treatments of the story began to reflect a wider interest in the general principles of interactive psychology. Gower, for instance, divorces the incident from its Jewish origins and makes it a moral parable illustrating the sloth of parental love in comparison with the daughter's unlimited love for her father, and he extracts considerable pathos from her predicament.

In early Tudor times, Buchanan takes this further: he suppresses the girl's plea to be allowed time with the other maidens to mourn the fact that she will die barren, because he feels it would blur the determination of her character, and constructs his play on Greek principles, making the climax a messenger's speech describing her death, in which her heroic calm, in the face of the laments of the crowd and her father's last-minute indecision, provides an impressive picture of a spirit too noble to suffer the fears and regrets of the majority of mankind.

Buchanan's play, in its turn, encouraged Theodore Beza, the French Calvinist, who greatly admired it, to update the story of Abraham and Isaac by treating it in a similar way. He rejects medieval typology, jettisons the Isaac of the old plays, who is touching and brave in his tiny, childish way, and presents us with a young man who is well aware of all the issues involved, obedient and unafraid, a character who arouses admiration for his capacity to rise above the baser human emotions in order to obey a divine command, and yet is psychologically believable enough to support such an interpretation.

In these alternative treatments of Biblical subjects, which reflect a general trend, we can clearly see the shift to reliance upon personal faith and self-examination which makes them distinctively Protestant and therefore acceptable to the reformed Churches. Yet, by their very insistence on psychological realism, they also become indistinguishable from the more secular drama around them, and it is only too obvious that an important period of religious drama is drawing to a close.

At which point this survey ends, somewhat beyond the confines of its period. However, we have brought the European theatre to a crossroads where it was finally throwing off its medieval heritage. Intellectually it was becoming involved in a greater psychological realism, and physically it was about to introduce the picture-frame stage and painted perspective scenery – through the agency of the court masque – and these two developments were destined to dominate drama for the next three hundred years.

# NOTES ON THE INDIVIDUAL
# CHAPTERS

The sources for the chapter are given first, and, where they are not specific, may be found by referring to the recommended background reading under the writer's name. Notes are appended on a few points of particular interest, and a clear indication is given where the opinions presented are those of the author.

## 1 THE PASSION OF JESUS CHRIST

SOURCES: Huizinga (1924), Auerbach (1953), Jungmann (1951), and Hardison (1965).
A fuller explanation of symbolic methods of thinking in the Middle Ages can be found in Huizinga (1924), Tillyard (1943), and Auerbach (1953).

## 2 CHRISTIANS VERSUS PAGANS

SOURCES: Chambers (1903), Carcopino (1941), Beare (1950) and Axton (1974).
What little is known about the absorption of the mimes into the minstrel troupes can be found in Chambers (1903).
Axton (1974) covers very thoroughly what little evidence we have of mimed dance-drama accompanying minstrel narration.
Kahrl (1974) notes that by the fifteenth century the terms *mimi, ministrales* and *histriones* had all come to mean 'minstrels', while *lusores, ludatores* and *homines ludentes* were used for 'actors'. The linking together of mimes, minstrels and general entertainers suggests the composite nature of minstrel troupes.

## 3 FROM RITUAL TO DRAMA

SOURCES: Chambers (1903), Young (1933), Jungmann (1951), and Hardison (1965). For the musical details, I have used *The New Harvard Dictionary of Music* (1968) and *The New Grove Dictionary of Music and Musicians* (1980). A detailed description of Amalarius' interpretation of the Mass will be found in Hardison (1965).
The reconstruction of the popular practices surrounding early performances of the *Quem quaeritis?* was arrived at by conflating a number of accounts from Winchester and Laon, and incorporating the simple version of the trope from St Gall.

## 4 THE CHURCH AS A THEATRE

SOURCES: Chambers (1903), Young (1933), and Konigson (1975).

'Baldaquin' is pronounced '*bal*-dakin', stressed on the first syllable.

The popular pronunciation of Mary Magdalene's name as 'Mary Maudlin' gave us the modern meaning of the word, on account of the character's tearful self-indulgence.

## 5 THE LANGUAGE OF THE PEOPLE

SOURCES: Chambers (1903), Auerbach (1953), and Hardison (1965).

Axton (1974) summarises the action of the *Auto de los Reyes Magos*.

## 6 THE VILLAGE AND THE COURT

SOURCES: Chambers (1903), Welsford (1927), Brody (1969), and Wickham (1972). I have also called upon Sir James Frazer's *Golden Bough* (1890) and Sir Charles Oman's *History of War in the Middle Ages* (1898).

I tread here on dangerous ground, currently the subject of fierce dispute between traditional, ritual-favouring, 'folk-lorists' (see Brody (1969)) and modern anthropologists who claim that the case for a ritual drama is pure hypothesis (see Thomas Pettitt's article 'Early English traditional drama: approaches and perspectives', *Research Opportunities in Renaissance Drama* 25 (1982)). After reviewing the arguments, I still accept the 'ritualist' case for the early existence of a fertility play centring upon the death and resurrection of a 'King of the Year', because the pattern of action in the existing folk-plays of the last two centuries – challenge, conflict, death, lamentation, resurrection and rejoicing – is anticipated by the 'Memphitic drama' of 2500 BC from Egypt (translated by Theodor Gaster in his *Thespis* (1950)), and reflected in so many of the Greek myths (as Robert Graves has shown in his commentary to *Greek Myths* (1955)). It seems that the re-enactment of death and rebirth in symbolic terms appeals to unconscious longings in our psyches, as Vince (1984), quoted in the text, observes.

It is rather surprising to find Glynne Wickham accepting the notion that mumming was silent. This is presumably because the *Oxford English Dictionary* has doubts of the derivation of the word from the Teutonic *mommen*. However, some Renaissance scholars were clearly aware of the true roots of the word: for instance, Jean Savaron (1608) writes: 'the proof that the Devil is the originator of masques and mummeries is to be found in the true source of the words *momon* and *masque*: *mommo* in Greek [and] *masca* in Tuscan and Lombardian speech, signify at the same time both *a demon* and *a vizard*'. He obviously did not know the Germanic word *mommen*, but the Greek *mommo* is closely related to it.

## 7 THE COMING OF CORPUS CHRISTI

SOURCES: Jungmann (1951), Kolve (1966), Woolf (1972), Nelson (1974), and Roberts (1980).

'Reredos' should be pronounced '*rear*-doss' and 'retable' '*ree*-table', with stress on the first syllable in each instance.

In most texts the Feast of Corpus Christi is assumed to fall somewhere between

23 May and 24 June – but this is wrong! It was Bevington (1962) who first noted that the *old calendar* was still in use.

## 8 AN ACUTE SENSE OF SIN

SOURCES: Owst (1933), Russell (1940), Rossiter (1950), Hardison (1965), Potter (1975), and Roberts (1980).

Hardin Craig supposed the cycles were simply liturgical plays translated from the Latin and rearranged, while Mary Marshall felt liturgical plays must have established the *methods* of dramatising sacred history, but Kolve's and Hardison's pioneering work has shown they were both wrong. Edmund Chambers first advanced the 'crowded church' theory, which was later espoused by Nicoll and others, but that too has been discredited by Hardison and can only be partially true, at best.

It was A. G. Little who claimed that *compulsory* private confession could never have been enforced without the friars.

The strong emphasis on the Black Death as a catalysing agent is entirely my own, and, though speculative, is, I think, justified. Its influence on play presentations can be seen from the phenomenal increase in new religious guilds, many of which produced plays reminding men of their mortal sin and the urgent need for redemption. John Coldewey (in Briscoe and Coldewey (1989)) observes that 63 per cent of the religious guilds who registered their existence in 1389 claimed to have been founded since 1360.

## 9 THE STRUCTURE OF THE CYCLES

SOURCES: Chambers (1903), Auerbach (1953), Kolve (1966), and Woolf (1972).

## 10 STAGING THE CYCLES ON SCAFFOLDS

SOURCES: The illustrations mentioned in this chapter are all extremely well known and can be found in almost any theatre history. I have used Tydeman (1978) for details of French productions.

My view of the staging of *The Castle of Perseverance* does not coincide with that of Southern (1957). Despite the clear indications of the sketch, and its accompanying notes, Southern reckons the ditch was *outside* the earthen bank, as in the Cornish rounds, and assumes the audience mingled with the actors in the Place, being controlled there by the 'stytelers'.

Natalie Schmitt (*Theatre Notebook* 23), suggests the ditch formed a 'moat' close to the castle near the centre of the Place, and quotes Sloth's attempt to divert the waters with a spade, but this would have been very inconvenient for the actors.

*The Martyrdom of St Apollonia* does not *necessarily* represent a performance in the *round*. It could easily be a *semi-circular* arrangement, intended to be seen by the bulk of the audience from the artist's viewpoint. Presumably, though, the customary view is correct, and there was essentially a cruciform arrangement around the Place, the scaffold of Apollonia (omitted in the picture) confronting that of the Emperor, so Spiritual Power challenged Earthly from south to north, and Heaven confronted Hell from east to west, strongly recalling the use of a church building.

The details of the production of *The Mystery of the Three Masters* at Romans is drawn from Volume 1 of Wickham (1972).

## 11 STAGING THE CYCLES ON WAGONS

SOURCES: Chambers (1903), Salter (1955), Wickham (1972), Nelson (1974) and Tydeman, (1978 & 1986). Also drawn upon are Alexandra Johnston's and Margaret Dorrell's articles in *Leeds Studies in English* 5 & 6, Meg Twycross's analysis of the positioning of, and attendance at, the stations in York ('Places to hear the play: pageant stations at York 1398-1572', *Records of Early English Drama Newsletter* 2), and articles by Richard Rastall and Meg Twycross in Neuss (1983).

The material in this chapter has been interpreted by many gifted scholars, so my only aim has been to present what seem to be the facts and to emphasise the probable use of platforms as acting extensions to the pageants, an idea originally proposed by Nelson and Wickham and, to my mind, since that time unfairly discounted. The interpretation of the 'rolls of tree' in the York account is entirely my own, but it seems legitimate in view of the other information.

Kahrl (1974), amongst others, discounts the suggestion of extra platforms on the grounds that even York's Micklegate was not more than 35 feet wide and 'no matter how narrow one imagines the waggons to have been' there would not have been room for two placed side by side *and* an audience to fit into the width of the street, in addition to which 'overhanging buildings built out over the street further restricted the available space'. But the 'jutty forward' used to shed rain water into the street was usually 10 inches, as in the Fortune contract, reducing the width of the road by only a foot, and it is, in fact, *crucial* how narrow we imagine the wagons to have been. Kahrl suggests 10 feet as a 'good working hypothesis', but a breadth of 8 feet would have been quite feasible and would have greatly aided the shifting of them from place to place. What is more, the additional platforms need not have been even that wide, since in some illustrations of street theatres the actors apparently have a depth of little more than 6 feet to act on. Assuming both wagon and platform to have been 8 feet broad, and granting a 1-foot clearance to avoid overhang, only 17 feet of the Micklegate width is taken up, leaving a full 18 feet for the audience.

When Rogers refers to 'scaffolds and stages', he definitely means that *two quite different things* were built at the sites where the plays were performed. A 'scaffold' was originally a platform on which you displayed something - an execution, or the king and his party at a tournament, or, if it was Shakespeare's 'unworthy scaffold', a play - while a 'stage' was something on which you stood. By 1620 these two words had more or less reversed their meanings, but they still implied two different things. A 'stage' was now the structure on which something was shown, and the scaffold was something to sit or stand on - defined, at the Whitehall production of *Gorboduc* in 1561, as 'scaffolds to sit upon', so there should be no mistake. Rogers therefore definitely means both some kind of stand *and* a stage at each station.

It was Nelson (1974) who proposed a single performance of the plays at York, suggesting the acting venue may have been indoors, protected from the weather, and that the plays may even have been given on a different day from the procession - which would certainly accord with the usual German practice, as outlined by Neil Brooks, 'Processional drama and dramatic procession in Germany in the late Middle Ages', *Journal of English and Germanic Philology* 32 (1933) - yet Johnston and Dorrell have marshalled an impressive amount of evidence to prove that public processional staging took place. It is they who suggest that perhaps the number of plays given was limited, but this contradicts the guild accounts.

It is Tydeman's suggestion that the plays may have been performed in groups of four. This might have greatly speeded the presentation of the last two performances in the main part of the town, if the pageants could be moved from station to station through linking streets. The same thing could have happened between the first four stations on Micklegate and the next four stations on Coney Street if the ferry to the north of the Ouse bridge was large enough to take carts, as on German rivers. This would also avoid the awkward right-angle, mentioned by Tydeman, at the east end of the bridge.

## 12  PRODUCING THE CYCLES

SOURCES: Chambers (1903), Nicoll (1927 & 1931), Southern (1957), Wickham (1972) and Woolf (1972), and articles by Richard Rastall and Meg Twycross in Neuss (1983) and by Tydeman in Meredith, Tydeman & Ramsay (1985).

Rey-Flaud (1973) made the estimate of attendance at the French mystery plays, using all sorts of indirect evidence. He believes that the 5,000-a-day attendance was only exceeded on three occasions: at Reims in 1490, where he estimates an audience of about 5,600, at Autun in 1516, and at Bourges in 1536. He does not venture an estimate for the last two venues.

## 13  THE MORAL DIMENSION

SOURCES: Lewis (1936), Rossiter (1950), Bevington (1962), and Potter (1975).

Axton (1974) describes an impressive Latin morality play written by Hildegard of Bingen in about 1155, but, although brilliant, it is too idiosyncratic to be considered part of the tradition.

## 14  MORAL INTERLUDES IN ACTION

SOURCES: Chambers (1903), Bevington (1962), Craik (1967), Wickham (1972), Southern (1973), and Potter (1975).

Touring of amateur productions certainly occurred in East Anglia, and *The Castle of Perseverance* may have been toured as some kind of 'civic' production, despite its large cast, though it could never have paid its way professionally. Part of the argument in favour of touring derives from the fact that, like the N-Town cycle, the document recording the play's banns has a space left, apparently for the insertion of the names of different towns, and there are also hints in the *Castle* plan that more than one venue was envisaged by the presenters; but it seems more likely that the *playscript* of these plays (accompanied by the design in the case of the *Castle*) was passed from town to town, allowing the local guilds to produce them individually.

## 15  NEWS FROM THE COURT

SOURCES: Chambers (1903), Welsford (1927), Nicoll (1931 & 1938), and Wickham (1972).

The observer of the Feast of the Pheasant was Mathieu d'Escouchy.

## 16  MYSTERIES' END

SOURCES: Gardiner (1946), Woolf (1972), and articles by Coldewey and Clopper in Briscoe & Coldewey (1989).

# NOTES ON THE ILLUSTRATIONS

I deliberately re-drew my illustrations, because this forced me to consider the practicalities of the settings – where, for instance, in the Valenciennes mysteries were buildings in the background modelled in three dimensions, and where were they merely painted on to a large canvas flat, in perspective? If you inspect the original engraving, you can see where the 'moulded' buildings come down to a single flat horizontal line at the bottom, implying a long run of flats and *trompe l'oeil* painting. Similarly, the curtains in Pilate's judgement hall seem to be painted, where the curtains in front of the Temple look as if they are a practicable blind, that could be dropped and raised at will.

This kind of consideration made the exercise worth undertaking. In other cases, like my impression of the Fouquet miniature of *The Martyrdom of St Apollonia*, I have still to see a photographic reproduction which brings out clearly the detail of the original.

## SOURCES AND DESCRIPTIONS

### Figure 1  A booth stage in Holland, *c.* 1550 (p. 109)

An impression of a well-known painting by Peter Balten.

### Figure 2  The east end of Lucerne wine-market, set up for the play, 1583 (p. 111)

An imaginary re-creation, based on the plan for the first day of the play, and the sketch of the wine-market which it includes. The other end of the market is less interesting, consisting almost entirely of a large stage, probably with booths at the back for different characters, and stands for spectators, although it did have what looks like a very entertaining Hell Mouth. Shown are the platform for God at the back, Mount Sinai and the garden of Paradise (back right), the hut of the Annunciation (back left). The River Jordan, which is the long thin carpet stretching from the front of the picture to the gate at the back beneath the stand. The table for the Last Supper (on the extreme left), the platform for Cain and Able's sacrifices (straddling the Jordan), the platform for Abraham's sacrifice of Isaac (nearer), and, at the front, the golden calf on its pillar (with altar and sacrificial pit) and the brazen serpent on its cross, while to the extreme right is the temple.

**Figure 3 The Castle of Perseverance set up in a small round, c. 1450 (p. 114)**

An imaginary re-creation, based on the original ground-plan. We are looking north-east over the central castle at Covetyse's scaffold; at the back right, to the east, is Heaven, at the back left, to the north, Belial's scaffold, at the front left, to the West, Mundus' (the World's) scaffold, and at the front right, to the south, Caro's (Flesh's) scaffold. The figures – two stagehands arguing – are for scale.

**Figure 4 The martyrdom of St Apollonia, c. 1460 (p. 116)**

An impression of the famous French miniature by Jean Fouquet, as accurate as I can make it.

**Figure 5 The St Lawrence Play (Laurentius) at Cologne, 1581 (p. 119)**

Based on a contemporary drawing of the stage. A fascinating feature here is the way in which the floor-cloth is laid in a series of 'pathways' to help guide the actors.

**Figure 6 The Valenciennes mystery play, 1547 (p. 120)**

Based on a contemporary engraving of the stage.

**Figure 7 Side elevation of a pageant-wagon, 1615 (p. 128)**

An extraction, for the purposes of greater clarity, of the main features of the Car of the Nativity from the picture *The Triumph of Isabella*, described in some detail in the text. It is particularly interesting to notice the slanted farm-wagon-like stern, which reduces weight, and the fact that the corners of the 'house' structure are located over the wheel-bases, in order to distribute the weight. The figures – a couple of pageant-masters checking the structure – are merely there to provide scale.

**Figure 8 Preparing a small hall stage at any time between 1550 and 1700 (p. 176)**

The main objective of this imaginary reconstruction is to show how simple an interlude's 'setting' could be, and how much the emphasis was placed on the actor. Some of the detail is from the frontispiece to Francis Kirkman's *The Wits; or Sport Upon Sport*, 1672. The hall might equally well have had two doors and two or more candelabra, since private halls varied widely.

# RECOMMENDED
# BACKGROUND READING

Anderson, M. D. (1963) *Drama and Imagery in English Medieval Churches*, Cambridge.

Auerbach, Eric (1953) *Mimesis: The Representation of Reality in Western Literature*, trans. Ralph Manheim, Princeton, NJ.

Axton, Richard (1974) *European Drama of the Early Middle Ages*, London.

Beare, W. (1950) *The Roman Stage*, London.

Bevington, David M. (1962) *From 'Mankind' to Marlowe*, Cambridge, Mass.

Briscoe, M. G. & Coldewey, J. C. (eds) (1989) *Contexts for Early English Drama* Bloomington, Ind.

Brody, Alan (1969) *The English Mummers and their Plays: Traces of Ancient Mystery*, London.

Carcopino, Jerome (1941) *Daily Life in Ancient Rome* New York.

Chambers, Sir E. K. (1903) *The Medieval Stage*, 2 vols, Oxford.

Craik, T. W. (1967) *The Tudor Interlude*, Leicester.

Davenport, W. A. (1982) *Fifteenth-Century English Drama*, Woodbridge.

Elliott, John R. (1989) *Playing God: Medieval Mysteries on the Modern Stage*, Toronto.

Frank, Grace (1954) *The Medieval French Drama*, Oxford.

Gardiner, H. C. (1946) *Mysteries' End*, New Haven, Conn.

Hardison, O. B. Jr (1965) *Christian Rite and Christian Drama in the Middle Ages*, Baltimore, Md.

Huizinga, J. (1924) *The Waning of the Middle Ages*, trans. F. Hopman, London.

—— (1949) *Homo Ludens*, London.

Jungmann, Joseph (1951) *The Mass of the Roman Rite: Its Origins and Development*, New York.

Kahrl, Stanley J. (1974) *Traditions of Medieval English Drama*, London.

Kolve, V. A. (1966) *The Play Called Corpus Christi*, London.

Kongison, Elie (1975) *L'Espace théâtrale médiéval*, Paris.

Lancashire, Ian (1984) *Dramatic Texts and Records of Britain; A Chronological Topography to 1558*, Cambridge.

Leacroft, Richard (1973) *The Development of the English Playhouse*, London.

—— (1984) *Theatre and Playhouse* (with H. Leacroft), London.

Lewis, C. S. (1936) *The Allegory of Love*, Oxford.

Mâle, Emile (1902) *L'Art religieux du treizieme siècle en France*, Paris.

—— (1908) *L'Art religieux à la fin du moyen âge en France*, Paris.

Meredith, P., and Tailby, J. E. (eds) (1983) *The Staging of Religious Drama in Europe in the Later Middle Ages*, Kalamazoo.

—— Tydeman, W., and Ramsay, K. (1985) *Acting Medieval Plays*, Lincoln.

Nagler, A. M. (1976) *The Medieval Religious Stage* New Haven, Conn.

Nelson, Alan (1974) *The Medieval English Stage: Corpus Christi Pageants and Plays*, Chicago.
Neuss, Paula (ed.) (1983) *Aspects of Early English Drama*, Woodbridge.
Nicoll, Allardyce (1927) *The Development of the Theatre*, London.
—— (1931) *Masks, Mimes and Miracles: Studies in the Popular Theatre*, London.
—— (1938) *Stuart Masques and the Renaissance Stage*, London.
Owst, G. R. (1933) *Literature and Pulpit in Medieval England*, Cambridge.
Potter, Robert (1975) *The English Morality Play*, London.
Purvis, Canon J. S. (1969) *From Minster to Market Place*, York.
Rey-Flaud, Henri (1973) *Le Cercle magique*, Paris.
Roberts, J. M. (1980) *The Pelican History of the World*, Harmondsworth.
Rossiter, A. P. (1950) *English Drama: From Early Times to the Elizabethans*, London.
Russell, Bertrand (1940) *A History of Western Philosophy*, London.
Salter, F. M. (1955) *Medieval Drama in Chester*, Toronto.
Southern, Richard (1957) *The Medieval Theatre in the Round*, London.
—— (1962) *The Seven Ages of the Theatre*, London.
—— (1973) *The Staging of Plays before Shakespeare*, London.
Tillyard, E. M. W. (1943) *The Elizabethan World Picture*, London.
Tydeman, William (1978) *The Theatre in the Middle Ages*, Cambridge.
—— (1986) *English Medieval Theatre 1400-1500*, London.
Vince, Ronald W. (1984) *Ancient and Medieval Theatre*, Westport, Conn.
Waddell, Helen (1927) *The Wandering Scholars*, London.
Welsford, Enid (1927) *The Court Masque*, Cambridge.
Wickham, Glynne (1972) *Early English Stages*, 2 vols, London.
Woolf, Rosemary (1972) *The English Mystery Plays*, London.
Young, Karl (1933) *The Drama of the Medieval Church*, Oxford.

## RECOMMENDED COLLECTIONS OF PLAYTEXTS

Especially recommended is:

Bevington, David M. (ed.) (1975) *Medieval Drama*, New York.
(This is an excellent selection of texts of all types of medieval drama, in parallel translation where appropriate. A most useful volume which provides all the general reader needs.)

Other useful collections for the general reader are:

Beadle, Richard (ed.) (1982) *The York Plays*, London.
Cawley, A. C. (ed.) (1974) *Everyman and Medieval Miracle Plays*, Everyman Library, London.
Happé, Peter (ed.) (1975) *English Mystery Plays*, Harmondsworth.
—— (1979) *Four Morality Plays*, Harmondsworth.
Rose, Martial (trans.) (1961) *The Wakefield Mystery Plays*, London.
Wickham, Glynne (ed.) (1976) *English Moral Interludes*, Everyman Library, London.

## MORE SPECIALISED DOCUMENTARY EVIDENCE

Any serious scholar of the subject should certainly also consult the Early English Text Society (EETS) editions of the plays, Lancashire (1984), and the output of the Records of Early English Drama (REED) project, founded in Toronto in

February 1975, under the general editorship of Alexandra Johnston with the express purpose of searching out all English information on early dramatic productions and making it generally available.

# INDEX

acting companies: boys' companies 170; interluders 21, 81, 160-1, 165, 168-9, 170-2; mimes 13-14, 18-21, 196; minstrels 18-20, 170, 196; permanent companies 168-70; *see also* regulation of actors in Rome

acting style: boys (choirboys, schoolboys) 165-6, 170, 177-8; early vernacular plays 54-5; interluders 21, 161, 163-5, 168-9, 172-8; later vernacular plays 106-7, 115-16, 131-3, 136, 139-40, 150-1; liturgical drama 31, 44-5; mimes 13-14, 18-21; minstrels 18-21; permanent companies 168-9; Roman pantomimes (actors) 10-13

Amalrius bishop of Metz 23-5, 31, 39, 71: desire to revitalise Mass 23; writings popular but condemned as heretical 26

aristocracy *see* nobility

Black Death 90-2, 198: appearance and progress 90-1; coming lends urgency to religious drama 90-1, 198; origin of Dance of Death 91; social effects, including new prosperity 90-2

bourgeoisie: celebrate king's successes with civic entries 69-70; cities' economic rise and growing prosperity 65, 69; cities encouraged to promote drama by Black Death 91-2; cities' economic decline affects support of cycles 188; city guilds and drama 65, 77, 91-2, 126, 132, 151, 188; protestant councils' views on plays differ 188, 190, 192

bread and wine 2-5, 7, 25, 71-2: *see also* Doctrine of the Real Presence, Host, Mass, Passover, species

Brotherhood of the Passion *see* Confrérie de la Passion et Resurrection

characterisation 50-1: in *Mystère d'Adam* 53-4; in *Seinte Resurrection* 52-3; simple in all medieval drama 51, 106, 156-7, 175; theological rather than psychological 53; the 'Vice' character in moral plays 158-9, 164, 166, 175

Christian disapproval of stage 10, 13-17, 22: *see also* decline and suppression of religious plays

Church of Rome 5-7, 9, 15, 23, 27: attempted reform of corruption 85-6; establishes feast of Corpus Christi 75-6; has doubts about religious drama 190, 193-4; *see also* Corpus Christi, friars, heresies

church building: early pre-Gothic building described 24; Gothic building described 71-5; important places for drama, centre of church 39-40; important places for drama, centre of nave 37, 39-42; symbolism of east end 'heavenly' 38-43; symbolism of north side 'good' 37-8, 41; symbolism of south side 'sinister' 37-8, 40; symbolism of west end 'worldly' 38-42; symbolism of western doors 'gates of Hell' 23, 36, 39-42; tribune at west end possibly extends action 39, 41

CPSIA information can be obtained at www.ICGtesting.com
Printed in the USA
BVOW01s0914300114

343496BV00003B/6/A